THE SELF-OVERCOMING OF NIHILISM

SUNY Series in
MODERN JAPANESE PHILOSOPHY

Peter J. McCormick, Editor

THE SELF-OVERCOMING OF
NIHILISM

*

NISHITANI Keiji

Translated by

Graham Parkes

with

Setsuko Aihara

STATE UNIVERSITY OF NEW YORK PRESS

The preparation of this volume was made possible in part by a grant from the National Endowment for the Humanities, an independent federal agency.

Published by
State University of New York Press, Albany

For information, address State University of New York
Press, State University Plaza, Albany, N.Y. 12246

Library of Congress Cataloging-in-Publication Data

Nishitani, Keiji, 1900–
    [Nihirizumu. English]
    The self-overcoming of nihilism   /   Nishitani Keiji : translated by
Graham Parkes with Setsuko Aihara.
        p.   cm. — (SUNY series in modern Japanese philosophy)
    ISBN 0–7914–0437–4 (alk. paper). — ISBN 0–7914–0438–2 (pbk. : alk
paper)
    1. Nihilism (Philosophy) 2. Philosophy, Modern—19th century.
3. Philosophy, Modern—20th century.   4. Philosophy, European.
5. Nietzsche, Friedrich Wilhelm, 1844–1900—Contributions in concept
of nihilism.   6. Heidegger, Martin, 1889–1976—Contributions in
concept of nihilism.   7. Philosophy, Japanese—20th century.
I. Title. II. Series.
B828.3.N513   1990
149'.8—dc20   90–31631
                                                                      CIP

10 9 8 7 6 5 4 3 2 1

Nanzan Studies in Religion and Culture

James W. Heisig, General Editor

Heinrich DUMOULIN, *Zen Buddhism: A History. Vol. 1, India and China.* Trans. by J. Heisig and Paul Knitter, 1988.

Heinrich DUMOULIN, *Zen Buddhism: A History. Vol. 2, Japan.* Trans. by J. Heisig and Paul Knitter, 1989.

Frederick FRANCK, ed., *The Buddha Eye: An Anthology of the Kyoto School.* 1982.

Winston L. KING, *Death Was His Kōan: The Samurai-Zen of Suzuki Shōsan*, with a Foreword by Nakamura Hajime, 1986.

Robert E. MORRELL, *Early Kamakura Buddhism: A Minority Report,* 1987.

NAGAO Gadjin, *The Foundational Standpoint of Mādhyamika Philosophy.* Trans. by John Keenan, 1988.

NISHITANI Keiji, *Religion and Nothingness.* Trans. by Jan Van Bragt with an Introduction by Winston L. King, 1982.

NISHITANI Keiji, *Nishida Kitarō: The Man and His Thought.* Trans. by Yamamoto Seisaku and J. Heisig, forthcoming.

NISHIDA Kitarō, *Intuition and Reflection in Self-Consciousness.* Trans. by Valdo Viglielmo et al., with an Introduction by Joseph O'Leary, 1987.

Paul L. SWANSON, *Foundations of T'ien-T'ai Philosophy: The Flowering of the Two Truths Theory in Chinese Buddhism,* 1989.

TAKEUCHI Yoshinori, *The Heart of Buddhism: In Search of the Timeless Spirit of Primitive Buddhism*. Trans. with Introduction by J. Heisig and a Foreword by Hans Küng, 1983.

TANABE Hajime, *Philosophy as Metanoetics*. Trans. by Takeuchi Yoshinori et al., with an Introduction by J. Heisig, 1987.

Taitetsu UNNO, ed., *The Religious Philosophy of Nishitani Keiji. Encounter with Emptiness*, 1990.

Taitetsu UNNO and James HEISIG, eds., *The Religious Philosophy of Tanabe Hajime: The Metanoetic Imperative*, 1990.

Hans WALDENFELS, *Absolute Nothingness: Foundations for a Buddhist-Christian Dialogue*. Trans. by J. Heisig, 1980.

Contents

Acknowledgments

Our gratitude needs to be expressed for the receipt of "seed money" for the translation project which we received in 1985 from the University of Hawaii Research and Training Revolving Fund. This grant enabled us to travel to Kyoto for a preliminary discussion of the text with Professor Nishitani. The bulk of the funding for the project came from a translation grant from the National Endowment for the Humanities: we should like to take this opportunity to thank the staff of the Texts / Translations Program at the Endowment for their efficient assistance and kind encouragement over the past few years. We are grateful for an award from the Research Relations Fund at the University of Hawaii, which provided the primary translator with a course-reduction for the semester following our six months of work on the translation in Japan. The release-time furnished by this award came at just the right time, and accelerated progress on the project considerably. We also wish to acknowledge the assistance of the NorthEast Asia Council of the Association for Asian Studies. A travel grant awarded in 1988 enabled us to return to Japan for final consultations with Professor Nishitani in Kyoto and Dr. James Heisig in Nagoya.

We are grateful to Jan Van Bragt, Director of the Nanzan Institute for Religion and Culture, for his meticulous reading of an early draft of the translation, as well as to James Heisig for his help in de- and reconstructing the manuscript at a later stage. Would that every translation project from Japanese could be blessed with such intelligent readers.

Throughout the course of the project Professor Horio Tsutomu of Ōtani University in Kyoto, a former student of Professor Nishitani's, provided invaluable assistance with unfailing serenity. Stefan Thumfart, who was engaged in graduate study at Kyoto University at the time of our first draft, was kind enough to let me (GRP) see a draft of his German translation of the chapters of Hishitani's book that deal with Nietzsche. He also provided references to the *Taishō Tripiṭaka* and German translations of the more opaque quotations from Chinese Zen sources (which he had it turn received from his friend Dr. Dieter Schwaller).

Gratitude is due to my colleague here in Hawaii, Virgina Bennett, who standardized the orthography of the proper names in the chapter on Russian nihilism. My friend Lee Siegel helped, at the eleventh hour, to eradicate some tenacious infelicities from the penultimate draft of the Introduction, which had already benefited from James Heisig's comments. Thanks, also, to Lori Kuriyama for her efficient typing of the entire draft of the translation.

I should like to take the opportunity to acknowledge Setsuko Aihara's invaluable contribution to the project, and to register awe at the facility with which she was able to wrest the most recalcitrant passages of Japanese into comprehensible English. Equally remarkable was the serene patience with which, in the earliest stages of the translation accomplished in the sweltering heat of a Tokyo summer, she would coolly remind me of what Nishitani's Japanese was actually saying in contrast to what I thought it ought to be meaning.

We should like, lastly, to thank Professor Nishitani himself, as well as his daughter, for the kind hospitality extended to us on our visits to his home in Kyoto over the past several years. The long conversations held in the quiet little room distinguished by the significant absence of any kind of clock, where time would pass as it rarely passes, linger in the memory as the most delightful feature of the entire project.

Abbreviations

Works by Nietzsche

AC	*The Antichrist*
BGE	*Beyond Good and Evil*
EH	*Ecce Homo*
GM	*On the Genealogy of Morals*
GS	*The Gay Science*
KGW	*Werke: Kritische Gesamtausgabe*
TI	*Twilight of the Idols*
UdW	*Der Unschuld des Werdens (ed. A. Bäumler [Leipzig, 1931])*
WP	*The Will to Power*
Za	*Thus Spoke Zarathustra*

Works by Heidegger

ER	*On the Essence of Reasons*
KM	*Kant and the Problem of Metaphysics*
SZ	*Sein und Zeit*
WM?	*What is Metaphysics?*

Others

KW	*Kierkegaard's Writings*
T.	*Taishō shinshū daizōkyō (Taishō Tripiṭaka in Chinese)*

Introduction

"But may I ask, first of all: just what would be the *point* of translating this book of mine into English?" I remained silent for a while, somewhat bemused by the question—addressed to me, as it was, by the author of a book entitled *Nihilism*. The main point of Professor Nishitani's text, which we had just begun to translate, had not yet penetrated so far as to prompt any question about the point of it all.

It was the first time we had met with the author after the decision to devote full time to the translation, and now his characteristic modesty was putting the whole enterprise into question by injecting an appropriate dose of what he would call "nihility" at its ground. Taking his question on the more restricted level, we learned that his concern was that an English translation of a book written forty years ago for a Japanese audience might not be of interest today to readers in the West. It consisted, after all, merely of a series of talks on a topic that happened to be rather fashionable at the time, and so was not endowed with any overarching structure or unified theme. But since the phenomenon of nihilism appears to have increased rather than diminished in intensity over the past four decades, I had simply assumed that the singular perspective from which Nishitani writes about what is traditionally regarded as a Western problem would render his treatment intrinsically interesting to the English-speaking world, where Japanese philosophical discourse is still largely unfamiliar. But perhaps, in deference to the author's concern with the value of a translation of the book, we might well begin by reflecting on where we stand with respect to the issue of nihilism.

I

What I am recounting is the history of the next two centuries.
Friedrich Nietzsche

Counting from when these words were written—just over a hundred years ago, in the unpublished preface to a manuscript Nietzsche sketched out under the working title *The Will to Power*—we find ourselves today no more than midway through the story of nihilism as foretold by that vatic raconteur. Halfway through this first half of the story, between 1936 and 1940, Heidegger lectured at length on Nietzsche's nihilism. Some of his reflections and projections were reorganized in the course of the ensuing years, and then committed to print as the essay, "The Word of Nietzsche: 'God is dead'."[1] This piece begins by characterizing itself as an attempt "to point the way toward the place from which it may be possible some day to ask the question concerning the essence of nihilism." A modest proposal, one might think, little more than a gesture in the general direction. But also a sobering indication of the difficulty of the question—so that one might well ask how far we have really come in resolving the problem of nihilism in the fifty years since Heidegger's musings.

In the audience during the first lecture cycle at the University of Freiburg in the late thirties was an inconspicuous visitor from Kyoto, who heard with a far ear and saw what was under discussion with a distant eye. From the cultural remoteness of Japan, the young philosopher was able to contemplate the course of European nihilism comprehensively, commanding a synoptic view of what Nietzsche had seen as a mighty stream gathering force with every passing decade: the upsurge—*après lui le déluge*—of nihilism. Ten years later, Nishitani would himself give a series of talks on the subject of nihilism to a small group of scholars and students in Kyoto. It is the text of those lectures, originally published under the Japanese title *Nihirizumu*, that constitutes the present book.

But let us turn back for a brief look at the history of European nihilism prior to Nietzsche.[2] Credit for the earliest development of the idea of nihilism in a philosophical sense is apparently due to F. H. Jacobi, who in an essay from the 1780s entitled "Idealism and Nihilism" argues that Kantian philosophy, especially as articulated in the *Critique of Pure Reason*, leads to a view of the human subject as "everything" and the rest of the world as "nothing." In a well known letter to Fichte in March 1799, Jacobi extends his criticism to include the idealism that dominated German philosophy at the time, and affirms his thoroughgoing opposition to it by branding it as *"nihilism."* Jacobi's position is nicely characterized by Otto Pöggeler in a play on the German word for faculty of reason: "The reason [*Vernunft*] of Idealism perceives [*vernimmt*] only itself; it dissolves everything that is given into the nothingness of subjectivity."[3]

Between the discussions of nihilism by Hegel and others among the German Idealists and the treatments of the issue by Stirner and Nietzsche, the major philosophical elaboration of the problem is to be found in a number of texts from the 1820s and 1830s by the theologian Franz von Baader. Baader's ideas were a major influence on Kierkegaard, and constitute another important chapter—one with which Nishitani was familiar—in the history of European nihilism. It is from the decline of Hegelian philosophy around this period that the author of the present study takes his point of departure.

Nishitani's interest in the topic coincided with a resurgence of concern with nihilism in Europe in the aftermath of the Second World War. Karl Löwith, a student of Heidegger's, had been the first to take up the question of nihilism again from an explicitly philosophical point of view. In a monograph published in 1933 he had undertaken an illuminating comparison of the engagements with nihilism of Kierkegaard and Nietzsche.[4] As the essay's subtitle suggests—"Theological and Philosophical Overcoming of Nihilism"—Kierkegaard's response is seen to remain within a Christian framework, albeit one radically transformed through that singular thinker's existential reflection, while Nietzsche's is understood as more strictly philosophical, grounded in the abyssal Dionysiac thought of "the eternal recurrence of the same." This monograph, which was surely a stimulus to Nishitani's work on the topic, remains a most valuable—though largely neglected—contribution to the field. Löwith went on to set the theme of nihilism in its broader historical and philosophical context in his monumental study *From Hegel to Nietzsche* (1941), which provides some valuable background for the themes of the first half of Nishitani's book.[5] And then in 1948, the year before these lectures were delivered, a long essay of Löwith's entitled "European Nihilism" (the appendix of which Nishitani discusses in one of his talks) was published in Japanese.[6]

The turn of the decade between the forties and the fifties saw the topic of nihilism become the subject of burgeoning interest. In Germany, an article on the subject of Nietzsche and European Nihilism appeared in 1948,[7] and the following year Ernst Benz published a slim volume entitled *Westlicher und östlicher Nihilismus (Western and Eastern Nihilism)*, which discussed from a specifically Christian perspective the phenomenon of nihilism as it had appeared in Russia as well as Western Europe.[8] The author begins with the observation that "a history of nihilism has not yet been written." It is a satisfying twist of intellectual history that such a history should be published by a Japanese philosopher that very year—from an even farther Eastern perspective. Two years later Helmut Thielicke's influential book *Der Nihilismus* appeared, which offered a response to the problem of nihilism in terms of Christianity.[9] This in contrast, however, with Nishitani's treatment, aligned as it is with Nietzsche's view, which sees Christianity as the major locus of nihilism—as the problem rather than the solution.

In the same year, 1951, a book appeared in France which took the overcoming of nihilism as the central task confronting humanity at mid-century, *L'Homme révolté* by Albert Camus.[10] In two chapters entitled "Absolute Affirmation" and "Nihilism and History," Camus discusses the ideas of Max Stirner and Nietzsche. While the discussion of Stirner (omitted, sadly, from the English translation of the book) is much shorter than Nishitani's, the treatment of Nietzsche is remarkably similar. Citing many of the same passages, Camus too views Nietzsche as a prophetic diagnostician of modern culture, and emphasizes the theme of *amor fati* and Nietzsche's method of undergoing the experience of nihilism so thoroughly that it finally overcomes itself.

II

I have come to understand things according to the Buddhist way of thinking.

Nishitani, autobiographical essay[11]

Nishitani began his intellectual odyssey by studying philosophy in European texts, only later finding himself drawn to the serious study of traditional East Asian ways of thinking. It is almost unheard of that someone in the West should start out with philosophy from another culture before coming to the study of Western philosophies. We tend to lack that dual perspective (*Doppelblick*, as Nietzsche would say), that sense of distance with respect to one's tradition which derives from being a latecomer to it. In an essay from 1967 entitled "Philosophy in Contemporary Japan," Nishitani writes:

> We Japanese have fallen heir to two completely different cultures. . . . This is a great privilege that Westerners do not share in . . . but at the same time it puts a heavy responsibility on our shoulders: to lay the foundations of thought for a world in the making, for a new world united beyond differences of East and West.[12]

Much of the author's work has been devoted to exploring and forging pathways between Eastern and Western thought, an enterprise he was engaged in long before it became fashionable on this side of the Pacific.

Nietzsche wrote that every great philosophy is "the self-confession of its originator and a kind of involuntary and unconscious memoir."[13] In Nishitani's case the confession and memoir are quite conscious, sincere, and open: he indicates clearly the original and sustained motive forces of his doing philosophy. It will be helpful to touch upon just a few of these motivations in order to provide some preliminary orientation.[14]

One feature of Nishitani's early intellectual development that has already been remarked deserves to be recounted again since it bears directly on the theme of the present work. He talks about it in the essay "My Philosophical Starting Point."

> Before I began my philosophical training as a disciple of Nishida, I was most attracted by Nietzsche and Dostoevsky, Emerson and Carlyle, and also by the Bible and St. Francis of Assisi. Among things Japanese, I liked best Natsume Sōseki and books like the Buddhist talks of Hakuin and Takuan. Through all these many interests, one fundamental concern was constantly at work, I think. . . . In the center of that whirlpool lurked a doubt about the very existence of the self, something like the Buddhist "Great Doubt." So it was that I soon started paying attention to Zen.[15]

A broad background in Western literature is by no means unusual among educated Japanese of Nishitani's generation (his mentor, Nishida Kitarō, was widely read in English, French, and German), but the early and decisive encounter with both Nietzsche and Dostoevsky in the context of nihilism stamped Nishitani's thinking with a unique character.

At the beginning of the same essay Nishitani characterizes this doubt concerning the self which originally motivated his philosophical quest quite explicitly as "nihilism," a mood of "nihility" occasioned by the deepest despair. In "The Time of My Youth" he writes of the utter hopelessness of that period and of his despair's being compounded by the death of his father when he was sixteen. Shortly thereafter, he was struck down by an illness similar to the tuberculosis that had killed his father. In an uncanny parallel to Nietzsche's situation some fifty years earlier, the young student felt "the specter of death taking hold" of him. It was the ensuing mental torment that led in his case, too, to the enterprise of philosophy as an attempt to plumb the experience of nihilism to its depths.

III

As a young man, I used to carry Thus Spoke Zarathustra *around with me wherever I went—it was like my Bible.*

Nishitani in conversation, 1988

While Nietzsche's influence on Japanese thought has in general been remarkably powerful,[16] Nishitani is distinguished from other members of the Kyoto School by the depth of his affinity with Nietzsche's thinking. Not only is Nietzsche the major presence in *The Self-Overcoming of Nihilism*, but the book also constitutes the first substantial introduction of Nietzsche's philosophical ideas to a general Japanese audience. (In fact it is difficult to meet a philosopher in Japan today who did not read *Nihirizumu* as a student; the book seems to have been, at least until recently, a more or less required text.) However, granted that Nietzsche scholarship in the West has come a long way in the past forty years, it is not impertinent to demand more and ask why it is relevant to study the book here and now, and in what respects Nishitani's reading of Nietzsche may illuminate our present understanding of that difficult thinker's ideas.

Firstly—and appropriately, in the context of Nietzsche—it is a matter of perspective. Nishitani's distance from the Western tradition, combined with his comprehensive grasp of the major trends in Western philosophy,[17] affords him a synoptic overview of Western intellectual history that is denied to thinkers who are thinking from within that tradition. Borrowing Nietzsche's image of the tradition as a river (which Nishitani elaborates in chapter three, below), one could say that while Nietzsche had to pull himself out of the current and yet leave one foot in it in order to understand it well enough to overcome it, Nishitani had the advantage of an overview from outside the current first, before stepping into it for a more intimate understanding. Nishitani's perspective has allowed him to see as more unified than Western commentators have generally done the current of nihilism which springs from the decline of Hegelian philosophy and runs through Feuerbach (with a branch off to Kierkegaard), Stirner, and Schopenhauer to Nietzsche and Heidegger.[18]

To speak of the advantages that accrue from Nishitani's standing outside the Western tradition is to express the value of his perspective as it were negatively. The source of the positive contribution of his view comes from his immersion in the tradition of East Asian Buddhist thinking—and in Zen in particular. The Zen standpoint brings into relief a nexus of issues surrounding the core of Nietzsche's thought: the idea of eternal recurrence in its connections with the notion of *amor fati*, love of fate.

There are earlier instances of interpretations of Nietzsche from a perspective influenced by Buddhist thought: the studies of Watsuji Tetsurō and Abe Jirō, for example, which appeared during the second decade of the century.[19] These two thinkers have been criticized for importing inappropriate conceptions from the Asian tradition into their readings of Nietzsche—and specifically for interpreting the idea of will to power as some kind of "cosmic self," suggesting that Nietzsche's program involves a transcending of the boundaries of the conscious ego in order to achieve participation in this universal self. Even if these interpretations are somewhat vague and sometimes extravagant, they can at least direct us to certain features of Nietzsche's thought that have received little attention in Western scholarship. In conversation, Nishitani has acknowledged the study by Watsuji in particular as being of central importance. He came upon the book early on, in his initial phase of avid Nietzsche-reading during his high school days in Tokyo, and sees it as having exerted a crucial formative influence on his understanding of Nietzsche. Some years ago he remarked in writing that it was Watsuji's book on Nietzsche that had prompted him to read and reread *Thus Spoke Zarathustra* "over and over again."[20]

Almost simultaneously with the publication of *The Self-Overcoming of Nihilism*, Nishitani's senior colleague, Tanabe Hajime, brought together the ideas of eternal recurrence and *amor fati* against the background of the Buddhist idea of *karma* in his discussion of Nietzsche in *Philosophy as Metanoetics*.[21] There he writes: "If we interpret the core of Nietzsche's eternal recurrence in terms of karma, the idea takes on a meaning of still vaster proportions" (p. 111). The suggestion is provocative, but the discussion is relatively brief and only sketches out the ground which Nishitani was working more deeply and thoroughly.[22] In general terms, consideration of the Buddhist idea of "networks of causation" (*pratītya-samutpāda;* Jap. *engi*) may serve to sensitize the reader to Nietzsche's conception of the interdependence of all things, an idea that is not immediately evident in the texts he himself published. And if in addition one comes at the idea of eternal recurrence from the perspective of

the Buddhist doctrine of "momentariness" (*kṣaṇikavāda*), one se-
cures a second advantage in tackling this almost impenetrable core
of Nietzsche's thought.[23]

The advantages of this kind of approach are clearly evident
from the treatment of Nietzsche in *The Self-Overcoming of Nihilism*.
Of particular interest is the fact that, when dealing with some of the
more difficult aspects of the idea of recurrence, Nishitani has especially frequent recourse to language that is rich with connotations
from Mahāyāna Buddhism. Some of the implications and connotations of this language are sketched in the relevant notes to the discussion of the major imagistic presentations of the idea of
recurrence in *Thus Spoke Zarathustra* (see below, chapter four, secs. 4
and 5).

But perhaps the most interesting feature of Nishitani's reading
of Nietzsche in this book is its appreciation of the radicality of
Nietzsche's undermining of the Western metaphysical tradition—especially when one contrasts it with Heidegger's estimation of Nietzsche's achievement. Through what one is tempted to call a "will-
full" misreading of the idea of will to power, Heidegger judges
Nietzsche's attempt to overcome metaphysics to have failed (thereby
leaving the way clear for Heidegger himself to be the first to succeed in this momentous enterprise). In spite of the fact that
Heidegger was giving lectures and seminars on Nietzsche's nihilism
throughout the time that Nishitani was studying with him, the latter's reading of Nietzsche in the present book remains independent
of the Heideggerian interpretation.[24] Nietzsche is seen here as having plumbed the abyss of the soul deeply and persistently enough
to have nihilism overcome itself—just as in Buddhism the relentless
engagement with nihility eventuates in an opening out into the
"field of emptiness."[25]

IV

*Here is the distinctively Heideggerian approach to the "fundamental
unity of creative nihilism and finitude" mentioned earlier in connection with Stirner and Nietzsche.*

Nishitani, from chapter 8 (below)

In the interests of establishing a context for the contribution of a
work that may at first glance look like a straightforward exposition

of a number of Western philosophers, it is appropriate to bear in mind the date of composition of Nishitani's text. Apart from the works of Löwith, no book on nihilism had been published in the West by 1949. The literature on Nietzsche up to that point had tended to be uncritically *pro* or *contra*, and Walter Kaufmann's *Nietzsche: Philosopher, Psychologist, Antichrist*, which did so much to get Nietzsche's work to be taken seriously as philosophy, was not to appear until the following year. The issue of nihilism in Nietzsche, so germane to an understanding of his thought as a whole, was not taken up at any length or depth until Heidegger's massive two-volume study, *Nietzsche*, appeared in 1961.

If the chapter on Heidegger in this book of Nishitani's appears at first sight somewhat pedestrian, one should reflect for a moment on the state of Heidegger scholarship in English in 1949.[26] The first English translation of any of Heidegger's works did not appear until that year, in the form of the collection of four essays edited and introduced by Werner Brock entitled *Existence and Being*. One factor behind the relative lack of discussion of Heidegger's ideas in English prior to this time was presumably Gilbert Ryle's review of *Sein und Zeit*, which had appeared in the journal *Mind* twenty years earlier.[27] The next major engagement with Heidegger on the Western front was Rudolf Carnap's well known "refutation," which appeared in *Erkenntnis* in 1931, "The Overcoming of Metaphysics through Logical Analysis." If Nietzsche's ideal was to philosophize with a hammer, to wield a blunt instrument as delicately as one would employ a tuning fork, Carnap's was apparently to turn Occam's razor into the pathologist's scalpel—except that he was operating on the wrong corpus.[28]

It was not until the early forties, with the founding of the journal *Philosophy and Phenomenological Research*, that articles began to appear in the United States showing some appreciation of Heidegger's philosophical project. Nevertheless, it is safe to say that by 1949 no major discussion of Heidegger's work had appeared in English. And yet it was by no means unusual that Nishitani should have devoted a chapter of his book to Heidegger, given the history of the reception of the latter's ideas in Japan. In fact this history is itself so little known in contemporary Western scholarship on Heidegger that it deserves a few sentences of exposition.[29]

The first Japanese philosopher to have studied with Heidegger was Tanabe Hajime, who went to Freiburg in the early twenties and in the course of the following ten years published several major essays on Heidegger's thought.[30] He was followed by such thinkers as Watsuji Tetsurō, Kuki Shūzō, and Miki Kiyoshi, whose subsequent writings helped to further the dissemination of Heidegger's ideas in Japan. A perusal of the chronological listing of the secondary literature on Heidegger in Sass's first bibliography shows that from the early twenties until the publication of *The Self-Overcoming of Nihilism* in 1949 dozens of substantive pieces on Heidegger were published in Japanese. The formidable volume of this literature, the flow of which continues unabated to this day, derives in part from the speed and diligence with which the Japanese have traditionally produced translations of Heidegger's works. The first translation of *Sein und Zeit* into a foreign language was *Sonzai to jikan*, published in Tokyo in 1939. Two retranslations had appeared in Japanese by the time the first (and, as yet, only) English translation was published in 1962, and a further *three* versions have appeared in Japanese since then.[31]

It is not surprising, given Nishitani's fundamental concern with religion, that he should have been interested in the philosophy of Kierkegaard, although the treatment in *The Self-Overcoming of Nihilism* does not give an adequate sense of the depth of that interest. What is remarkable, however, is his engagement with some of the ideas of Max Stirner, who was relatively unknown in Japan at the time. While Stirner has been largely neglected in the West, since the publication of Nishitani's book he has come to exert a persistent fascination on Japanese literati.[32] To the extent that the stereotypical view of Japanese society as suppressive of individualism is valid, it is not surprising that there should be such a strong intellectual interest there in the extremest advocate of the individual the individualistic West has produced. But the intriguing thing about Nishitani's engagement with Stirner is the way his approaching him from a Zen perspective offers an original reading of a number of key passages concerning the ideas of "creative nothing" and the "ceaseless perishing" of the ego.[33]

Given the recent outbursts of nationalistic sentiment from various quarters in Japan, Nishitani's short but rich chapter on "The Meaning of Nihilism for the Japanese" may be one of the most timely of the book. The author has actually been severely criticized for his "right-wing" stance in a round-table discussion that took place shortly after the outbreak of the Pacific War, transcriptions of which were published in the periodical *Chūō kōron*.[34] But a careful reading of the second section of chapter nine will make it clear that Nishitani's remarks concerning a reappropriation of the Japanese spirit are made in the spirit of a Nietzschean "redemption" of what is valuable in the tradition, and embody a stance that no more inclines toward nationalism than does that of Nietzsche—that proto-internationalist and "good European." And in fact the implication of this aspect of Nishitani's discussion, which makes it so relevant to the contemporary situation, is precisely that an outbreak of nationalism is a sure sign that the project of letting nihilism overcome itself has failed, that the experiential inquiry into the self has not gone deep enough.[35]

The discussion of Buddhism and nihilism at the end of chapter nine together with the reflections on atheism in the Appendix constitute a helpful introduction to the author's mature thought as articulated in *Religion and Nothingness*. In fact the present text is an indispensable aid to the full understanding of the later book, which is a more difficult work to fathom than an acquaintance with its surface might suggest. The two texts complement one another as records of a shift of emphasis in the author's thought. In the earlier book the primary themes stem from European philosophy, with Zen and Buddhist ideas constituting a background that is so unobtrusive as to be easily overlooked. In *Religion and Nothingness* the priorities are reversed. There the dominant ethos is of Zen, and the Western philosophical ideas constitute occasional connective elements and points of reference.

If the sentiment of nihilism was a sufficiently powerful, if largely subliminal, presence in the Japan of 1949 for Nishitani to have devoted a long series of talks to the topic, it is all the more so today as a result of the recent burgeoning of material prosperity in that country. It seemed fitting to be in Japan while preparing the first draft of the translation, since so many things about the world beyond the work-room confirmed the suspicion that Nishitani's ideas in this book have become even more vitally relevant to the present situation than they were when first proposed. Nor is this to suggest that the problem of nihilism has been faced, far less overcome, in the "postmodern" West—as evidenced in the way it has resurfaced in the mainstream of contemporary thinking on this side of the Pacific. A remarkable feature of the current resurgence of interest in Nietzsche is the number of studies devoted to his confrontation with nihilism, and in particular to the political and pedagogical implications of this confrontation.[36]

V

"The wasteland grows: woe to whomever conceals wastelands!"

Thus Spoke Zarathustra

In the final stages of preparing the manuscript for publication in the Nanzan Studies in Religion and Culture, the general editor of the series, James Heisig, and I paid a visit to Professor Nishitani's home in Kyoto to give a brief account of the state of the project. We sat for several hours, late into the night, in his small book-filled study, with the sounds of the early summer rain falling in the small garden just outside the opened sliding doors providing the perfect background to the conversation.

Much of our talk circled, appropriately enough, around nothing. In speaking of the Zen conception of the self, Nishitani quoted his favorite saying of Saint Paul: "It is no longer I who live but Christ who lives in me." " *Who* is speaking here?" is then his question—one he has been asking himself for decades. It is evidently not the "I" or the "me"; nor does it appear to be Christ either. Who, then, is it? "Just who is this self?"

Later in the evening, the question recurred in a different form. Always in this room, it seems, there is a single rose in a bamboo vase that stands on a shelf above the table. A piece of tape covering a crack in the bamboo contributes somehow to the "rightness" of the ensemble. Looking over at the rose, Nishitani asked in quiet puzzlement, "*Where* is the flower blooming? What about the locus of the unfolding of this rose? Where does it bloom from?" He went on to muse upon the notion of nature, especially in Spinoza's sense of *natura naturans*. And again it turned out to be the question of the self—not only the topic of the book we had just translated but the focal point of all the author's thinking.

Later still, he spoke of the Zen idea of "going to the mountain" in retreat from the world, remarking on the surprising power of the distractions even after an escape from the busyness of everyday urban life. Then the sound of the wind or the birds becomes every bit as disruptive to one's practice as the noise of the traffic or the neighbors was in the city. The final, most difficult task is to retain whatever understanding has been attained through contemplative isolation after the return to everyday life. Or, in terms of an example that suggested itself some time later: the ability to retain the security of the monk sunk in meditation in the mountain-top monastery while negotiating the rush-hour traffic after a trying day at work is the mark of one's being genuinely on the Way.

The differences between city and country do appear, however, to have an effect with regard to the *onset* of nihilism, to the kinds of experience that might put one underway in the first place. In an environment of relatively untouched nature, what Nishitani calls the "abyss of nihility" is less likely to yawn; the question of the point of it all is not acutely pressing. Things in nature are what they are, and do what they do "without why"; the drives of life operate simply, and perpetuate themselves, without there being any external *telos*, any end or point to the process. In the realm of natural phenomena, in the midst of the grand cycles of nature, nihilism is not even possible, let alone actual.

If certain features of the modern city are especially conducive to nihilism—even while at the same time covering it over—they operate in Tokyo (site of the first phase of the translation) at full pitch. In a city where such a huge population does so much—and so much moving—in the course of a day, and in an environment so distanced from the natural, nihilistic moods are more likely to arise in the event that any kind of break occurs in the routine. In the ineluctable awareness of the active presence of multitudes of one's fellow human beings devoting their energies toward work and recreation—both as means to survival and distraction—the question of the point of it all is more apt to arise with some force. One comes to appreciate Heidegger's saying that we exist for the sake of one "in-order-to" (*wozu*) after another, all the way down to the final "for the-sake-of-which" (*worumwillen*)—which may be ultimately in vain: for the sake of nothing at all.

Or, farther back, a classic but seldom cited aphorism from Nietzsche's *Gay Science* imparts a deeper resonance to Nietzsche's nihilism which finds its counterpart in Nishitani's thinking:

> *The thought of death*—It gives me a melancholy pleasure to live in the midst of this jumble of little lanes, needs, and voices: how much enjoyment, impatience, and desire, how much thirsty life and intoxication with life comes to light at every moment! And yet it will soon be so still for all these noisy, living, life-thirsty people! How his shadow stands behind each one of them, as his dark fellow traveler! . . . the hour is near, and the ocean [of death] and its desolate silence are waiting impatiently behind all of this noise—so covetous and certain of their prey. And each and every one of them supposes that the heretofore means little or nothing and that the near future is everything: hence this haste, this clamor, this drowning out and overreaching of each other! Everyone wants to be the first in this future—and yet it is death and deathly silence that are alone certain and common to all in this future! How strange that this sole certainty and common ele-

ment has almost no effect on people, and that nothing is *farther* from their minds than the feeling that they form a broth-
erhood of death! (*GS* 278)

This idea is echoed in the magnificent passage in *Religion and Nothingness* where Nishitani discusses the Zen saying "Death's heads all
over the field [of existence]." Invoking a double vision of places full
of life, such as the Ginza or Broadway, as being simultaneously
fields of death, he goes on to quote T. S. Eliot's lines from *The Wasteland* concerning the procession of the dead across London Bridge:

A crowd flowed over London Bridge, so many,
I had not thought death had undone so many.

The prospect of the torrents of the living and working being
pumped through the arteries of the big city of today is more overwhelming in mass and intensity than it was forty years ago, or than
the rush-hour crowds of London were in the thirties. And yet it is
that very mass which keeps the population from seeing, in Nishitani's telling image, "in double exposure, a picture of the dead"; and
that intensity which keeps them from hearing "the desolate silence
of death," from becoming aware of the "abyss of nihility" upon
which the whole world is so precariously perched.[37]

It is because these things do not pass, but rather persist or
recur, that nihilism was not merely a transient phase in the milieu
of post-war Japan. Recent conversations with Nishitani have served
to confirm that there is indeed a point not only to writing a book
about nihilism but also to translating such a work—especially if a
few readers are drawn to reflect upon the point of it all. Sitting and
talking in the beneficent presence of so cosmopolitan a soul, one
comes to appreciate more and more the point of translating that
voice's discourses on nihilism for a larger audience. The point is the
same as the one to be made by each individual self on its own—
itself something attained only through the persistent practice of letting nihilism overcome itself.

Graham Parkes
Honolulu 1989

Notes on Texts

A history of the text of *Nihirizumu* is given in the following translation of the Postscript to the latest edition of *Nihirizumu* (Volume 8 of
the *Collected Works of Nishitani Keiji*), written by the successor to
Nishitani's Chair at Kyoto University, Professor Ueda Shizuteru:

> For the publication of *Nihirizumu* in volume 8 of the *Collected
> Works*, the essay "The Problem of Atheism" has been included
> as an appendix. The history of *Nihirizumu* as a single volume is
> as follows.
>
> Beginning in May of 1949, Professor Nishitani gave several
> talks on nihilism to a small group. Out of these talks a mono-
> graph on European nihilism, focusing on Nietzsche, was pub-
> lished as a volume in the *Atene Shinshō* series by Kōbundō
> publishers in the autumn of the same year. This constitutes
> chapters 1 to 7 of *Nihirizumu* [*chapters 1–4, 6, 8 and 9 of the
> present translation*].
>
> After that there was a change at the publishers, and publica-
> tion was discontinued. During that period Professor Nishitani
> felt the necessity to expand the chapter on Heidegger, and in-
> tended to do so in view of the importance of the inquiry into
> the essence of nihilism in the later Heidegger. However, in
> 1966 the book was republished without modifications as a new
> edition of *Nihirizumu* by Sōbunsha through the International
> Institute for Japanese Studies in Nishinomiya. At that time the
> essay "Nihilism in Nietzsche—Existence," which had origi-
> nally been contributed to the volume *Niichie Kenkyū (Nietzsche
> Studies)* edited by Higami Hidehiro and published in 1952, was
> added as an appendix [chapter 5 of the present translation].
>
> From the ninth printing of the new edition in 1972, the es-
> say "Nihilism in Russia" was added [now chapter 7] to pro-
> duce the expanded edition of *Nihirizumu*. This essay had been
> published as a volume in the series *Atene Bunko* by Kōbundō in
> 1949. It was one volume of a planned series of three on the

topic of Dostoevsky's nihilism, from talks which were delivered after the talks on Western European nihilism mentioned above. Two further volumes were to trace the deepening of nihilism in Dostoevsky under the headings of nihilism "as action," "as being," and "as spirit," but they have not yet seen publication.

Of the three topics the author originally intended to cover when he began his talks on nihilism in May of 1949, "Nietzsche, Dostoevsky, and Buddhism," the section of Western European nihilism which focused on Nietzsche and about one third of the section on Dostoevsky together constitute the text of *Nihirizumu*. Many of Professor Nishitani's discussions of Dostoevsky's nihilism have remained unpublished, but the author's views on Dostoevsky are to be found in numerous places in the book *Kyōdō tōgi Dosutoefusukii no tetsugaku [A Discussion of Dostoevsky's Philosophy,* with Watsuji Tetsurō] (Kōbundō, 1950). The issue of nihilism and Buddhism is elaborated in a broader and deeper context in chapters 3 and 4 of the author's *Shūkyō towa nanika [Religion and Nothingness]* (Sōbunsha, 1961), "Nihility and Śūnyatā" and "The Standpoint of Śūnyatā," which is reprinted as volume 10 of the *Collected Works.*

The essay "The Problem of Atheism" was originally contributed to a volume of Collected Papers commemorating the fiftieth anniversary of the Department of Literature at Kyoto University in 1956.

The life-current of Professor Nishitani's thinking flows throughout the present volume which takes nihilism as the principal theme. As he himself puts it: "The fundamental task for me, before philosophy and through philosophy, has been, in short, the overcoming of nihilism through nihilism" ("My Philosophical Starting Point").

Ueda Shizuteru
August 16, 1986

The present translation is based on this latest edition of the text. The appendix on Nietzsche and Existence has been inserted, in the interests of continuity, as chapter 5, after the two original Nietzsche chapters. This transposition prompted the excision of several sentences here and there that would otherwise have replicated remarks made in the earlier two chapters. The logic and chronology of the argument suggested the insertion of the appendix on Russian nihilism as chapter 7, after the chapter on Stirner. The original final chapter (now chapter 9) and the Appendix on atheism provide an appropriate transition to the ideas to be developed in the later *Religion and Nothingness.*

For the translation of Nishitani's quotations or paraphrases from works in German, the original texts were used whenever they could be found. (The citation of sources has not traditionally been a major concern in Japanese scholarship.) Since most modern Japanese thinkers work primarily in European philosophy, when they write they frequently have in mind some technical term in German or French philosophy; the attempt simply to translate the Japanese term without "triangulating" through the European word of which it is a translation will often mislead or result in incoherence. In the present instance it was thought best to translate from the original European-language text while "inclining" toward Nishitani's Japanese rendering. In translating a passage from Nietzsche, for example, one checks the Japanese version at every step; often a particular word, or image, or phrase of the original could go in several directions in English—so that one can then let the choice of direction be guided by the Japanese. When the Japanese diverged too far from the original, the latter was given priority and the connotations of the Japanese remarked in an endnote.

In the case of Nietzsche's texts in particular, where ambiguity is often deliberately nuanced, this technique yielded some translations that were freshly illuminating—even to one already familiar with Nietzsche's works. Since some important features of Nishitani's reading of Nietzsche come across by way of his translations (all of which were his own), it was thought appropriate to incline to them rather than simply to use extant English translations of the relevant passages from Nietzsche.

The book as originally published contained no footnotes, the few references that there were being given in the body of the text. The author's references to passages from Schopenhauer, Kierkegaard, Stirner, Nietzsche, and Heidegger have been retained in parentheses, though they have been changed to refer to the best or most accessible English translations. Nishitani's references to Nietzsche's works are to the volume and page numbers of the *Grossoktavausgabe* of the *Werke* in twenty volumes, published by Kröner. Passages from the *Nachlass* have been referred to the appropriate section numbers of *Der Wille zur Macht (The Will to Power)* in cases where they can be found in this edition; otherwise the original references to the *Grossoktavausgabe* have been retained. References to works Nietzsche himself had published are to the title and aphorism number, so that they can be found easily in any edition. (In the case of *Zarathustra*, the Part is cited in Roman numerals and the chapter in Arabic.) References in square brackets and all the endnotes have been supplied by the translator.

The simple translation of the title of the original Japanese text would be *Nihilism*, but since several books of that name have been published in Western languages we thought it appropriate, with the approval of the author, to amplify it somewhat for the English edition. It was felt that the new title evokes the spirit of the text more fully—especially insofar as it obviates the impression that nihilism is to be overcome by means of something other than itself.

Preface to the First Edition[1]

In May of this year I had the opportunity to give several talks on the topic of nihilism. Initially I intended to focus on the three themes of Nietzsche, Dostoevsky, and Buddhism. When I was twenty, the figures of Nietzsche and Dostoevsky burned a lasting impression deep into my soul—as I suppose they may still do to many young people even today—and the tremors I experienced at that time have continued to make my heart tremble ever since.[2] The final theme, of Buddhist "emptiness,"[3] came to capture my interest more gradually. The connections among these three topics are not merely arbitrary or external. The nihilism that Dostoevsky plumbed so deeply has important connections with that of Nietzsche, as a number of critics have pointed out; and Nietzsche considers what he calls European nihilism to be the European form of Buddhism. Even though there may be in Nietzsche a radical misunderstanding of the spirit of Buddhism, the fact that he considered it in relation to nihilism shows how well attuned he was to the real issue. It was considerations such as these that inclined me toward these three themes in my discussion of nihilism.

When I actually began the talks, I found that my remarks on Nietzsche, as well as the discussions of Stirner and Heidegger (which were originally intended only as supplements), ended up being longer than expected, and the talk on Dostoevsky also went well beyond the scheduled limit. Upon publishing the talks in *Atene Shinshō*, it was decided to combine those dealing with Western European nihilism in a single volume. The reason for beginning with Nietzsche and not following chronological order was that I found the spirit of nihilism to be manifested most deeply and clearly in him.

The nihilism that I have made the issue here is no merely vague nihilistic feeling or trend; it is rather something that has become clearly self-conscious. Moreover, it is a nihilism that is in some sense the self-overcoming of what is usually called nihilism. In this sense the succession of nihilists represents a history of the all-out struggle of subjectivity against domination or suppression by something outside of subjectivity. In Dostoevsky and Nietzsche the struggle undertaken for the sake of the "I" intersects at right angles the struggle against the "ego." In this twofold struggle two new paths are opened up: in Dostoevsky the path toward "God," and in Nietzsche the way toward a new form of human being which goes beyond previous forms—namely, the *Übermensch.* Each of these approaches attempts to probe the standpoint in which the self itself can truly stand at the point where human nature is transcended in the crisis of the breakdown of modern humanism. As Berdyaev writes in his remarkable study of Dostoevsky:

> The works of Dostoevsky point not only to a crisis in humanism but to its very destruction and inner condemnation. In view of this his name merits renown as much as Nietzsche's. They have made it impossible to go back to rationalistic humanism with its self satisfaction. The path leads further toward Christ, the God-man, or the overman, the man-God, and one can no longer stand firm on the basis of things human.[4]

What these figures have in common—at least in the realm of spirit—with the medieval spiritualists is obvious. This is not to say that they are medieval; they are more modern than anything else. Dostoevsky and Nietzsche by no means solved everything, but there is no doubt that through their struggle they turned the European spirit in the direction of what is its profoundest dimension.

Each of the representative figures who mark the course of nihilism in Western Europe developed a quite different form of ideas. While the manifestations of nihilism are clear in each of them, a careful examination of their thought seems to reveal a basic common framework. I have attempted to draw out this framework as *the fundamental integration of creative nihilism and finitude.* From this standpoint I perceive signs of a new orientation forming in the depths of the spirit of modern Europe, and I also recognize that this spirit is beginning to open up a horizon for important contacts with Buddhism.[5] If there be any point to adding still another study to the many works on nihilism already existing in the West and in Japan, it is the attempt to pursue the ground of nihilism to the level of just such a standpoint.[6]

October 11, 1949

Chapter One

Nihilism as Existence

1. Two Problems

I have been asked to speak about nihilism, which has become something of a trend in the post-war era. The existential philosophies of Sartre, Heidegger, and others—which are major elements in contemporary intellectual history—also have connections with nihilism. I suspect that this accounts to a large extent for the desire to learn about the topic. But insofar as this approach to nihilism is not itself nihilistic, I sense that it may obstruct our understanding of the matter at hand. This fact itself is in some sense a symptom of nihilism—and particularly of nihilism in Japan. I shall begin, then, by focusing on these two points: the non-nihilistic nature of our way of inquiry, and the nature of nihilism in Japan which this reflects.

However appropriate a detached spirit of inquiry may be for other intellectual problems, in the case of existentialism and nihilism it is inappropriate. The attitude of wanting to know *about* nihilism, or the desire to know in order not to be left behind in conversation, means that from the start one is questioning from the standpoint of "society" and not from "the self itself." In other words, the questioning is no more than a topic of conversation. But if nihilism is anything, it is first of all a problem of the self. And it becomes such a problem only when the self becomes a problem, when the ground of the existence called "self" becomes a problem for itself. When the problem of nihilism is posed apart from the self, or as a problem of society in general, it loses the special genuineness that distinguishes it from other problems. Thinking about the issue by surveying it as an objective observer cannot touch the heart of the matter. This is what makes the question of nihilism the radical question it is.

1

However, to go a step further, even when it is made an important issue intellectually and the self is seen as the locus of the issue, there is still the danger that nihilism will after all be transformed into an objective issue within the self. No matter how much it becomes a problem of one's own self, as long as the standpoint of "observation" is present, the self remains split in two: the observing self and the self that is observed. The standpoint of observation remains, and to that extent neither the existential way of being nor the issue of nihilism can become present to the self itself.

Essentially, nihilism and Existence[1] break down the standpoint of the observing self in which the self that sees and the self that is seen are separated. When the existence of the self becomes a question mark, an unknown X, and when nihility[2] is experienced behind the existence of the self or at its ground, one can no longer afford to have two separate selves—the questioning self and the self that is questioned. The self is *compelled* to become one, and the self itself *resolves* not to conceal or evade this. In this resolve of the self, the self *becomes* one—it *becomes* the self as such. Only here does the actual existence[3] of the self become the question of the self. To put it another way: "I" stand on the standpoint of actual existence, which makes my own self an X. This is entirely different from an objective or reflective mode of thinking. One can follow Kierkegaard and Nietzsche in calling it a matter of thinking "with passion" (*leidenschaftlich*), or else Heidegger, when he tries to understand being through moods or *pathos* (*stimmungsmässig*). Here subjectivity in the true sense appears for the first time: the standpoint arises in which one strives resolutely to be oneself and to seek the ground of one's actual existence. It is also here that nihility is revealed for the first time. By being thrown into nihility, the self is revealed to itself. Only in such encounters does nihilism (like death) become a real question.

In short, nihilism refuses treatment as merely an *external* problem for one's self, or even *contemplation* as a problem internal to each individual self. This is the essence of nihilism. This is the most primordial and fundamental of the various refusals that nihilism presents. Nihilism demands that each individual carry out an experiment within the self. So much, in broad outline, on the first point, to which we shall return later.

The second point concerns the relation of nihilism to our present situation in Japan. From what has been said above, it would seem that the roots of nihilism reach down into the essence of what it is to be human, and as such it represents an eternal problem transcending particular times or places. Still, what we call nihilism today is a historical concept referring to a particular phenomenon, to something that arose in a place called Europe and in the spiritual situation of the modern era. It arose among Europeans in their attempt to understand the being of the self. Would it not then be a grave mistake for the Japanese, who are far from Europe and whose historical tradition and culture are different, to make an issue of nihilism only in personalistic terms? If so, can we do anything more than approach the issue from the outside and observe it, merely to satisfy our curiosity and intellectual desire?

The answer is relatively simple. While the spirit of nihilism has its origin in Europe, it is by no means unrelated to us in the modern era. We have been baptized in European culture, and European education has more or less become our own. The nihilistic mood of "post-war lethargy" and the vogue of existential philosophy and nihilistic thinking are no mere curiosity about new ideas in the world. Nihilism is also our own problem. But it is also true that behind this nihilistic mood and the vogue of nihilistic thinking there lurks the *unique* character of the issue of nihilism in Japan. This does not mean that we can dismiss the problem as the inevitable outcome of our appropriation of European ideas. This second issue is at once the point of departure and the final destination of our inquiry.[4] Let us now look more closely at the implication of these two points.

2. Nihilism and the Philosophy of History

On the one hand, nihilism is a problem that transcends time and space and is rooted in the essence of human being, an existential problem in which the being of the self is revealed to the self itself as something groundless. On the other hand, it is a historical and social phenomenon, an object of the study of history. The phenomenon of nihilism shows that our historical life has lost its ground as objective spirit, that the value system which supports this life has broken down, and that the entirety of social and historical life has loosened itself from its foundations. Nihilism is a sign of the collapse of the social order externally and of spiritual decay internally—and as such signifies a time of great upheaval. Viewed in this way, one might say that it is a general phenomenon that occurs from time to time in the course of history. The mood of post-war Japan would be one such instance.

When these two viewpoints are integrated, and nihilism as a general historical phenomenon is investigated right down to its philosophical ground, it becomes the object of the *philosophy of history*. This third step is unavoidable. As soon as the ground which has supported historical life both within and without begins to be perceived as something unreliable, an immense void[5] begins to open up within history. Profound anxiety shakes the foundation of human being; and the more foundational the supporting ground had been, the greater the void and the deeper the anxiety. If the ground is an ultimate one—if it has to do with a goal for human existence, a direction for life, a doctrine on the meaning of existence, or any similarly basic metaphysical issue—then its loss ushers in an abyssal nihility at the basis of human history.

In this kind of nihility, "being" itself is now transformed into a problem. Up until this point human existence had a clear and eternal meaning, a way in which to live. To follow that way or not was a matter of personal choice. But now existence is deprived of such meaning; it stands before nihility as having been stripped naked, a question mark for itself. And this in turn transforms the world itself into a question. The fabric of history is rent asunder, and the "world" in which we live reveals itself as an abyss.[6] From the bottom of the self the world and the self together become a question—at the same time a historical and a metaphysical question.

Such a fundamental question belongs to the philosophy of history, but in such a way that the very nature of the philosophy of history and its previous standpoint itself becomes part of the problem. In seeking the reasons for the occurrence of nihilism as a historical phenomenon, the philosophy of history must dig down to its ultimate ground. There it will question the metaphysical and to this extent transcendent ground of history that is essentially rooted in human existence. And with this the metaphysical foundation of history, becomes a problem. The nihilism of various epochs is "experientially understood"[7] as the problem of the self, and thus the issue of nihilism becomes the issue of the philosophy of history by way of philosophical anthropolgy. Here nihilism is disclosed as a universal phenomenon—appearing, for example, at the end of the ancient period or the medieval period in the West, and in Japan in the *mappō* thinking of the Kamakura period.[8] Karl Jaspers categorizes various stages and forms of nihilism in his book *Psychologie der Weltanschauungen*, and some aspects of his treatment correspond to my discussion above.[9] But does this approach do the question full justice?

The philosophy of history understands nihilism as a historical *phenomenon*, its approach being by way of *historical*-philosophical understanding. But it also has to do with the nature of human existence within history, and thus displays features of *philosophical-historical* understanding. The way the philosophy of history understands nihilism means that these two aspects are one in the *self* of the philosopher of history, who experiences the problem of the essence of "humanity" as a problem of the self, and thereby understands both history and humanity philosophically. The philosopher of history pursues historical problems to their philosophical ground as problems about the essence of being human. The metaphysical essence of human existence and its historical manifestations are correlatives, whose connections are is gradually opened up with the "self" of the inquirer. In spite of this, inquiry in the philosophy of history has remained within the standpoint of reflective observation: the one who observes and the one who is observed have been separated. Even though traditional philosophy of history may approach its subject matter from out of the lived experience of the self, its standpoint remains one of *observing*. The habit of separating essence and phenomenon is a residue of just this approach. Even when life is taken as the central problematic of history, there is still a chance that one is not yet questioning in a truly *historical* way.

Thus, in the fourth place, there must be a way of inquiring into history that is fundamentally different from the way the philosophy of history has been conducted up until now. The questioning itself must be *historical* and the inquirer unified within history. What is more, the inquiry must be conducted "with passion" and existentially, so that the relationship between essence and phenomenon in history and humanity is realized existentially and thoroughly within historical Existence. In other words, the great historical problems need to become a problem of the self. In Nietzsche's terms, the history of humankind has to be made the history of the self itself, and history has to be understood from the standpoint of Existence. The great problems of history must find a place of "passionate" confrontation within the self.

In such an existential understanding of history the fundamentally historical nature of human existence, or what Nietzsche calls its essentially temporal nature, discloses itself for the first time, and the true significance of history as the locus of the "transhistorical" and metaphysical comes to be realized. What we call "history" becomes an encounter with external problems, and this encounter constitutes historical Existence.

In shifting away from a standpoint of observation to one of Existence, history becomes a locus of existential encounter with the metaphysical, and the philosophy of history makes genuine contact with history. Only in this context can we ask after the meaning of nihilism; and only with the emergence of nihilism is this standpoint of philosophical-historical inquiry as Existence realized.

3. European Nihilism

It was in modern Europe that the question of historical reality and its metaphysical ground, the philosophical ground of historical life, came to be asked *historically*. The reasons for this are manifold. First of all, what is called *historical consciousness* emerged largely from the modern spirit of Europe. The connection between metaphysics, the inquiry into the ground of being, and historical consciousness had been made since the eighteenth century through the philosophy of history, and subsequent metaphysical inquiry into the ground of being came to be conducted within the explicit context of history. Principles such as nature, reason, *idea*, and so on came to be seen as concretely realized only within history. This approach, needless to say, reached its consummate expression in Hegel. But both before and through Hegel these metaphysical principles historically concrete through they were, were still considered fundamentally transhistorical—whether derived from a transhistorical God or, as in the case of Spinoza, through nature's being equated with God. Beneath it all lay the old metaphysics handed down from the Greeks, with its emphasis on contemplating the world of true, transtemporal Being that lay concealed behind the world of temporal becoming. As long as this view held sway, the questioning of the ultimate metaphysical ground of history could not become genuinely historical.[10] Historical consciousness required a second stage of development.

After Hegel, there began the rapid collapse of metaphysics and moralities based on God or a world of "true Being." The worldview that had supported the spiritual life of Europe for more than two thousand years was all at once thrown into question. Faith in God and the eternal world and their accompanying conceptions became no more than historically conditioned ideas. What had once been considered transhistorical now began to be seen as products of history. With this an abyssal nihility opened up at the ground of history and self-being, and everything turned into a question mark. Sincerely to acknowledge this kind of despair as despair and at least to try to live in sincerity without avoiding or diverting it—or, like Nietzsche, to carry out its consequences voluntarily and thoroughly on one's own, and to seek to confront the spirit that had controlled all of history up until then—this would be nihilism.

In other words, nihilism is the transition from the standpoint of observation to that of "passionate" Existence. It means taking the entirety of history upon oneself as a history of the self, shifting the metaphysical ground of that history to the ground of the self, and saying "No" to it in this ground. It is at the same time to deny oneself the ground of the being of the self given by history and voluntarily to demolish the ground which has become false, turning the being of the self into a question mark. To disclose the nihility at the ground of the self is to live in sincerity, and within such sincerity the self becomes truly itself. When the idea of a transhistorical world of "true Being" has become a mere chimera, then the passion for the "nihility" which negates that world points to sincerity and the standpoint of Existence.

When nihility took the place of transhistorical true Being, fundamental inquiry into history became possible for the first time. It also became possible for the self that questions the ground of history and the self to overcome its reflective duality and to be unified in full existential *pathos*. This kind of self-conscious and resolute nihilism appears in its greatest and profoundest form in Nietzsche, and is represented in Stirner before him and Heidegger after him. Philosophy of history from the standpoint of Existence became possible only when it had arrived at nihilism by way of the two-stage development of historical consciousness discussed above. The disclosure of nothingness[11] at the deepest transcendent ground of history and the self makes a metaphysics of history from the standpoint of Existence possible.

Nihilism as we understand it today is the product of a particular epoch, the modern period in Europe. It represents the current achievement of the European spirit, a provisional outcome of the whole of history in a modern European expression that set itself up against everything that had gone before. The problem of how to live came to be fused with the problem of how to interpret history, in particular European history. The point at which the two questions converged became the historical-existential standpoint. The inquiry into history was wholly metaphysical and yet in no way detached from history. Metaphysics itself became a problem of history and of the epoch itself. The eternal inquiry into what it means to be a self was transfigured into an inquiry into historical actuality, and Existence became *fundamentally* historical. Such was the state of affairs that came to light in nihilism, whose standpoint is philosophical not in spite of its being entirely historical but because of it.

The historical-existential standpoint also gave European nihilism its dual quality as a nihilism that overcomes nihilism. On the one hand, it was an "active" nihilism whose basic critique undermined the very ground of history and the self. On the other, this "Nothing," without God or Truth actually harbored within itself the seeds of a turn to a great affirmation in which existential nothingness replaced God as the creative force.

It seems to be in Dostoevsky and Nietzsche that European nihilism was first articulated in this full and fundamental sense, with all its historical and a metaphysical implications. Nietzsche in particular pursued the consequences of nihilism relentlessly and without faltering—an achievement in which he took considerable pride. In the Preface to *The Will to Power* he speaks of himself as "the first consummate nihilist in Europe, who has himself already lived nihilism through to the end in himself—who has it behind him, beneath him, outside of him" [*WP*, Preface, § 3]. Accordingly, it is with Nietzsche that our account of nihilism's rise to consciousness will begin.

Chapter Two

From Realism to Nihilism:

Hegel, Schopenhauer, Kierkegaard, Feuerbach

1. Hegel's Absolute Idealism and Radical Realism

Around the middle of the last century in Europe, from 1830 until 1850, symptoms of a profound crisis began to appear in everyday life and in the spiritual life. In terms of intellectual history, the period is generally considered to represent a turn from idealism to realism and positivism. The trend came to the fore throughout philosophy, politics, ethics, and the arts. People of the time summed up their basic attitude toward life in the word *Realität*, a catchword of the age.

It was in Germany that this *Realität* was most radically and keenly pursued—and for good reasons. Hegel had developed idealism to the point of an absolute idealism, leaving realism no choice but to assume a radical—and even violent—form in its counter claims. Such was the atmosphere of the period marked by thinkers like Feuerbach, Bruno Bauer, Stirner, Marx, and Nietzsche—as well as Kierkegaard. And even today their radical realism remains an issue for us.

The absoluteness of Hegel's absolute idealism comes down, roughly speaking, to this. Hegel's philosophy is a philosophy of *spirit*, where spirit in its self-conscious aspect contains reason, whose content in turn is the Idea (*Idee*). The activity of spirit consists in the actualization of the Idea, which is something like the content of the self-consciousness of spirit. On the one hand the Idea stands as the transtemporal or transhistorical "Concept" [*Begriff*] which partakes of eternity, and on the other the Concept makes itself concrete in temporal or historical reality. The integration or identification of temporality and transtemporality is what Hegel calls the Idea. On this view things that are merely ideal, in the sense of not being actualized, are not truly Ideas. The Idea is not something subjective, thought about in the mind, or contained within consciousness. Conversely, reality is grasped as truly real Being only when it is grasped as the actualization of the Idea. Hegel sums up this view in his famous statement: "*What is rational is actual, and what is actual is rational.*" For him, the Idea is "the synthesis of the concept and existence."[1] This synthesis is the result of a dialectical movement in which the transtemporal is first realized (*realisiert*)[2] as actual things and events, and then from within real Being becomes aware of *Idealität* as its essence.

In general Hegel's philosophical system is not clear in its overall integration, but if one can take his *Logic* as developing the transtemporal aspect of the Idea, the aspect in which the Idea is established as the thought-content of divine reason, works like the *Philosophy of History* and *History of Philosophy* develop the aspect of the realization or actualization of the Idea in history. The integration of the two is his philosophical system itself, at whose apex stands the *Philosophy of Religion*. In Hegel's absolute religion (Christianity), God is manifest as Spirit and the human being rises to a standpoint of spirit corresponding to that Spirit. This highest stage is the world of pure spirit, which is the ultimate realm of Hegel's metaphysics. This is not, however, a world apart from history but a world actualized in and through history. The relationship between God as Spirit and human individuals as spirit is eternal life actualized within history. At the basis of this scheme lies the Christian religion with its Revelation of God in history and its belief in the communion of the divine and the human in the Spirit. It is here that Hegel's philosophy culminates, in a truth whose content realizes itself most fully in philosophy and religion.

In short, Hegel's view at once exhausts the inner dynamic in the "essence" of things to full actualization, as well as the dynamic in real Being that drives it to essentialization. More concretely, it is the historicization of the eternal and the eternalization of the historical. Speculation and philosophical thinking in Hegel see everything as the self-unfolding of the Idea from a standpoint where eternity and history are one. This is in some sense an idealization of real Being, but not an idealization or abstraction in the ordinary sense. It is a view of ideality in which the ideal promotes the real even at the cost of suppressing itself, mediates itself to reality, and thereby mediates and absorbs the real into itself from its ground. Ideality is absorbed into real Being in its self-denial, and from there essentializes Being and resurrects in the fullness of an ideality containing real Being. The relative standpoints of reality and ideality are made to negate one another, in order to be superseded[3] and integrated on a higher level. From the standpoint of such an absolute ideality, everything is the activity of "spirit," and everything comes to be seen as a world of the spirit—of individual subjective spirit, of objective spirit as ethical institutions such as law, society, or state, and of absolute spirit which manifests itself in art, religion, and philosophy.

Against such a standpoint of absolute spirit and thoroughgoing absolute ideality, it was clearly impossible for an ordinary realism to insist on its *Realität*. In Hegel's idealism, the standpoint of realism as formerly understood had been subjected to a radical negation, mediated, and taken up into *Idealität*. Only an equally extreme and radical realism could take a stand against it; and this meant an absolute negation of the ideality that had been projected on to reality as its eternal essence. It meant a radical self-negation of *Realität*, a kind of "purging of the blood," or self-deconstruction of the "spiritual" framework that had been erected within it. To put it more forcefully, *Realität* had to negate from within itself the very ideality that had elevated it to the status of divine thinking. A reality submitted to such absolute self-negation would have to be of the simplest and rawest nature. It would remain among things regarded as real Being, without itself being essentialized or idealized, as the "beingness" of real Being. It would have to be grasped as something immediate and simple within the most ordinary things.

Perception and its objects, impulses, and the fantasies that arise when impulses are not satisfied, the blind *will* to live, the *facticity* of a thing's actually existing, labor for the production of food—all these are instances of this simple and immediate *Realität*. To accommodate this fundamental reality, absolute idealism had held itself in check in order to enter into the real, encompassing it and giving it life in order to mediate it to the spiritual, rational, or conceptual domains of *Idealität*. In the end, the real was idealized, and what appeared to have been given life was actually most deeply suppressed. The ultimate line of resistance was the simple immediacy in reality—perception, matter, the blind will to live (Schopenhauer), freedom for evil or the facticity of experience (Schelling), Existence, or life. But the way to grasp such simple and immediate things could not itself be simple and immediate. To confront absolute *Idealität*, it must embrace a *Radikalität* fundamental and extreme enough to invert the Hegelian absolute mediation by passing through it. This standpoint of *Realität*, poised at the opposite pole of simple immediacy, was possible only after Hegel had made it necessary. An opposite dialectic was called for to push headlong against Hegel's dialectic based in God and absolute spirit, or else to attack it from the rear.

. The idea that the roots of radical realism lay in a subversive of Hegel's absolute idealism is common to Kierkegaard and Marx, as well as Schopenhauer and Nietzsche. To reclaim *Realität*, they conceived it by assuming a posture of radical paradox or irony with respect to absolute idealism.

The confrontation with absolute idealism was effected by "nullifying" the basic framework of absolute idealism. The standpoint of "spirit," which had evolved out of the metaphysics of reason inherited from Greek Platonism and the communion in Spirit (*pneuma*) that Christianity had established between God and humanity, was a key element in this framework. It was demonstrated how the whole standpoint was based on the most irrational and nonspiritual—that is, most simple and immediate—ordinary things, albeit in such a way that the resulting standpoint was unaware of the fact. This kind of ironical genealogy of the component elements of absolute idealism sought to undermine its claim to ultimate foundations—God, spirit, Idea—by exposing them as fictions and illusions arising out of the most earthly of things. With the insertion of the lowest and shallowest principle at a stratum just below the "highest" and most "profound" foundation of absolute idealism, the latter turned into empty nothing and collapsed into simple reality.

In Hegel, God as Spirit is understood as the highest essence, the supreme being (*Wesen*), and all else is considered mere appearance (*Schein*) as the self-projection of God's radiation of himself into himself. This is how the relation between *Schein* and *Wesen* is conceived in Hegel's *Logic*, where essence is the ground (*Grund*) of appearance. The more this relation internalizes itself, and the more appearance expresses essence, the more it returns to its ground and collapses into it (*zu Grunde gehen*).[4] Finite things decline into God and thereby reveal him. Now this very logic was turned against Hegel: God, the "highest essence," is considered mere appearance, and what was "mere appearance" becomes the most essential. This is the nature of the irony and paradox that radical realism opposed to Hegel's idealistic dialectic by itself assuming the form of a dialectic.

2. Schopenhauer—Will as Real—The Nullity of Existence

Thinkers like J. F. Herbart are remembered in the history of philosophy as having set up a philosophy of realism in opposition to German Idealism. But the more radical orientation we have been speaking of moved in three directions represented by Schopenhauer, Kierkegaard, and Feuerbach. Each of these currents gives voice to the deep crisis of the European spirit that lay behind the "breakdown" of Hegelian philosophy. Their critiques of idealism, each to a greater or lesser degree, helped precipitate and consummate that crisis. At the same time, Schopenhauer's metaphysics of will with its new possibility of "emancipation," Kierkegaard's existentialism with its new possibility of "faith," and Feuerbach's anthropology with its new possibility of "humanity" all tried to propose a way to overcome the crisis.

This is not the place to detail how this crisis came about. Among the probable causes we may mention the changes in political consciousness which followed in the wake of the French Revolution, the social anxiety over changes in the economic system resulting from the Industrial Revolution, and the rise of "liberalism." At a deeper level, the development of the natural sciences had brought a naturalistic worldview into prominence; the metaphysical worldview that had hitherto held sway was losing its credibility; and belief in Christianity was beginning to totter. Centuries before, Saint Augustine, under the influence of Platonism, had seen that visible, material things subject to birth and decay are not true beings, and that invisible, ideal things are. This had prompted him to abandon his skepticism and enter the Christian faith. The unity of Platonism and Christian faith in Augustine then became the basis of the European spirit throughout the medieval period and into the modern era. This basis now began to crumble. The positivistic-scientific spirit and social reform movements joined hands in the critique of religion and the Christian morality that had grounded social structures. The philosophy of Hegel represented the highest achievement of metaphysics up until then; it was, as Feuerbach put it, "the last rational supporting pillar of theology." The collapse of Hegel's philosophy therefore signalled the gradual encroachment of "nihilation" into the European spirit and was a portent of the nihilism to come. Insofar as the dark shadow of nihilism began to fall over radical realism as well, the latter may be understood as a resistance to its advance.

The emphasis that Schopenhauer places on the notion of "the real" in his philosophy is evident from the way he sees the history of modern philosophy mainly from the perspective of "the ideal and the real."[5] For Schopenhauer, the maintaining of the clear distinction between *das Ideale* and *das Reale* was the point of departure of all true philosophy. The reason he esteemed Kant so highly was

that Kant grounded reality in that which could not be totally idealized—the "thing-in-itself." Fichte, however, "eliminated the real entirely, leaving nothing but the ideal"; and Schelling "in his system
of the absolute identification of the real and the ideal declared the
whole distinction to be empty." Finally "the nadir," the philosophy
of Hegel, stepped in to claim that "what is thought *in abstracto* is as
such and immediately one with what objectively exists in itself . . .
Thus, everything that floats around (*spuken*) inside the skull would
be immediately true and real."[6] This then gives rise to "the dialectical self-movement of the concept," as expressed in the contention
that "it is not *we* who think, but concepts alone which carry out
the process of thought." This is the context for Schopenhauer's
claim that "the characteristics of my philosophical speculation
[consist in pursuing] what is ultimately and really given," and in
trying to reach the "ground" of things. Further, according to
Schopenhauer, the theism of Christianity conceived of will as transcending the things of the world and governing them through intellect, and named this will "God." By contrast, pantheism calls
God the will that works internally in all things. But will is not
something that works from the outside or the inside of things: all
things are themselves a manifestation of will as such. This will is
blind and without intellect, a "will to life" (*Wille zum Leben*), and
things are the appearance of will in visible form. This blind will to
life is therefore the ultimately real; it is nothing other than what
Kant calls the "thing-in-itself." This unitary will to life takes visible
form in the multiplicity of individual things, with time and space
serving as its principles of individuation as it were. From the perspective of will, which forms the innermost core of the world, the
visible "world as representation" is mere appearance, like images in
a dream.

　　From there, Schopenhauer goes on to emphasize the *nullity* of
all existence (*Parerga and Paralipomena* II, chap. 11 deals in particular
with this *Nichtigkeit*). Within time, "everything becomes nothing
under our fingertips at every moment." That everything passes
away in this manner reveals the nullity of the strivings of the will to
life. The will to life appears as desire in the individual things that
are its phenomena, and this desire harbors profound dissatisfaction.
As long as the will to life is operative, dissatisfaction arises ceaselessly from within. Therefore, life is essentially *suffering (Leiden)*.
Now when the desired is attained and dissatisfaction is momen-
tarily held in check, what has been attained becomes a burden.
Boredom (Langeweile) "attacks like a bird of prey that has been hov-
ering in wait." Boredom is insight into the essentially void nature of

our existence and the existence of all things, into their insubstantiality and nullity. Schopenhauer says further that human social intercourse also has its source in boredom, and that what we call "killing time" is the essential basis of social interaction. Existence, which is completely null, assumes the *appearance of reality* by enduring briefly within time; but even this endurance is no more than a succession of present moments, which ceaselessly turn into nihility. For all our pursuit of happiness, at the moment when our life comes to its end in death, it is all one and the same (*einerlei*) whether our life has been happy or unhappy. This is how Schopenhauer sees the nullity of existence grounded in the will to life. "The *will* to life exhibits itself in mere phenomena which all become absolutely *nothing*. However, this nihility together with phenomena remain within the will to life and subsist on its ground." Herein lies the *finitude* of all existence.

The idea of the world as the projection of the will, of the striving of the will as essentially null, and of the things of the phenomenal world as void, valueless, and not worth pursuing, is a tranquilizer for the will. The will is illuminated at its ground, and there the negation of the will to life can take place. Schopenhauer sees this negation as emancipation, and as the equivalent of *nirvāṇa* in Buddhism. Within nature, there is no way to escape the bonds of the necessity of cause and effect imposed by the will to life. Only by acknowledging these bonds can an order entirely different from that of nature open up for us. The key to this is the unreality—ideality— of time and space. This is the key to all true metaphysics, as Kant taught in his theory of *a priori* intuition. According to Schopenhauer, the rigorous distinction between the real and the ideal is the precondition for understanding ourselves and the essence of things as blind "will to life," and also for *intellect* to be truly liberated from that blind will in the direction of ideality. Herein rests true metaphysics and philosophy, as well as the basis for true morality (a point to which we shall return in connection with Nietzsche). For now, I would simply note that for Schopenhauer blind will and emancipation from it are connected with *pity (Mitleiden)* for suffering, or with the highest *askesis (Askese)*—that is, with a morality of the complete negation of the will. This is the morality of Christianity, where, however, it is based on a fantastical fiction. In addition to remarking that "faith in this fiction is gradually disappearing," Schopenhauer claims that a comparable morality can be grounded rationally through a philosophy of the interconnection of all things. He therefore presents his metaphysics, which shows the way to a Buddhist *nirvāṇa*, as a true grounding for Christian morality.

This summary should give a sense of Schopenhauer's realism and its clear tendency toward nihilism, as also of its ironical attitude toward German idealism in general and Hegel in particular. By distinguishing clearly and completely what is ideal from what is real, and by recognizing the blind will at the ground of what is real, the intellect can for the first time actually escape from this will and become free. This is true philosophy. If, as in the case of German idealism, one negates or blurs this distinction, the intellect is left to deal with what is real only in the head, and thus remains in the realm of fantasy. The intellect can only churn around in vain, and cannot become truly free. In other words, intellect remains fettered to the controls of blind will. As Schopenhauer writes in the appendix of *Parerga and Paralipomena* I:

> The basic reason why [Fichte, Schelling and Hegel] could not achieve anything substantial in philosophy is that in them *the intellect did not become free*, but rather remained under the control of the *will*. In such a condition the intellect can achieve an extraordinary amount for the will and its purposes—but in philosophy, as for art, nothing.

When intellect is pressed into the service of the will, it loves truth only so long as it corresponds to self-interest, the will of one's superiors, the doctrine of the Church, or the prejudices and tastes of one's contemporaries. This is no more than a case of "loving oneself" rather than "loving wisdom." Philosophy as love of wisdom can only occur in an intellect that has been liberated from the will; what the idealists pursue as philosophy lacks "sincerity, honesty, and integrity." In this way Schopenhauer tries to show how a standpoint like that of Hegel's absolute spirit is really no more than the product of an intellect that has not broken free of blind will, an intellect in which self-love lurks and whose very foundations harbor a moral problem of basic honesty. Such is the irony Schopenhauer employs to undermine Hegel's philosophy.

3. Kierkegaard—Becoming and Existence

Radical realism, an ironical attitude toward absolute idealism, and the struggle within the self over the consequences of a nihilism brought about by irony as absolute negativity are clearly visible in the thinking of Kierkegaard as well.

Hegelian philosophy dissolves all contradictions into the eternal from the standpoint of seeing things *sub specie aeternitatis*. Within the abstractness of speculative thinking the philosopher takes refuge in the illusion of being elevated to eternity through pure thought. But is he, Kierkegaard asks, a human being who *exists* in reality? "When he is asleep or blows his nose," Kierkegaard asks, "does he himself exist under the aspect of eternity?" (*KW* VIII, 5).[7] Pure thought is devoid of the temporality or becoming (*Werden*) of existence, and of the need, or necessity (*Not*), of one who exists. Idealism is unable to grasp real being in its reality. Pure thought mediates the way from the finiteness of the real to the infinity that is the ideality of thought itself. This is the standpoint of the *ideal identity* between reality and ideality, the standpoint of *sowohl/als* (both/and). For the person who exists, however, *sowohl/als* is a point of departure for *entweder/oder*(either/or) and not a destination. "A person who exists *is* as such finite *and* infinite as a person who exists, and *becomes* either finite *or* infinite."[8] This either/or is the standpoint of the *real contradiction* between reality and ideality: "the absolute decision of how to *become*." While the abstraction of speculative thinking moves from becoming to being and from contradiction to identity, existence moves, in contrast, from being to becoming and from identity to contradiction. "It is not that identity supersedes [*hebt . . . auf*] contradiction, but rather that contradiction supersedes identity, or (as Hegel so often says), it makes it 'collapse' (*zu Grunde gehen*)" (*KW* VII, 377). The existence of the concrete individual, which signals the collapse of this kind of speculative identity, pursues through the despair and suffering of the consciousness of guilt (*Schuld*) or sin, and by way of a so-called paradoxical dialectic, a way of being in which "the individual as an individual stands in absolute relation to the absolute."[9] In this emphasis on existence as real being itself, we see Kierkegaard's radical realism take shape.

In Schopenhauer's philosophy, life was said to be boredom: "Behind any kind of *need* there is *boredom*" (*PP* II, 146). Beginning from the basic necessities of clothing and food, life is filled with urgent matters to attend to, and from these some kind of meaning is given to life. Daily work and amusement are its inherent meaning; they divert the boredom that is its essence as "pastimes" that help one forget life's abyssal nihility. One pays attention to this meaning, "orients" oneself by it and thereby forgets life. Thanks to its meaning, life becomes something worth taking an interest in, acquires some kind of structure, and the aspect of infinite nihility recedes into the background. But for one who is aware of life's nihility, life becomes meaningless and stands revealed as the bare life that it is. Such persons seek some transcendent meaning through religion or metaphysics in order to escape life's *ennui* and despair. Having lost its inherent meaning, life is thereby restructured from a transcendent ground and given a purpose. Finally, in time of crisis when even religion, metaphysics, and morality are perceived as null, life becomes *fundamentally* void and boring. The radical realists belonged to an age that was approaching just this kind of crisis; and it follows as a matter of course that boredom bulked large for them.

Kierkegaard devoted a section of his early work *Either/Or* exclusively to the topic of boredom (*Langeweile*).[10]

> [Boredom] can be traced back to the very beginning of the world. The gods were bored; therefore they created human beings. Adam was bored because he was alone; therefore Eve was created. Since that moment, boredom entered the world and grew in quantity in exact proportion to the growth in population. . . . Boredom is the root all of evil. . . . There is the idea of convening a consultative assembly. Can anything more boring be imagined, both for the honorable delegates as well as for one who will read and hear about them? [*E/O* I, 286]

Just as Schopenhauer moved from a pantheism that sees divine will within all phenomena (which is how he viewed the philosophies of thinkers like Hegel and Schelling), to a pessimism that sees all phenomena as an empty and tedious objectivization of blind will, for Kierkegaard, too, boredom takes the place of a pantheistic god as the essence of all phenomena. He calls boredom "the demonic pantheism" [*E/O* I, 290].

> Pantheism ordinarily implies the quality of fullness; with boredom it is the reverse: it is built upon emptiness, but for this very reason it is a pantheistic qualification. Boredom rests upon the nothing that interlaces existence; its dizziness is infinite, like that which comes from looking down into a bottomless abyss. [*E/O* I, 291]

Kierkegaard understands boredom as the encounter with the infinite void of the abyss resulting from God's withdrawal from the center of the totality that connects all phenomena horizontally. The situation he describes is not unlike what Nietzsche meant by saying that "God is dead." Existence, having lost its center, is dissipated; life, which has become pure boredom, "distracts" itself among "excentric" (that is, peripheral) pleasures. This distraction of the mind is at ground pure boredom; what evades the void is itself void. Such is the depth of this kind of void.

Kierkegaard continues in this vein:

> That the eccentric diversion [*exzentrische Zerstreuung*— peripheral dissipation, an extraordinary scattering of the mind] is based upon boredom is seen also in the fact that the diversion sounds without resonance, simply because in nothing there is not even enough to make an echo possible [*E/O* I, 291].

From within our nihility not even so much as an echo arises— which is precisely why it is a nihility. To escape nihility one has to make life interesting somehow or other. Meantime, nihility dissipates any kind of *Interesse* and takes away all distractions. Since nihility reverberates no echoes, life is left without support. In the encounter with absolute nihility, the question of how any kind of "interest" is possible became for both Kierkegaard and Nietzsche a philosophical problem of the very foundation of Existence or life. The question of "aesthetic existence" which Kierkegaard pursues in the first volume of *Either/Or*, is concerned with how it is possible for "something accidental [to be] made into the absolute and as such into an object of absolute admiration" [*E/O* I, 299–300]. It has to do with things like "regarding everything in life as a wager." In this case the possibility of living becomes the possibility of pleasure. Matters such as "the moment," "things of interest" (*das Interessante*), and "arbitrariness" become the essential problems. The moment when something entirely *accidental* is *absolutized as something of interest* that anchors life—the "moment" in aesthetic existence. Arbitrariness as a free living that appears from the depths of nihility to break a "length of time" (*Langeweile*) of boredom at the moment of pleasure represents precisely aesthetic existence. This kind of existence has as its background the crisis of the history of spirit, the symptom of which is the collapse of Hegelian philosophy, and the lurking shadow of nihilism. Its significance lies in its confrontation with the metaphysical question of the nihility of life revealed in that crisis.

The reason children at play begin to misbehave is that they become bored; even in small children boredom can set in. The chief qualification of a nursemaid is the ability to make the child play; personality is secondary. The selection of a nursemaid, Kierkegaard says, is done not from the ethical but from the aesthetic viewpoint [*E/O* I, 285–86]. Aesthetic existence is a struggle against boredom,

"the root of all evil." *Langeweile*—"lasting long"—derives from temporality, which is essential to existence itself. The surfacing of the
contradiction that this temporality contains nihility in its ground—a
self-contradiction contained in existence as temporality—is boredom. Aesthetic existence represents a first attempt to resolve this
self-contradiction, by way of simply avoiding it.

The felt need to move from aesthetic up to ethical existence,
and from ethical to religious existence, represents a confrontation
with historical and metaphysical nihilism. According to the later
Kierkegaard, the individual in aesthetic existence "relates himself
absolutely to a *relative telos* [goal, purpose]."[11] This means that "a
being who is made to face eternity devotes all its strength to cap-
turing the ephemeral." The ephemeral is essentially nihility, and
"the moment of sensuous enjoyment" is "the moment within time
filled with emptiness." This moment "expresses the farthest isolation from the eternal." Therefore, existence pursued as a temporality floating on an absolute nihility that has lost God cannot remain
in aesthetic existence. Kierkegaard's ideas of ethical and religious
existence are well enough known not to bear repeating here.

The dizziness at the brink of the abyss of nihility is now deep-
ened into irony, anxiety, and despair. Irony means, on the one
hand, opposing from the standpoint of "subjectivity" the entirety of
historical actuality which has as its background the manifold world-
historical process—the world of reality to which the self belongs—
in order to insert infinite negativity behind it and so establish
nihility at its ground.[12] This view of existence as possibility is the
infinite negation of all actuality. It reveals the nihility of the historical world and the self, and at the same time faces the metaphysical
nihility—nihility as the absolute—at the ground of history. On the
other hand, in irony the self that takes its stand on nihility returns
within itself and is transformed into subjective inwardness. The
abyss of nihility is brought into the subject to actualize subjectivity
and its freedom. In irony, the nihility behind the self-will of aesthetic existence is appropriated within the subject.

The essence of subjectivity is revealed as *anxiety* when the self,
as a realm of infinite possibility within absolute nihility, sets out to
become itself in will and decisiveness, when the subject tries to exist actually in its subjectivity. Just as boredom represented the dizziness of life peering into the abyss of nihility, anxiety represents
"the dizziness of freedom" on the brink of the abyss, where the
self, in the desire to grasp and become itself, looks into the abyss as
the infinite possibility within itself. In the attack of dizziness the
self grasps its finitude and preserves itself by clinging to it, and in

that dizziness freedom falls to the ground. This is the self of "self-ishness," wherein the self becomes finite by putting itself to the test of a nihilistic view of life. Thus "at the moment" when the self, in the very effort of trying to attain the infinite self, falls into finitude, "everything is changed, and freedom, when it again rises, sees that it is guilty [*schuldig*]. Between these two moments lies the leap."[13]

When the self becomes selfish by trying to become itself through its own freedom and strength, the indebtedness (*Schuld*) and original sin buried in the depths of freedom come to the surface.[14] At the same time, the self in its depths no longer faces the abyss of absolute nihility; it stands before God. The anxiety of standing before God as one who is a self by virtue of carrying the burden of original sin is *despair*. When anxiety deepens into despair, the self penetrates through to and unites with its ultimate depths and finitude, and thereby becomes an "individual." This is nihilistic Existence. Here the nihility of the self, and of humankind and its history, is most clearly revealed. The nihilism of despair, lurking all along within aesthetic existence, now begins to emerge from the depths. The self is most radically pulled away from God at the point where it most radically touches God. The point at which eternity as eternity and time as time diverge is the "moment" in religious existence. In this moment of anxiety, time and eternity confront one another as complete opposites and the temporality of existence becomes plain.[15]

Anxiety as despair also becomes the medium for redemption. This turn of "paradoxical dialectics" marks the resurrection of the self to a new life through faith in the forgiveness of sin and through voluntarily dying to sin, and is also the "leap" of becoming in existence. The moment appears not as an atom of time but as "an atom of eternity," or "the first reflection of eternity in time."[16] This is death and at the same time the transcendence of death.

As the moment becomes an atom of eternity within time, the flux of existence becomes a "repetition" of life penetrated by death. Repetition is true transcendence and true immanence; it is true temporality grounded in the revelation of eternity.[17] Only insofar as the moment becomes repetition is there true life. The nihility that exists within life as boredom and dissipation (*Zerstreuung*)—for Kierkegaard, the nihility of life without God—is overcome. Radical engagement with the nihility within nihilistic existence, and a thoroughly existential confrontation with original sin and the finitude and death rooted in it, enable us to escape the abyss of nihility at the ground of life. This is the way to overcome nihilism offered by Kierkegaard's existentialism.

4. Feuerbach—Critique of Religion, Philosophy, and Ethics

In Schopenhauer we saw a realism opposing absolute idealism in the form of a "metaphysics of will"; in Kierkegaard it took the form of a new basis of faith through existentialism; in Feuerbach, realism emerges as a new "anthropology."

Feuerbach, like Kierkegaard, criticizes Hegelian philosophy for its "abstractness," its failure to grasp the concrete in its concreteness. Here, too, the critique is an expression of radical realism. It is true that Hegel made *Realität* an issue; in a sense he tried to grasp the real in its reality more than any previous metaphysics had done. Indeed, the bulk of his criticism of previous metaphysics was directed at its standpoint of merely intellectual "reflection" and its abstract ideality. Seen from a different perspective, however, Hegel ended up by completely idealizing the real, including the essence of its *Realität*. Kierkegaard characterized reality in Hegel as "thought reality" (*Gedanken-Realität*), demanding that one throw oneself into nihilistic existence and become ironical in order to escape it and return to being a person who exists *actually*. Feuerbach's critique of Hegel is not without an ironical character of its own. For example, he writes in his *Principles of a Philosophy of the Future:*

> Hegel is a *realist*, but he is a *purely idealistic* or rather abstract realist—a realist in the *abstraction from all reality*. He *rejects* thinking, abstract thinking, and yet this rejection is *itself a case of abstract thinking*, so that the negation of abstraction is itself an abstraction.[18]

Here, too, realism is presented in the form of an ironical dialectic in which realism, while negating Hegelian philosophy from a diametrically opposite standpoint, is at the same time its natural consequence.

> The new philosophy which recognizes the *concrete* as the true, *not in abstracto*, but rather *in concreto*, the real *in its reality*, and therefore in a way which *corresponds to the essence of the real*, and elevates it to the *principle* and the object of philosophy, is the *truth* of Hegelian philosophy, *the truth of modern philosophy in general*. [*Grundsätze*, § 31]

The ironical character of this realism shows up in the claim, contrary to what we might have expected, that it is precisely in the understanding of reality within the real that the truth of Hegelian philosophy lies. This idea is tied in with Feuerbach's critique of religion, which in fact accounted for his greatest impact on European thought at that time and also has the most connections within nihilism.

As is well known, Feuerbach sought the origins of religion in the egoistic "striving for happiness" and the fictitious structure of the power of imagination associated with it.[19] "Self-love is the ultimate ground of religion. . . . Human happiness is its purpose." Primitive societies, living under constant threat of nature and the force of circumstances, lacking any control over the vicissitudes of life, fabricated in imagination beings endowed with the power to overcome the unpredictable arbitrariness of life and to answer the prayers of mere mortals suffering from a surplus of unfulfilled desires. According to Feuerbach, gods are created by the unsatisfied drive for happiness of primitive people projected through imagination into their objective satisfaction in the natural world.

With Christianity, God is conceived of as a transcendent spirit above and beyond nature—as the essence of beings (*das Wesen der Wesen*), or as the supreme being (*das höchste Wesen*). God is absolute Being, independent creator of the world. Human being came to be seen as spirit associated with God, and as belonging to "the world of spirit" which is beyond the world of the body and the senses. The body and the senses become illusory phenomena lacking true being. The ideas that God is a being who transcends the world, and that the essence of human being lies in a realm of spirit, beyond the body, are mutually supporting.

In Feuerbach this kind of supreme being is also the result of an idealizing of human nature, a supposed supreme essence within us which has been objectified as a personal God. The human being is seen as one whose self is dependent on this God, and who must therefore believe in it. This means that the self is the object of a God who is the idealized objectification of the self's essence. In other words, the essence of the self is idealized and then realized through being projected on to a divine ideal. In such a religion, God as absolute Lord becomes the grammatical subject, and the human being as spirit becomes the creature who obeys that Lord and the predicate which belongs internally to the subject. However, if this God is merely the objectification of the supreme human essence, the actual relationship is reversed so that the human being is the subject and God the predicate. By means of this kind of explanation of the origin of religion, Feuerbach argued that theology is absorbed into anthropology. It is not that God is the transcendent supreme being, but rather that "man"—his own "humanity"—is the internal supreme essence. This is why he can claim that "Man is God for man" (*homo homini deus*). By reversing the subject-predicate relationship between God and humanity that governs theology and the idealistic philosophy that is its philosophical counterpart, the correct standpoint, free of illusion, is achieved. It is said that "God is love," but actually "love is divine"; it used to be that "God became man" in Christ, but now "man" has become God. Needless to say, Feuerbach's critique shook the intellectual world of the time to its foundations.

Feuerbach's anthropology was a critique not only of religion but also of idealism, and in particular the Hegelian philosophy that stood at its apex. Behind Hegel's idea of the "Concept" as the essence of things, lay the theological view of God as absolute Spirit, the supreme essence of all things, and of the essence of the human as spirit corresponding to that of God. But for Feuerbach, to call the Concept the essence of things is tantamount to saying that "the skeleton has more reality than the living human being," that blood and flesh are superfluous additions. But it is this living flesh that is the true essence of human beings, primordially sensuous beings that we are. Even if we say that reason regulates sensation, it does so only according to the prescriptions laid down in advance by sensation; the ground of the unity of reason and sensation is itself sensuous. Thus for Feuerbach, sensation came to assume the status of an ontological and metaphysical principle. His "sensation-ism" set itself up as a standpoint of dialectical irony against the metaphysics of reason.[20]

In addition to his critiques of religion and philosophy, Feuerbach proposes a critique of morality. With God as the supreme being and transcendent supreme essence, morality takes form around love of this God as its center. But since humanity is the supreme essence for human beings, for Feuerbach the highest law of morality is the love of one human being for another. The essence of human being is to be found in "the unity of one human being with another, a unity which depends on the reality of the difference between I and Thou . . . The unity of I and Thou is God" [*Grundsätze*, §§ 59–60). "It is not that God is love, but love of humanity is divine. . . . Religion must become ethics. Only ethics is religion." In this way Feuerbach tries to find a new religion within the ethics of humanity through his critique of ethics. This kind of approach was not uncommon among people of the period coming out of idealism to positivism—as in the case of in Comte in France—and as such it mirrors the transitional nature of the era.

Although Feuerbach's realism tended toward materialism, it did not leave the confines of anthropology, for which it became the subject of Marx's criticisms. It is not necessary to go into this issue here, except to cite a section of Marx's critique as summarized in the *Theses on Feuerbach:*

> The major failing of all materialism (including Feuerbach's) is that the object [*Gegenstand*], actuality, and sensuousness are grasped only under the form of the object [*Objekt*] or intuition; and not as human sensuous activity, as *praxis*, and subjectively. . . . Feuerbach does not understand human activity itself as objective [*gegenständlich*] activity. (§ 1)
>
> The coincidence of a change in circumstances and human activity [or self-change] are understood only as *revolutionary praxis* [*umwälzende Praxis*] and also rationally. (§ 3)

The subjective interpretation of object, actuality, and sensibility as praxis, objective activity, and revolutionary praxis forms the basis of the philosophical development from Feuerbach to Marx. From this perspective Feuerbach's critique of religion is further criticized:

> Feuerbach starts out from the fact of religious self-alienation, the doubling of the world into a religious, imagined world and a real world. His task consists in dissolving the world into its secular foundation. . . . But the fact that the foundation lifts off from itself and establishes itself as an independent kingdom [in the clouds] is to be explained only from the self-splitting and self-contradiction of this secular foundation. (§ 4)

Here realism develops from the standpoint of the human as a real "being" to that of the "real ground" of history in Marx. For example, in *The German Ideology* we read:

> This totality of the various powers of production which any individual or generation finds as something given, the various items of capital and the various forms of social intercourse, is the real ground of what philosophers have represented as "substance" or as the "essence of the human," the ground of that which they have deified and struggled against, and this is the real ground which cannot be in any way disturbed in its action or influence on the development of humanity through the rebellion of these philosophers against it as "self-consciousness" and "individual."[21]

"Self-consciousness" here refers to the standpoint of Bruno Bauer and "individual" to Stirner—about whom I shall say more later. At any rate, the standpoint of Marx's critique is that of *historical materialism* connected with revolutionary praxis. He criticizes Feuerbach as follows: "as long as Feuerbach is a materialist, there is no history in him. As long as he is concerned with history he is in no way a materialist. In him, materialism and history are mutually exclusive." From this perspective Marx locates the reality of human existence not in sensation but in the "totality of the variety of social relationships." In the *Theses* he writes as follows:

> Feuerbach dissolves religious being into *human* being. But human being is not something abstract which exists within the particular individual. In its actuality it is the whole ensemble of social relationships. Feuerbach, who does not go into the criticism of this actual being, is therefore compelled: (1) to abstract from historical process and to determine the religious temperament itself and to presuppose an abstract—*isolated*—human individual; and (2) thus human being can be understood only as "*species*," as the inner, mute universality which connects the multiplicity of individuals merely *naturally*. (§ 6)
>
> Feuerbach, therefore, fails to see that the religious temperament is itself a *social product*, and that the abstract individual which he analyzes belongs in actuality to a certain form of society. (§ 7)
>
> All social life is essentially practical. All mysteries which turn theory into mysticism find their rational solution in human praxis and the comprehension of this praxis. (§ 8)

In the end, Marx reaches the conclusion that "Philosophers have only *interpreted* the world in different ways; the task, however, is to *change* it" (§ 11).

The realism that develops between Feuerbach and Marx appears to be free of the shadow of nihilism—with the exception of Stirner's thought. Their materialism seems to have already overcome nihilism. But this is precisely the problem, in that nihilism is neither understood subjectively nor overcome in the struggle within the subject. Marx says that the essence of human being is not "something abstract" that exists within the individual (his so-called abstract-isolated human individual), but is rather the totality of social relationships. However, does this not amount to a dissolving of the essence of human being into its real basis, that is, "the totality of the various forces of production, elements of capital, and social intercourse," just as Feuerbach had dissolved the religious essence (God) into the essence of the human? From this standpoint, "religious temperament," for example, would have to be understood as a social product and "be extinguished theoretically and practically" (§ 4).

The standpoint of not considering the individual merely as the "abstract-isolated human individual" takes an opposite position. With Kierkegaard, Dostoevsky, or Nietzsche we can claim that insofar as the individual is from the beginning understood only in its social aspect, insofar as it is seen only from the perspective of dissolving into "the totality of social relationships," it is seen merely "abstractly." For them the individual is to be found only in Existence—as one who cannot be socially abstracted, as one who by free will resists this kind of trend as a "single" or "isolated" individual. Conversely, they find in socialism, atheism, and materialism manifestations of the nihilism rampant in the modern era. (For example, Nietzsche considers socialism a kind of modern nihilism, though it is unaware of the nihility that lurks in the background.) They seek to bring out the nihilism concealed in the foundations of history into the interior of the self, to live it subjectively, and overcome it. For them nihilism has to so with a confrontation of Existence with God: for Kierkegaard and Dostoevsky it is the search for the Christian God, and for Nietzsche, the search for a "new religion" of the Antichrist. In either case "religious temperament" is not merely a social product, and the issue of the confrontation of Existence with God is not a problem that can be "solved rationally." They are fundamentally irrationalists, and they all—including Nietzsche—fight the battle against nihilism in the arena of religious "mystery." While each of them fought against the religion and morality of the bourgeoisie, at the same time they opposed the "progressive" tendency to dissolve Existence into the totality of social relationships, and also claimed to be "conservative" in a fundamental sense. Their conservatism is not a political conservatism; they did not fail to see the shadow of spiritual "regression" which was following in the footsteps of modern "progress." This tendency toward fundamental human degeneration was a more important issue for them than any other. They fought against regression as hard as they fought against the idea of "progress" that pervaded bourgeois liberalism and socialism.

The opponents of Hegel we have been looking at were not operating from a truly nihilistic nihilism. Of course, Schopenhauer and Kierkegaard advocate the nullity of existence, but this was not yet based on the kind of critique of history we shall see in Nietzsche's "European nihilism." Nihilism had not become a historical question within the history of the actual, a question regarding the transcendent ground of history; nihility had not become an issue of nihility in the ground of actual history itself. These thinkers showed a way to overcome the nullity of existence just before reaching the point of nihilism; and they were therefore not nihilists, but rather realists in the broad sense. Thus the *Realität* with which they proposed to fill the immense void left after the collapse of absolute idealism still retained remnants of the past, in contrast to the nihilists who came after them. Their radical realism was in this sense a precursor of nihilism, although it may be too much to say that the transition from this realism to nihilism was inevitable. The fact that Stirner came out of Feuerbach, and Nietzsche out of Schopenhauer, and Heidegger from the lineage of Kierkegaard—in other words, the fact that nihilism came out of every major spiritual and intellectual movement after Hegel—may be no more than mere coincidence. However, if we consider that the standpoint of the radical realists contains a radical negation of the ground of traditional spirit, we may see a kind of logical and at the same time psychological consequence in the fact that their views tended toward nihilism. This is also evident in the fact that Russia, where socialism actually appeared in the form of nihilism, was the scene of a more radical nihilism developed by Dostoevsky through his confrontation with this phenomenon. I shall take up each of these matters in the chapters that follow.

Chapter Three

Friedrich Nietzsche:
The First Consummate Nihilist

1. The Significance of Nihilism in Nietzsche

Nietzsche's nihilism, developed in the last years of his career, centers around the idea of will to power.[1] *The Will to Power* is also the title of a posthumous manuscript which he may have intended to be his greatest work, and the subtitle of which was to be *Attempt at a Revaluation of All Values*. The framework of the connection between the standpoints of radical revaluation and nihilism is clearly outlined in the Preface to *The Will to Power*.

The Preface consists of four short sections. The opening section reads: "Great things demand that one remain silent about them or else speak greatly [*gross reden*—talk boldly]: 'greatly' means cynically and innocently."[2] "Cynical" here has the same sense as the term "ironical" in the preceding chapter. It is a matter of setting up what desecrates the holy and violates values in opposition to the holy and to received values or ideals, and then of reducing the latter to the former. It is to dig beneath the holy and beneath values to pull up their roots. Moreover, this wicked act should be something "innocent"—about which more later.

In the second section Nietzsche writes:

The story I have to tell is the history of the next two centuries. I am describing what is coming, what can no longer come in any other way: *the advent of nihilism*. This history can now be related already, for necessity itself is at work here. This future already speaks in a hundred signs. . . . The whole of our European culture has for a long time been moving in tortured

tension . . . as if rushing towards a catastrophe: restlessly, vi-
olently, precipitately: like a river that wants to reach *its end*,
but no longer reflects, that is afraid to reflect upon itself.

If the advent of this kind of nihilism is so violent a necessity as
to leave no room for self-reflection on the part of those who are
carried away by its torrent, then how on earth could Nietzsche,
who records it, become aware of this process? Was it in his capacity
as a historian or social scientist analyzing and studying past history
or contemporary society? Or was it perhaps in his capacity as a philosopher of history? The answer is—neither. In the third section of
the Preface, Nietzsche himself offers a straightforward answer.

The one who speaks here has—rather than recounted—done
nothing up until now other than to *reflect upon himself*: as a
philosopher and a hermit by instinct, who finds his advantage
in withdrawing to the side, in standing outside, in patience, in
hesitation, in lagging behind; as a daring and (re)searching
spirit (*Versucher-Geist*) who has already lost himself once in every labyrinth of the future; as the spirit of a bird of prophecy
who *looks back*, when he narrates what is to come . . .[3]

It is in this context that he speaks of himself as "the first consummate nihilist in Europe, who, moreover, has already lived nihilism
through to the end in himself—who has it behind him, beneath
him, outside of him."

History pushes ahead relentlessly to its end without time to
reflect upon itself or catch its breath. To stand outside this stream of
history and reflect at some remove does not mean simply detaching
oneself from history. It means reflecting not upon history as it is,
but up where it is headed. It does not mean to observe the reality
of history and its ideas objectively as historians or philosophers of
history do, but to experiment with history within oneself. It is to
experiment with the future tendencies and issues of history by making the self one's laboratory. This activity discloses the end of history lurking in its ground by tempting the self to venture into every
labyrinth of the future, which is to lure the ending out of history
and into the self. This is the meaning of "living nihilism through to
its end" and the standpoint of "one who is a philosopher and a
hermit by instinct." It is in this sense that Nietzsche claims to be
doing nothing other than reflecting upon himself.

Such philosophy of history takes the self as its experimental
subject. The mystics of the past attained direct experience of God by

intersecting with God within God, a process they called "experimental knowledge" (*cognitio experimentalis*). They sought God through the laboratory of the self, by luring the interior of God into the interior of the self. They were in this sense "experimenters" with God. It is in a similar sense that Nietzsche was a philosopher of history—not in the sense of philosophizing about history, but rather of living history within history experimentally and philosophically, and in such a way that the self lives in history and history lives in the self. As he himself describes it: "*Experimental philosophy*, as I live it, tentatively [*versuchsweise*] preempts the very possibilities of fundamental nihilism . . ." (*WP* 1041). To philosophize is to experiment within history and to preempt various possibilities of the future; that is, to elicit these possibilities from the depths of history into the depths of the self. Hence for Nietzsche philosophizing means *Existenz* in the midst of history, *historical* Existence within history. In this way all the great events of the past, present, and future become events within the Existence of the individual who has become an experimenter in the depths of history.[4] This explains the necessity for the philosopher in Nietzsche to become a "hermit."

Nietzsche's Zarathustra became such a hermit, pulling himself out of the mighty river of the current of history to engage in self-reflection. For Nietzsche, Existence as "the relationship in which the self relates to itself" meant becoming absolutely "solitary" (*der Einsame*) by diving down to the depths of actual history. His was, as it were, a deep-sea solitude. In this way, living nihilism through to the end could for the first time mean the overcoming of nihilism, the ability to place what must come in the future behind the self. His was the spirit of the bird of prophecy that looks back when it foretells the future as something already overcome within the self. The philosopher who is historical-existential must not only be an experimenter but must also have the spirit of prophecy. And the philosopher who has the spirit of prophecy must also—as one who has put beneath and behind him the necessity of what is to come— be a legislator.

Such a philosopher will be a founder of new values. As Nietzsche says in section 4 of the Preface:

I hope that the meaning of the title with which this gospel of the future would be named will not be misunderstood. "*The Will to Power*. Attempt [*Versuch*] at a Revaluation of All Values": with this formula a *counter-movement* is given expression, with respect to its principle and task; a movement which will in some future or other slough off that consummate nihilism; and yet which *presupposes* it, logically and psychologically, and can actually only come *to that nihilism and out of it.* For why is the advent of nihilism now *necessary?* Because it is our values hitherto which are themselves drawing their ultimate consequences in it; because nihilism is the final logic, thought through to the end, of our great values and ideals—because we must first live and experience nihilism in order to get behind (*dahinter kommen*) and learn what the *value* of these "values" really was. At some point we need *new values.*

The ground of received ideals and values has become hollow. As Nietzsche puts it elsewhere, "God is dead."[5] The advent of nihilism consists in the gradual crumbling of these ideals and values, as well as of the entire structure of European life, so that nihility can emerge from the depths. The nihilist is one who experiments with nihilism as the logical consequence of these values and ideals, anticipating it psychologically. In this anticipation there arises a counter-movement against the current history rushing headlong toward nihilism. *Psychological* reflection on the *logical* consequences of the values and ideals that have formed the basis of historical life up until now is not any kind of abstract understanding that merely reflects the logic of historical circumstances into consciousness; this would not be historical Existence. *Psychological* reflection as Nietzsche understands it "comes around behind" the values in question. On the one hand this "coming around behind" reveals the hollowness at the ground of these values; it is a revelation of nihility. This draws nihilism out of the self as "consummate" nihilism, allowing one—as Nietzsche says—to "slough [it] off." On the other hand, it is a matter of critically evaluating these values, and thereby engaging in the establishment of new values. Since the values and ideals in question are based in Christian morality, which in turn rests on a total negation of life, to come around this kind of total negation from behind leads to a thoroughgoing affirmation of life, to a standpoint of life that affirms life itself. This is precisely what Nietzsche means by will to power.

The movement to present nihilism in its consummate form eventually comes together with its counter-movement—which is what Nietzsche means by a movement "to it and out of it" (*auf ihn und aus ihm*). To live nihilism through to the end in this sense eventually leads to its overcoming. This is what Nietzsche means by "cynically and innocently." "Cynical" refers to the disclosing of the back-side of all previous values, and "innocent" to the standpoint of life that affirms itself directly. The radical negation of historical life is the direct affirmation of this life. This what is meant by "speaking greatly about great things"—taking decisive judgment in a great crisis. At the same time, Nietzsche is speaking from the midst of actual history. To present the standpoint of will to power by anticipating nihilism was, for Nietzsche, a counter-movement toward the goal of Europe's one day reaching a mature and ripened nihilism and becoming aware of the necessity for new values.

2. Radical Nihilism

We may distinguish three aspects to the way Nietzsche approaches his task as a nihilist. The first concerns what nihilism itself is; this is presumably the issue of European nihilism that was to constitute the first book of the work *The Will to Power*. The second concerns the self-reflection of the philosopher who lives nihilism through to the end; this appears concretely in the second book, entitled "Critique of the Highest Values Hitherto." The third concerns the standpoint of will to power as the counter-movement that emerges from the critique; this would constitute the topics of the third and fourth books, "Principle of a New Positing of Values" and "Discipline and Training." We must begin with the first issue, concerning the nature of nihilism.

In the first section of "European Nihilism" Nietzsche gives a general definition of nihilism; in the next section he further defines what he calls "radical nihilism"; and in the third section he touches upon the morality of Christianity.[6] In the first, general definition of nihilism, he characterizes it as the condition in which "the highest values lose their value." Before inquiring into the nature of Nietzsche's radical nihilism, however, we need to look briefly at his discussion of Christian morality, since the former has to do with an interpretation of values for survival that had come from the latter. The question, then, is how the Christian value-interpretation results in nihilism, in the highest values losing their value.

In the third section of "European Nihilism" Nietzsche gives a general description of the benefits wrought by Christian morality. First, in the ephemeral stream of becoming, the human individual is a small and accidental being; but Christian morality granted the human absolute *value*. (Nietzsche probably had in mind here the idea of humanity as bearer of the "image of God.") Second, in spite of the fact that the world is full of suffering and evil, Christian morality recognized the quality of *perfection* in the world, including the "freedom" that can render evil *meaningful*. (This probably refers to the idea that the world is the creation of God, that the "essence" of all things is rooted in him, and that all events are governed by divine Providence.) Thirdly, Christian morality provided human beings with *wisdom* concerning absolute value, so that they came to think themselves capable of *adequate knowledge* of the most important things. Fourth, it prevented people from despising themselves for their humanity, from rebelling against life and despairing of knowledge; that is, morality became a *means of self-preservation* (a preservative). Nietzsche concludes: "To sum up: morality was the great *countermeasure [antidote] against practical and theoretical nihilism*."

In another note, entitled "The Meaning of Religion," he writes: "People who are failures or are unhappy must be preserved and by improving their mood (hope, fear) be prevented from committing suicide" (XIII, 300). Although this refers to religion in general, Christian morality is again singled out for its view of human beings as weak and contingent beings within the flux of becoming, and of suffering and evil as inextricably bound up with the world. If this were all, human life would be worthless and the world meaningless; one would "despise [oneself] as human and rebel against life." This is "practical (or praxis-oriented) nihilism." However, even if value and meaning are given, if human beings are unable to know them they will "despair of knowledge" and fall into "theoretical nihilism." But Christian morality, in opposition to this kind of practical or theoretical nihilism, granted absolute value to the human, gave meaning to the world, and left room for wisdom and knowledge about these things. What Nietzsche calls "European nihilism" was a revolt against this kind of value interpretation. It was for him a logical consequence of a radical psychological reexamination of the very Christian morality that had originally been a countermeasure to nihilism. Hence this "European nihilism" is different from the kind of nihilism that arises *immediately* from human life. It is, so to speak, a *higher* nihilism that appeared as a result of the breakdown of the very institution—Christian morality—that was supposed to overcome "immediate" nihilism. This is probably why Nietzsche called European nihilism a *radical* or "extreme nihilism."[7]

Under the title "Collapse of Cosmological Values" (*Hinfall der kosmologischen Werte*) Nietzsche discusses *nihilism as a psychological condition* and distinguishes three forms of it [*WP* 12]. The first arises when the view that the transiency and becoming of the world have a definite, fundamental *purpose* ends up in disillusionment. Once the world-process is seen to have a purpose of some kind and to be heading toward a goal, all events within it are considered meaningful. On the view that everything has some kind of purpose or ideal toward which it is heading, human beings, as central agents of the process (or at least as collaborators in it), may also be able to feel that life is worth living and to discover meaning in their lives. Once one has seen through the giving of purpose to life as an illusion, once it has become clear that we are searching for meanings that do not actually exist, then life loses all significance and anguish over the vanity of the search supervenes. It is here that the first form of nihilism as a psychological condition arises.

The second form has to do with the conviction that the totality of events in the world forms a systematic whole. This belief binds human beings to a great totality that transcends the self, gives them a profound sense of dependence on it, and enables them to devote themselves to the welfare of the whole. But if this totality that gives meaning to life is seen to not actually exist—to be merely a fictitious construct that we have imagined in order *to believe in the value of the self*—then we lose all faith in our own value. Thus the second form of nihilism emerges, the nihilism that brings with it a loss of faith in unity.

These two forms of nihilism as a psychological condition have to do with the ephemeral world of becoming, with "this world." What Nietzsche refers to as totality, or universal being, may be something like the God of "pantheism," immanent in the world. At any rate these two forms of nihilism arise as a result of our seeking a purpose and a unity in the events of this world, only to arrive at the insight that these efforts are in vain. It is probable that the "practical and theoretical nihilism" mentioned earlier, the countermeasure to which was said to be Christianity, also establishes itself on this kind of standpoint.

The third and final form of nihilism Nietzsche describes is somewhat different in its nature from the first two. It has to do with the final *refuge* that remains even after the disillusion of the first two. Here nihilism consists in "condemning the entire world of becoming a deception, and inventing a world which lies beyond this one as the *true* world." The issue is now transposed to a realm one level higher. The erection of a true world, a *Hinterwelt*, beyond the present world is nothing other than the worldview of Christianity combined with Platonism. Here Christianity again provides a ground for teleology and unity—about which one is bound to despair if one remains only on a this-worldly standpoint within the world of becoming—from out of the transcendent world beyond. Metaphysics and Christian morality were thus established as higher-level theory and morality respectively, the latter to serve as a countermeasure against practical and theoretical nihilism.

The idea that the first two forms of nihilism belong to one realm and the third to another, and that their negations operate at different levels, is not without precedent in other post-Hegelian thinkers. Schopenhauer and Kierkegaard distinguish pantheism from theism; Feuerbach distinguishes the ancient idea of nature-gods from the Christian idea of a transcendent God. Similarly Stirner—as we shall see later—distinguishes the natural world as the realm of truth for primitive peoples from the spiritual world of Christianity's truth. All of these correspond in some sense to the distinction I am drawing between forms of nihilism in Nietzsche.

As soon as we "see through" (*dahinterkommen*) the fact that the higher realm is constituted simply by various psychological desires, and that we have no right to believe in such a realm,

> the final form of nihilism arises, which includes the *disbelief in a metaphysical world*—which denies itself belief in a *true* world. In this standpoint one recognizes the reality of becoming as the *only* reality, and forbids oneself every kind of escape to other worlds and false divinities.

Nietzsche concludes that one then *"cannot endure this world, which one yet does not want to negate."* It is this inability to tolerate the ephemeral world of becoming, all the while knowing it to be the only reality, that is the final form of "nihilism as a psychological condition." I shall return later to the significance of this condition and what it means to say that ephemeral becoming is the only reality. For now, the important thing is to see that disillusionment with respect to the "true world," the collapse of the standpoint of seeking the truth beyond the transience of becoming, is a higher-level nihilism. The collapse of faith in such a "true world," combined with the loss of Christian morality as the final countermeasure to practical and theoretical nihilism, constitutes radical nihilism.

In the second section of "European Nihilism" Nietzsche characterizes *"radical nihilism"* as "the conviction of the absolute untenability of existence, when it is a question of the highest values one recognizes" [*WP* 3]. What he means is that for us to exist in the world there has to be some ground, some foundation of highest values without which our lives would be a meaningless void. We may find value in existence through its connection with "God" or "the true world" or something of the sort. Of course many people can survive without such ultimate values: they may find some degree of satisfaction in eating, drinking, having a family, doing business or politics, being involved with social "praxis" or with scholarship, and so on. But even for these, the fundamental void of existence cannot be filled by such things alone, and in the end they will find that they "cannot endure this world"—any more than they could believe in the "highest values." Existence thus becomes absolutely untenable; and this is radical nihilism.

Nietzsche goes on:

in addition, there is the *insight* that we have no right whatso-ever to set up a world beyond or an in-itself of things that would be 'divine,' or morality incarnate (*leibhaft*).

By "morality incarnate" he means that the world of the thing-in-itself, or *idea*, the "intelligible" world beyond—indeed everything normally referred to as "divine"—are actually projected images of a morality that has assumed concrete form. It is the same union, in Christian faith, of higher theory and the metaphysical world, and of higher praxis and its morality, that we referred to above. The integration of all the highest metaphysical, moral, and practical principles grounds the manifold of European culture, including even positivism and socialism which may appear at first glance to negate Christianity. It is disbelief in any kind of true world and insight into the grounds for this disbelief that constitute radical nihilism and the *absolute* untenability of existence.

3. Nietzsche's Interpretation of Christianity

We turn now to Nietzsche's confrontation with the nihilistic tendency in Christian morality, and with the "modern nihilism" of democracy and socialism that is its continuation into the modern era.

Nietzsche criticizes Christianity repeatedly and from a variety of perspectives. There is no need to examine these criticisms in detail here, but since his confrontation with Christianity touches the very roots of his nihilism and represents a task he pursued to the end of his work, it is only fitting to highlight a few of its main points. Firstly, Nietzsche holds that Christian morality and the modern spirit that is based on it, as exemplified by democracy and socialism, are all grounded in a *decline of life*. Secondly, their principles are *hostile to life* (*lebensfeindlich*). And thirdly, this very will that negates the will to power is after all a will to power that is masked and inverted. Let us look at each of these points in turn.

Nietzsche writes in aphorism 15 of *The Antichrist* that the world of Christianity is "a purely fictional world," and that "neither [its] morality nor religion has any point of contact with reality." What are taken to be the basic entities in Christianity—"God," "soul," "ego," "spirit," "free will" (also "unfree will")—he claims to be all entirely imaginary; and therefore also "sin," "redemption," "grace," "punishment," "forgiveness of sins" are equally phantastic concepts. Further, "repentance," "pangs of conscience," "temptation of the devil," "nearness of God," "the kingdom of God," "the Last Judgment" and "eternal life" are equally phantastic concepts. If this is so, we want to know how such an entirely imaginary world came to be fabricated. Nietzsche sees its source in "the *hatred* of the natural." For him, the imaginary world of Christianity is an expression of deep dissatisfaction with the real world. He speaks in a number of places of the "denaturalization" (*Entnatürlichung*) perpetrated by Christianity, by which he means its tendency to see all values rooted in the instincts of natural life as non-values, to consider the negation of natural values—that is, denaturalization—to be rather a "sacralization." In other words, "God" is imagined as something opposing nature, so that for the first time "natural" becomes synonymous with "reprehensible."

Holiness, which had been achieved by depriving the natural of its holiness, is a "holy lie". Who needs such a lie?—those who *suffer* from reality (*die Leidenden*) and whose lives are not going as they wish (*die Missratenen*). These lives evoke the fictitious world of the beyond, and mark a fundamental decline of life as such. The essence of life is the will to the growth of life itself and to the surmounting of life—namely, "will to power." Essential to will to power is the feeling of pleasure (*Lust*), the innocent desire for power of the lion and the light-hearted freedom of the bird. But suffering (*Leiden*) blocks the desire that is essential to life, and the feet become heavy. This indicates a weakening and decline of life—which is for Nietzsche the essence of *décadence*. He concludes the aphorism by saying: "The preponderance of feelings of unpleasure over feeling of pleasure . . . however, yields the formula for *décadence*." In this *décadence* lie the foundations for the fictitious world of Christianity, and of the morality and religion it gives rise to.

Nietzsche's perception of the weakening and decline of life in Christianity has profound implications. He holds that Christianity singles out those who suffer and deems them morally better than those who are healthy, thereby obstructing the natural development of life and according unnaturalness the status of a norm and moral rightness. It not only advocates the weakening of life, but also presents life's negative and reactive aspects as a positive principle. This is not simply a case of a "minus direction" running counter to life, but of positing the "minus direction" as a "plus direction" and then consciously opting for it. Nietzsche characterizes Christianity as hostile to life, but depicts its stand as that of a warrior wielding a spear held the wrong way round.

There seems to be a contradiction here. On the one hand, Nietzsche says that Christianity is the consummate proponent of the negation of life, which inclines it to nihilism. On the other, he says that it encourages the self-preservation, resistance, and resentment of the weak against the strong, which is a masked and inverted form of will to power. These dual aims to negate life and preserve it are simply two aspects of the same basic standpoint of Christianity. The same duality can be seen in Nietzsche's view of pity, or sympathy, a basic Christian virtue which derives from a "pessimism of weakness."

In another aphorism of *The Antichrist*, Nietzsche calls Christianity "the religion of pity" (*AC* 7). Pity (*Mitleiden*), he says, spreads the contagion of powerlessness that is the essence of suffering (*Leiden*). It preserves everything that manifests the weakening of life, everything that should be left to decline and decay, and gives it the means to affirm itself. This points to a latent drive to obstruct the instincts that aim at the preservation of life and the enhancement of its value. At the ground of the religion of pity lies what Nietzsche describes as "a nihilistic philosophy that inscribes the negation of life on its banner." Such a philosophy goes so far as to "make pity *the* virtue, the ground and source of all virtues." He goes on:

> Pity is the *praxis* of nihilism . . . a major instrument of the heightening of *décadence*—Pity talks us into *nothingness!*[8] Except that one does not say 'nothingness': one says instead 'the beyond,' or 'God,' [or '*true* life,'] or Nirvana, redemption, bliss.

Thus Christian pity or love of humanity ends up as no more than a solidarity in which the weak can preserve each other.

Nietzsche's ideas here overlap with certain aspects of the theory of evolution. Whatever the direct influence, it is clear that evolutionary theory gave a sharper edge to his confrontation with Christianity [*WP* 246]. He stresses that the human species constantly demands selection; or conversely, that it is the demand of the species that elements representing regression and a weakening of life should perish. On this view, Christianity is set up as the absolute counter-principle to natural selection and as the fundamental obstacle to the destiny of humankind, since its foundational standpoint values the interests of individuals more highly than those of the species. Therefore, Christianity's so-called love of humanity is a "solidarity of the weak" or mass egoism (*Massen-Egoismus*) of the weak. True love of humanity, in contrast, demands the sacrifice of the self in favor of the best of the human species; the human species can survive only through a love of humanity that demands self-sacrifice for the sake of the highest. Moreover, Christianity, in contrast, argues the extreme position that nobody may be sacrificed— even those who most ought to sacrifice themselves voluntarily. For Nietzsche this is not genuine "humanity"; indeed it is not any kind of humanity at all [*WP* 246].

From Nietzsche's perspective the view that all souls are *equal* before God is the most dangerous of all possible valuations.[9] It grants to all souls an absolutely equal degree of perfection, the same ideal, and the same way to salvation. This is the most extreme form of making equality a right, in which the importance of the self is inflated to the point of meaninglessness. In such an equality of rights, the order of rank (*Rangordnung*) that Nietzsche sees as essential to life—the distance between higher beings and lower—is eliminated. Each one becomes aware of the importance of his or her own self to a ludicrous extent, thus reducing everyone to the lowest common denominator. This is the danger of the situation in which what should be left to perish is preserved and the destiny of the human species is ignored.[10]

This kind of Christian valuation and its danger for humankind still pervade the entire modern era. For Nietzsche the French Revolution, which was stimulated by the ideas of Rousseau, represents the continuation of such Christian ideals.[11] While the modern era has lost the ridiculous self-importance of the equality of all before God, the value of "man" is now sought in an idealism that sees all people as gradually approaching some ideal human being. This view contains residues of the "optical habit" of the Christian perspective which ignores the destiny of the species in favor of the interests of the individual. This optical habit takes its stand on the negative direction of life and marks a decline of the human species [*WP* 94, 339].

The moralities of democracy and socialism, as extensions of Christian morality in the modern era, also conceal the will to transform the negativity of life into a positive principle. The decline of life itself has, as it were, become will. Those who stand higher in the order of rank are distinguished by will to power in the fundamental sense described above; but the moralities of democracy and socialism teach hatred and contempt for such a will. In this sense, such moralities stem from a transformation of the *décadence* of life into a positive principle of will—the will to reduce life and humanity to the lowest common denominator. These two features constitute what Nietzsche calls "slave morality."[12]

According to Nietzsche the essence of life itself is an instinct for growth, for the accumulation of strength, for power. Those who lack this will to power necessarily perish [*AC* 6]. The highest values based on Christian morality have so far lacked such a will, crowning instead various nihilistic values of *décadence* with the names of the holiest and letting them reign supreme. Beneath this phenomenon lurks a denaturalized naturalness, a life that tortures itself, an instinct that sees life itself as an enemy, a hatred and resentment toward the order of rank that is essential to affirmative life. This nullification of actual life lies at the very ground of the awe-inspiring world that Christianity, in its self-deception of weakened life, imagines to lie beyond this world. Insight into this state of affairs divests the world beyond of its awe-inspiring splendor and uncovers the fundamental nullity of actual reality. What then appears is true, self-conscious nihilism, and not the unconscious or merely latent nihilism of Christianity or democracy and socialism. Schopenhauer and other pessimists, and certain *décadents* of the modern era, were precursors of this kind of nihilism [*WP* 765]. The reason why the pessimism of Schopenhauer, who negates the will to life even though he opposes Christianity, considers *Mitleid* a virtue is that it still clings to the spirit of Christianity. The *décadence* of European literature and art as a whole—"décadence from St. Petersburg to Paris, from Tolstoy to Wagner"—also rests on pity. Of this, Nietzsche writes:

> Nothing is unhealthier, in the midst of our unhealthy modernity, than Christian pity. To be a physician *here*, to be merciless *here*, to ply the surgeon's knife *here*—that is *our* task, that is *our* kind of human love, that is how *we* are philosophers, we Hyperboreans![13]

4. The Concept of "Sincerity"—"Will to Illusion"

Nietzsche's view of Christian morality and the *décadence* of modern culture come from his own nihilism, from his having lived through all these forms of nihilism, anticipated their endings, and "looked

back" at them from the "hyperborean" standpoint that had reached
the end of the end of nihilism. At that very end, at the North Pole
within Nietzsche himself, nihilism consummates itself and is
sloughed off. It swells to a round ripeness within him, and then
drops like a fruit from a tree. For Nietzsche, to live through nihilism
is to produce an interpretation of it (auslegen) in this way.[14] His is an
existential interpretation—cultivated within himself and then expressed—that is at the same time negation and creation.[15] Here interpretation is confrontation and confrontation is interpretation.
The movement into nihilism is also the counter-movement against
it—the "to it and out of it."

What made such an interpretation of Christianity possible for
Nietzsche? What was it that prompted him to go beyond Christian
nihilism to his hyperborean nihilism? In his own words, it was
nothing other than the sincerity (Wahrhaftigkeit) cultivated by Christianity that allowed him to pursue psychologically the logical consequences of Christianity's becoming nihilism. Nietzsche writes at
the end of the short section on "radical nihilism" that the idea that
the highest values are mere fictions is "a consequence of 'sincerity'
that has been fully cultivated: and thus itself a consequence of faith
in morality" [WP 3]. He explains in a subsequent passage: "Among
the forces that morality cultivated fully was sincerity: this finally
turns against morality itself . . ." [WP 5]. What does it mean to say
that sincerity negates morality, its foster-parent? What is the dialectical character of this sincerity?

Sincerity, in a word, means to be honest, both toward oneself
and toward others. Christian morality, however, fabricates a "true
world" and sets up the self to be eternalized as the self before God.
It further establishes an idealistic self by having it approach but
never reach an ideal image. It sees the self through a distance-
perspective, as it were, holding up a mirror before it from afar. An
eternal and divine world is set up in opposition to actual reality,
and such illusions as an ideal society of ideal people, and the kind
of selves that would exist in such a world, are held up as models for
the self in reality. It is here that the standpoint of trying to be infinitely sincere toward oneself and others originates. In a note entitled "The Problem of Sincerity" Nietzsche writes: "The first and
most important thing here is the will to illusion [Schein], the setting
up of perspectives, the 'laws' of optics, which means the positing of
the untrue as true, and so on" (XIV, 89). He seems to have in mind
here the setting up of illusion as true Being, the fabrication of a
model for the self, and the establishment as "truth" of the "law"

that regulates this kind of seeing.

In another note on this topic, Nietzsche writes: "Nobody has yet grasped the problem of sincerity. The things that are said against lying are the naiveté of a schoolmaster—especially the commandment: 'thou shalt not lie!' " (XI, 261). On this view, what is primary is a "will to illusion" (*Wille zum Schein*) that would take what is not true and set it up as truth; and the realization of this will is the foundation from which sincerity arises. Nietzsche says that sincerity is cultivated by our trying to have "God" and "conscience." Though we shall discuss this in more detail later, we may mention here that he considers lies as permissible creative acts for will to power to be fulfilled, and illusions of various kinds as necessary for the preservation and enhancement of humanity. He also says that in order for us to be able to act and have knowledge, the source of illusion must be maintained (XIV, 87). The will to illusion is actually backed up by will to power, and is in this sense an important expedient. Will to power strives to reach the truth of the self by constantly shattering falsehoods.[16] However, things that are fixed as "truths" again become falsehoods and illusions, and this hinders the growth of life and puts an end to the becoming of will to power. This negates will to power. That is, if will to power can see through this truth of the self within "the truth" and can reflect the self in it, it is able to see the self in the perspective of distance. This is the self-deception of will to power that lies behind all "truths." Only when this self-deception comes to awareness, and illusion is understood as illusion, is a further, broader and deeper perspective opened up. This, too, is the fruit of sincerity. Only with the final realization that everything that is being objectified by will to power, everything that is being set up as true reality, is illusion, does sincerity come to term.

Nietzsche expresses this idea in another fragment by saying: "The sincere person ends up by understanding that he is always lying" (XII, 293). This kind of sincerity was actually cultivated by Christian morality in its idea of conscience, according to which there is not a single thing that is not false when it is placed before God. But then this sincerity is turned against Christian morality, the womb from which it sprang, and unleashes the power to carry out psychologically the logical consequences of escaping from morality and ending up in nihilism. This is a case of getting behind Christian morality to discover the will to illusion supporting it. Sincerity thereby reaches its "end" in Nietzsche—or, as he says: "sincerity finally (*endlich*) turns against morality itself."

Nietzsche develops the theme of "radical nihilism" further:

> now insight into this lie that has for so long been carved into
> our flesh, and that we despair of getting rid of, works pre-
> cisely as a stimulant. We now confirm in ourself needs im-
> planted in us by moral interpretations, over a long time, that
> now appear to us as needs for what is untrue. [WP 5]

All of what has been regarded as the need for the true or the good
has come to be seen as actually a need for the untrue—a will to
illusion. An antinomy then arises between our not valuing what we
acknowledge as true and our no longer being permitted to value
what we would like to deceive ourselves about. This kind of situation sets in motion a process of dismantling. As long as we believe
in a morality as the only basis upon which we can live, we cannot
approve of our own existence. We are caught in the contradiction
that Christian morality, conceived as a countermeasure to prevent
our lives from falling into nihility, ends up by leading us into nihilism. To reveal this kind of antinomy is precisely the meaning of sincerity, whose dialectical process dismantles the Christian morality
that gave it birth. This dialectic is the psychological carrying out of
the logical consequences mentioned earlier, a philosophizing about
the consequences in historical and existential fashion. It means un-
covering the nihilistic tendency at the basis of Christian morality,
willing nihilism affirmatively, and willing to demolish what needs
to collapse. This is where the distinction between passive and active
nihilism is to be found. So far, we have focused on the former. In
the next chapter we turn to the latter, in connection with Nietzsche's ideas of *amor fati* and eternal recurrence.

Chapter Four

Nietzsche's Affirmative Nihilism:

Amor Fati and Eternal Recurrence

1. Value-Interpretation and Perspectivism

The world does not exist apart from our "value-interpretation" of it. There is no such thing as a "true" world that has nothing to do with us; conversely, what we interpret as the world is always an illusion,[1] and this illusory world a "perspective" of will to power. Nietzsche's view that *the world is illusory* and is to be *affirmed absolutely* is most clearly illustrated in the following passage from the posthumous notes:

> That the *value of the world* lies in our interpretation [—that perhaps elsewhere other interpretations than just human ones are possible—], that interpretations hitherto have been perspectival evaluations by means of which we can preserve ourselves in life, that is, in will to power and for the growth of power, that every *enhancement of humanity* brings with it the overcoming of narrower interpretations, that every strengthening and broadening of power that is attained opens up new perspectives and calls for belief in new horizons—this idea runs throughout my writings. The world that *concerns us* is false; that is, it has no factual substance to it, but is rather a poetic filling in and rounding out of a meager sum of observations; it is "in flux," as something becoming, as a constantly sliding and shifting fabrication that never approaches the truth: for—there is no "truth." (*WP* 616)

The broadening of perspectives continues to be false no matter how far it is carried out, and so the world we cognize is always

false. Nonetheless the broadening of perspectives is a new illuminating of the world and thus strengthens and enhances humanity.
The roots of this idea of Nietzsche's lie in his "epistemology."

As we saw earlier, Nietzsche spoke of the collapse of the "cosmological values" of purposiveness, unity, and truth—that is to say,
of the view which supposes that the world-process has some kind
of meaning or purpose, that the variety of the world in its entirety
forms an integrated system, and that there is a "true world" apart
from the transient world of becoming. These values are categories
of reason, and things in which previous philosophy had recognized
standards of truth and reality. An absolute standard was established
apart from the flux of becoming, and things were distinguished as
true or false, real or unreal, according to whether they did or did
not measure up to the standard. The world of becoming accordingly
came to be considered a world of mere appearance, while a "true
world" beyond was assumed to be the truly real world.

According to Nietzsche, these values are fabricated by the will
in order to control the actual world and make it easier to deal with.
They are, as it were, a kind of handle that the will has attached to
the world to manipulate it. At the basis of the scheme lie hidden
considerations of utility and the human instinct for self-
preservation. The purpose is efficient self-deception. The resulting
falsehoods are falsehoods "*of principle*": their fabrication is indispensable for human survival. Nietzsche's idea may be easier to understand if we compare it to Hegel's thought. For Hegel, logic and
the categories of reason belong to divine reason, and at the same
time to the self-consciousness of human reason, which ultimately
reverts to divine reason. For Nietzsche, however, it is "the *biological
utility* of this system of *lies of principle*" [WP 584] that grounds the
categories of reason. This will to deceive the self efficiently is an
expedient (*Mittel*) employed by will to power, functioning here as a
"will to deception" (*Wille zur Taüschung*).

The idea that human beings can live only through illusion is
one that Nietzsche held from early on. As he says: "Knowledge as
such is impossible within the flux of becoming. In that case, how
then is knowledge possible? As an error about oneself, as will to
power, as will to deception" [WP 617]. In other words, there is in
the incessant flux of becoming no such thing as knowledge *as such*
about determinate "being" in determinate forms. Knowledge is
possible only through will to power, which constantly engages in
efficient self-deception. By contrast, when "truth" is seen not as
something at the service of life but as the value-standard of life—
and this is where moralistic interpretations enter in—and when life

and becoming are measured against some totally separate truth, then a "will to truth" appears which seeks determinateness. This signals the *"impotence of the will to create"* referred to earlier.[2]

To return self-consciously to the will to deception by negating the will to truth, to revolt against the creative will and lie against life, constitutes sincerity toward life. This also means, as I said before, that the story of the progress of interpreting the value of the world, a string of lies all the way to the end, arrives at a new perspective and opens on to a new horizon. What Nietzsche calls the constant fabrication of new lies is therefore a new development of becoming. Life is not tied down to any fixed truth, nor does becoming hold fast to "Being." There is a leap toward further, broader horizons, and the emergence of *new possibilities* for humanity; in this sense, "deception," "illusion," and so on are always expressions of human power and potential. With insight into the world as illusory and something to be affirmed absolutely from this kind of perspective, the will to deception realizes itself as will to power.

Elsewhere Nietzsche talks about two conditions in which art appears within human beings as a natural power: the dream-vision of Apollo, and Dionysiac intoxication. Of the former he says: "The will to mere appearance (*Schein*), to illusion (*Illusion*), and to deception, becoming, and change is deeper, more 'metaphysical' than the will to *truth* or reality or Being."[3] This suggests an identification of the "will to illusion" and "will to deception" with the will to Apollinian dream-vision, and of the will to power as Dionysian will. It would also allow us to see a consistent theme running through Nietzsche's works from the time of *The Birth of Tragedy*.

At any rate, the return to the standpoint of will to power takes a person of strong will who can stand existence in a world without "purpose, unity, or truth," a world of becoming where everything constantly shifts, flows, perishes or is born—in short, one who can stand up to the absolute nihility of "the death of God." It requires relentlessly tracking down and negating all idealistic and otherworldly worldviews and moralities in oneself and others; such a one must, in Nietzsche's own words, be "the murderer of God." Only thus can one come to an absolute affirmation of life and human destiny. Such a person can, through a sudden reversal of perspective, look into the abyss of the nihility of the absence of God and truth and see the creative will there and the horizon of infinite possibility and power behind the entire fabrication. From such a standpoint of depth one can see the reality of this world. In a fragment quoted from earlier, Nietzsche writes: "Becoming as inventing, willing, negating the self, as self-overcoming: no subject, but a

doing, a positing, creative . . ."[4] The standpoint at which one shat-
ters the nihility of the absence of God and lives in creative will,
regarding this fictitious world without meaning or purpose as the
only reality—in effect, a "new religion" with a Dionysian "new
god"—is similar in some respects to the standpoint of Meister Eckhart who speaks of living "without why," within the "God"-less
"desert" of divinity.[5] It also bears affinities to the Zen Buddhist
observation that "the willow is green and the flower red."[6] When,
for example, a Zen master was asked: "It [buddha-nature, presumably—tr.] is purely primordial; how does it then bring forth in
an instant mountains, rivers, and the vast earth?" his reply was
simply, "It is purely primordial; how does it then bring forth in an
instant mountains, rivers, and the vast earth?"[7]

2. The Problem of *Amor Fati*

When one sees the world perspectivally in this way the world-
process takes on the necessity of *fatum*. The world appears as the
"playful" activity of will to power and at the same time as fate.
Nietzsche says that when an "other world" is posited behind this
world of becoming, it gives the impression that this world *could be
otherwise* than it actually is. This thereby "annuls necessity and fate"
in the world, and renders it useless "to *submit*" to its necessity and
"*to conform oneself to it.*"[8] After the other world has disappeared, in
what do the necessity and fate of the world consist? And what does
it mean to submit oneself (*sich ergeben*) to fate?
  Nietzsche acknowledges Schopenhauer's understanding of the
"thing-in-itself"—which had hitherto been considered necessary,
good, and true—as will, but at the same time criticizes him for not
deifying this will. Schopenhauer, he claims, had not yet broken free
of Christian values, and thus he understood the thing-in-itself as
will and not as God, and so considered it absolutely evil and to be
negated. "He did not understand that there can be infinitely many
ways of being-able-to-be-different [*Anders-sein-können*], and even of
being-able-to-be-God."[9] Nietzsche is saying here that will to power
can be different infinitely. While there is no "other world" besides
this world, and even though this world *cannot be different*, will can
differ infinitely. However, this will at the same time demands that
we submit to the utmost necessity and fate of the world and conform ourselves to it. The standpoint of *amor fati* demands that the
will, which can differ infinitely, conform itself to the world, which

cannot be different. This standpoint is deeply bound up with the idea of the illusory nature of the world, with the interpretation of the world as self-deception of the will throughout, and with the absolute affirmation of this illusion and self-deception. Love of fate therefore means understanding the world as a play of the multiple perspectives of will to power. Against this backdrop we may look more closely at Nietzsche's ideas of fate and of love.

In the present "godless" era the divine Providence of Christianity has ceased to be believed in and fatalism has stepped in to take its place. While Nietzsche says that fatalism is "the contemporary form of philosophical sensitivity" [*WP* 243], it is clear that his "love of fate" is not fatalism in the ordinary sense. It rather pushes the fatalistic viewpoint to the extreme, purifying it and imparting a profound *turn* to the meaning of fate. In the same note, he speaks of the way in which

> the [disastrous] belief in divine providence—the most *crippling*[10] belief to the hand and reason there has ever been . . . continues to exist under various formulas guises such as ["nature,"] "progress," "perfection," or "Darwinism" . . . Even *fatalism*, our contemporary form of philosophical sensitivity, is a consequence of that *oldest* belief in divine providence, an unconscious consequence . . .

In the ordinary sense of fatalism each individual is seen as merely a particular *modus* of a single absolute being; fatalism thus retains traces of divine Providence even after having denied it. It is, Nietzsche adds, as if the course of all things were being conducted "independently of *us*."

However, in another note he writes: "The highest fatalism is identical with chance and the creative" (XII, 405). In opposition to ordinary fatalism, which makes the world-process necessary in such a way as to destroy chance or creativity, Nietzsche advocates a fatalism in which they are as such immediately identical with necessity. The identity of necessity and chance, of fate and the "play" of will, is possible only by virtue of the creating self. If divine Providence is there instead, necessity means no more than control by Providence; chance and the self-creation connected with it cannot but disappear. This is why Zarathustra says: "What would it then mean to create, if there were—gods!" [*Za* II, 2]. Only from the standpoint of the creative self can chance and necessity come together as one. This is also expressed in Nietzsche's idea that "*self is fate"* (*ego fatum*). While he says that all concurrences of things and events are "enormously *coincidental*" (*ungeheuer zufällig*), he continues by saying:

> *from this* it follows that *every* action of a person has an *infinitely great* influence on everything that is to come. The same reverence which, looking back, one gives to the entirety of fate, one must at the same time give to one's own self. [XIII 74]

And then he adds the words "self = fate" ["*ego fatum*"].

In the absence of both divine Providence and fatalism in the ordinary sense, occurrences assume the character of utter chance. Every action of the self in this context is influenced by all things and in turn influences all things. All things become the fate of the self, and the self becomes the fate of all things. At such a fundamental level the world moves at one with the self, and the self moves at one with the world. This idea is close to the Buddhist idea of *karma*, although in Nietzsche the standpoint of self as fate is a fundamentally creative one.[11] The ego itself becomes *fatum* insofar as the creative standpoint is one of will to power. This means that the world of becoming itself reveals its inherent form as a manifestation of will to power and as a multiplicity of perspectives; and at the same time that the self which exists within this world becomes the will to power that is inherent to the self. In the midst of the world of becoming the self turns the world and its "necessity" into its own will and affirms it; it affirms the world and its chance nature as necessity from out of creative will to power.[12] Nietzsche characterizes the standpoint of *amor fati* as "attaining height and a bird's eye view in observation" [*WP* 1004]. He explains this by saying that there "one understands how everything actually goes *as it should go*: how every kind of 'imperfection' and the suffering due to it belong together in the *highest* desirability." To say "yes" in this sense (*Ja-sagen*) is precisely *amor fati*;[13] and this means that "self = fate." That love of fate should be "*self* = fate" demands more careful investigation.

3. Love of Fate as "Innermost Nature"—Suffering—Soul

In the Epilogue to *Nietzsche contra Wagner*, Nietzsche calls *amor fati* "my innermost nature":

> I have often asked myself whether I am not more deeply indebted to the most difficult years of my life than to any of the

others. As my innermost nature teaches me, everything necessary is, when seen from a height and in the sense of a *great
economy*, also useful in itself—one should not only bear it,
one should *love* it. *Amor fati*: that is my innermost nature. [And
as far as my long period of illness is concerned, do I not owe it
infinitely more than I owe my health?] I owe it a *higher* health,
[one that becomes stronger from everything that does not kill
it!]—*I also owe my philosophy to it*. Only the great pain is the
ultimate liberator of the spirit, as the teacher of the *great suspicion*. . . . Only the great pain . . . forces us philosophers to descend into our ultimate depths and to disabuse ourselves of all
trusting, of everything good-natured, concealing, mild, medi-
ocre, in which we have perhaps placed our humanity up until
now . . . [and] out of the abyss of the *great suspicion* one returns newly born . . .[14]

What Nietzsche calls "the abyss of the great suspicion" and
"the ultimate depths" of the philosopher is nihilism. In this rebirth
from the depths "with a higher health" and "with a second and
more dangerous innocence" one's innermost nature bursts forth
like a natural spring from which the covering debris has been re-
moved. At this point the spring proclaims as its liberator the sharp
pick-axe of necessity that has pierced down through the debris and
brought it pain. Nietzsche writes in another passage about "taking
suffering more profoundly as a means of transformation" (XIV,
301). Here suffering is seen from a higher vantage point and affirmed as useful from the perspective of the "great economy"
(*grosse Ökonomie*) of life. And ultimately the spring will come to affirm even the debris it burst through and which now floats in it.[15]
Absolute affirmation affirms even the deceptions that had blocked
it, and which themselves are part of that "great economy" through
their biological usefulness as lies of principle. Even that which negates and obstructs life is affirmed as useful for life. This standpoint
of life as absolute affirmation is *amor fati* in the sense of love of what
is inevitable.

For Nietzsche, to endure the inevitable is a way of returning to
the self itself. The very act of submitting to fate is a returning to
one's own innermost nature. It is to become oneself, shaking off
what is not oneself and what prevents one from becoming oneself.
To call this innermost nature wherein one becomes oneself *amor fati*
means that what is not oneself—what has prevented one from being oneself—is appropriated into the self and transformed into
something uniquely one's own (*eigen*).

Under the compulsion of the need or necessity (*Not*) that prevents one from becoming oneself and from becoming free, one is forced to descend into the abyss within. But once one is freed within the abyss, the need is turned into an element of this life of freedom. When Zarathustra calls his own soul "turn of need" (*Wende der Not*) and "fate" (*Schicksal*),[16] he means that the turn of need, in which necessity is turned into an element of the life of the free soul, is the soul itself. In this case necessity becomes one with the creative. When Zarathustra says, "instead of loving your neighbor love yourself" [I, 16; III, 11–12], this love of self means a love of fate and necessity—or rather it means that one *becomes* fate itself. It means loving all things that are not the self, and which obstruct the self, as one's own, in the pleasure (*Lust*) of a self-transformation that overcomes suffering through suffering (*Leiden*), rather than through pity (*Mitleiden*) or sympathy. This Nietzsche calls "great love" (*grosse Liebe*).

In *Ecce homo*, after speaking of his long neglect by the Germans, Nietzsche writes:

> I myself, however, have never suffered as a result of all that; what is *necessary* does not hurt me; amor fati is my innermost nature. This does not, however, prevent me from loving irony, even world-historical irony. ["The Case of Wagner," §4]

World-historical irony here refers to the overturning of former ideals and values in the face of the abyss of nihilism. For Nietzsche, the solitary mountain peak harbors the abyss, or, rather, the abyss and the peak become one [*Za* III, 1]. Zarathustra says to his soul: "Oh my soul, I gave you the right to say No like the storm and Yes as the open heavens say Yes" [III, 14]. To say No like the storm is active nihilism and its accompanying world-historical irony; and to say Yes like the open heavens is *amor fati* and will to power. Both of these spring from the same source, namely from the soul that has returned to will to power as the principle of the world. "Oh my soul," Zarathustra continues, "I taught you the contempt that does not come like the gnawing of the worm, the great and loving contempt which loves most where it despises most." What is to be despised is anything that blocks *amor fati* and will to power, anything that obstructs the soul on its way to itself. And what obstructs most profoundly is worthy of the profoundest contempt. Only when the obstructions are eliminated does *amor fati* becomes true *amor fati*— the soul itself—and only then is the innermost nature of the self revealed. Such a soul loves what has caused it suffering; it turns its need, and loves most where it most despises.

Zarathustra also calls his soul "encompassure of encompassures" (*Umfang der Umfänge*)[17] and "umbilical cord of time" (*Nabelschnur der Zeit*) and "azure bell" (*azurne Glocke*). With respect to this final appellation we recall Zarathustra's earlier comment:

> I have become one who blesses and says Yes. . . . But this is my blessing: to stand over every thing as its own heaven, as its round roof, its azure bell and eternal security. [III, 4]

Here we are close to the standpoint that embraces what is not-self as self, the standpoint of love of fate. "Encompassure of encompassures" means something similar. Zarathustra goes on to say:

> Oh my soul, there is nowhere a soul more loving and more embracing and more comprehensive than you! Where would future and past lie more closely together than in you? [III, 14]

This is the soul as "great love" and love of fate, where future and past are embraced as one in the soul.[18]

When fate is brought into identity with one's innermost nature in this way, and the world becomes the perspective of the great love and the will that embraces all possible comprehensive horizons, this will then comes to move as one with the world in such a way as to be able to generate "world-historical irony" and become fundamentally creative. This is a radical reversal of the meaning of fate in ordinary fatalism, in that fate is made one with the self's creative will and all residues of the idea of divine Providence have been eliminated. But if the meaning of *fate* is radically transformed through being brought into identity with the self, there must also be a radical transformation of the *self's* mode of being as a result of its equation with fate. The meaning of this can be clarified by considering the idea of the eternal recurrence.

4. The Idea of Eternal Recurrence: The "Moment" and Eternity

The idea of eternal recurrence did not come to Nietzsche as a consequence of theoretical reflection: it was more like a bolt of lightning that struck him from direct experience of the world. So profoundly did it spring from his very being that it was difficult even for him to explain. I shall consider it here first as a direct experience of the nature of eternity, then with respect to its "momentary" nature, and finally in its connection with fate.

Eternal recurrence may be called the intuitive experience of insight into eternity from within this world of becoming. The search for eternal life in another world that transcends the world of becoming is, of course, negated by Nietzsche in his radical pursuit of the nihility that such an other world hides from view. For him only the world in which all things are in ever-changing flux remains. The world of flux, of impermanence, comes to be seen as the activity of bottomless will, an activity without any transcendent meaning or purpose; it becomes the play (*Spiel*) of bottomless will in the joy (*Lust*) of life which is absolute affirmation. That all things are ceaselessly changing and passing away is a source of suffering and grief; yet this suffering and its source can, just as they are, be transformed into joy. Thus Nietzsche has Zarathustra sing in "The Drunken Song"[19]: "Suffering says: 'Pass away!'" and *"all joy wants— eternity!"* This joy does not exist apart from suffering:

> Pain too is a joy, cursing is also a blessing, so rich is joy that it thirst
>   after pain, for hell, for hatred,
> for shame, for the cripple, for *world*—for this world, oh you know it
>   well! . . .
> For all joy wants itself, and therefore it also wants suffering in the
>   heart! . . .
> Joy wants the eternity of *all* things, *wants deep, deep eternity!*
>
> (*Za* IV, 19, §§ 10–11).

When joy, the innocent play of life, wants itself, all phenomena of the world are dissolved into this joy and innocent life. This is the absolute affirmation of life, the form of life that affirms itself absolutely. *There* is the eternity in the midst of the transiency of becoming; *there* is divine life in a new and Dionysian sense, in a world without God.

The direct experience of this eternity is the "moment." Nietzsche speaks of the points at which new gods reveal themselves in different ways as "those timeless moments that fall into life as if from the moon, in which one simply does not know how old one is and how young one will yet become" [*WP* 1038]. Such an experience of the timeless moment may be similar to what the ancients called *ekstasis*; and some such experience is probably the basis of the insight of eternal recurrence.

In a letter to his friend Peter Gast, Nietzsche reports that the thought of recurrence struck him in August of 1881, as he was walking in the woods along by Lake Silvaplana in the Upper Engadin. He wrote it down on a piece of paper with the inscription "6000 feet beyond humanity and time."[20] The idea of eternal recurrence is the major theme of *Zarathustra*. In the chapter entitled "On the Vision and Enigma," Zarathustra confronts the *spirit of melancholy*—the "spirit of gravity"[21]—and speaks of the idea as his "abyssal thought" [III, 2]. In the speech "On the Spirit of Gravity" this spirit is characterized as that which makes one weary of the world (*weltmüde*): "Earth and life are said to be heavy for [human beings]; and thus the spirit of gravity *wills* it" [III, 11, §2]. Nietzsche then enumerates all the things that make human life tiresome, which he dubs values of *décadence* and nihilism. At their foundation is a spirit that excavates a cavernous nihility in the ground of the life of this world and drags life down into it. But what exactly is the nature of this spirit?

At the beginning of "On the Vision and Enigma," where Zarathustra first speaks of eternal recurrence, he tells of how, as he climbed up the mountain, the spirit of gravity made his feet heavy and "dragged [them] downwards, down toward the abyss." He calls this spirit his "arch-enemy" and "devil."[22] It sits on Zarathustra's shoulder in the form of a dwarf who lets thoughts drip like drops of lead through his ear and into his brain.

> "Oh Zarathustra, you philosopher's stone . . . you threw yourself so high—but every stone that is thrown—must fall!
>
> Condemned to yourself and to your own stoning: oh Zarathustra you threw the stone far—but it will fall back on to *you!*"
>
> Then the dwarf fell silent, and that lasted long. But his silence was oppressive; and in being two people like that, one is truly more solitary than when alone!
>
> I climbed and climbed, I dreamed, I reflected—but everything oppressed me. I was like an invalid made tired by his torture, and whom an even worse dream wakens from his eventual sleep.

The spirit of gravity is the force that makes one fall back to one self no matter how high one may throw oneself. It prevents one from becoming, as Nietzsche says, "free as a bird, and light, and one who flies."[23] In one of his poems he writes: "one must have wings if one loves the abyss . . ."[24] The essence of the spirit of gravity is that one can never escape the boundaries of the self no matter how much the self tries to elevate itself or how far one tries to fly away from oneself. It is the gravity that anchors the self to itself. To escape this kind of gravity was Nietzsche's final and most difficult battle.

As we saw earlier, when God dies and the true world is shown to be an illusion, the resolve to nihilism becomes a necessity, and the standpoint of will to power is attained. To make this standpoint one's own means to love the whole of necessity—all suffering, shame, and hell, indeed everything that goes against one's will—and to *will* it. In this way, everything turns to joy. At this point some doubt may arise as to whether this love of fate may not simply be a state of mind in which one finds nothing but the self no matter where one turns. Is this not a frozen hell of solitude where everything has turned to ice? If so, the only way to avoid this state of affairs would be through pity, which could still remain even after the death of God. To turn away from the deep pit of solitude is to end up in pity. The relationship of nihility and pity was, as we saw, one that concerned Schopenhauer, and it will turn up again as a problem for Dostoevsky. But the love of fate of which Nietzsche is speaking is not such a hell of solitude.

Zarathustra was, to be sure, a solitary. His world was in the cold, clear heights, where the air is thin and pure, where glaciers shine in strong sunlight, and where clouds sometimes gather at their base and lightning strikes. From such a world Nietzsche hurled his bolts of lightning into the gloomy and oppressive spirit of Europe; yet his was not a world of death and freezing cold. Zarathustra strained to hear the distant call of the voice of the one who is to come—the *Übermensch*—and went forth to welcome him. Within the will to power, which is the source of all things, he waits confidently for the advent of those who are his equals, of his children, of those who have overcome "man." And because he is oriented toward such figures, he is able to affirm everything and love everything with a smile—including even what is meanest and ugliest. The figure of the one to come is projected as if in a mirror in the will of Zarathustra, who stands at that summit of life. His creative will, through which he seeks his children and strives to give birth to the *Übermensch*, is itself evidence for the *Übermensch*'s advent. Such conviction and self-confidence strictly negate love of the closest person, of the neighbor, as well as pity. In their place, a love of the farthest is advocated—a love of the self, which is love of everything, including the meanest things—and this accounts for the source of the absolute affirmation in love of fate. This kind of self-love is not a hell of solitude; it is life that can affirm everything as it is and as it becomes. This is the season when the spring breeze brings everything back to life, melting the ice that had held it frozen. But we must return to Zarathustra's confrontation with the spirit of gravity in "On the Vision and Enigma," to the point where he finally challenges the spirit of gravity with the thought of eternal recurrence.

5. Eternal Recurrence and Overcoming the Spirit of Gravity

Zarathustra counters the spirit of gravity, which is pulling his climbing feet downward, with courage. He uses courage (*Mut*) to oppose melancholy (*Schwermut*).[25]

> Courage strikes dead dizziness at the edge of the abyss: and where does the human being not stand at the edge of the abyss! Is seeing not itself—seeing the abyss?
> Courage is the best slayer: courage slays even pity. Pity is however the deepest abyss: as deeply as one looks into life, so deeply does one also look into suffering.
> Courage which attacks is the best slayer: it strikes dead even death, for it says: "*That* was life? Well then! Once again please!"

Here we see the thought of eternal recurrence as the source of this courage. Zarathustra challenges the spirit of gravity by saying: "Dwarf! I or you! But I am the stronger of us two! . . . you cannot bear my most abyssal thought!"

Zarathustra and the dwarf are soon standing in front of a large gate. Two roads meet at this gate, roads that no one has ever walked to the end. One road leads back to an eternity, and the other road also leads to an eternity. On the gate the name *Moment* is inscribed. Standing at the gate, Zarathustra says:

> Look at this moment! From this gate a long, eternal ring-road runs *back*: behind us lies eternity.
> Of all those who *can* run, must they not have run this ring-road once already?

All transient things are said to have passed through this moment once before. This strange intuition of Nietzsche's must have come from an experience of a timeless moment or of the eternal present. For if the moment is the eternal present, everything that is past must have passed through this moment. In this sense the eternal present is the eternal past and each moment of that past. At this present moment the eternal past is all pulled back into the present. The eternal future, too, passes through this moment. At this present moment, both the eternal past and the eternal future are pulled back into the present in their entirety, from opposite directions, in such a way that they overlap.[26] What has not yet come is what has already existed, and what is past is also what is to come some time. The eternal past and eternal future are tied together in the present, and time becomes a ring: "the path of eternity is curved." Things past and to come have gone around this ring already innumerable times; they have already passed the present moment innumerable times. The ring of time has already overlaid itself repeatedly, and from now on will continue to overlay itself:

> Everything goes, everything comes back: eternally rolls the wheel of Being. Everything dies, everything comes up again, eternally runs the year of Being.[27]
> Everything breaks, everything is put together anew; eternally the same house of Being builds itself. Everything parts, everything greets itself again; eternally the ring of Being remains faithful to itself. In every now Being begins; around every here rolls the ball of there. The middle is everywhere. The path of eternity is curved. [III, 13]

The eternal present is something that numerous mystics of the past have experienced. One thinks, for example, of the idea of the "One" in Plotinus, who speaks of the experience of union with the One as an *ekstasis*, a standing out from the self. Or again, there is the famous passage in the *Confessions* of Saint Augustine concerning the ecstatic experience of touching eternity within the present moment.[28] Augustine's theory of time understands the past as present and the future as present in the eternal present of God. Since Augustine many mystics have spoken of this kind of experience, of the moment in which one tastes eternity directly while in time. But for the godless Nietzsche, not even the eternal present can be based on something that transcends time, even though the point is still to break free of the bonds of time. His concern is with liberation from the human way of being, carried along by the stream of time and suffering under impermanence and change. But to transcend time, for Nietzsche, would mean getting caught in another illusion. Instead, one needs a standpoint from which living time in a truly temporal way, within time, becomes a liberation from the bonds of time. This eternity is not an eternity posited outside of time, but a ring of time turning eternally.

This "ring of time" turns out to be nothing other than will itself and life. Nietzsche's eternity is a this-worldly eternal life: "*This* life—this *eternal* life."[29] As Zarathustra says: "*That* was life? Well then! Once again please!" The will to will this way makes time curved and eternal in nature, and lets one live time in its full temporality. Here the eternal recurrence, the self-overlapping of ring-like time, opens up the standpoint of the will to affirm life absolutely, the will to love of fate, and itself becomes the content of this absolute affirmation. This helps us to see why Zarathustra called his soul the "umbilical cord of time": time and Being begin from a standpoint within the ring of time turning around in overlapping layers of eternity, from a moment of affirming and seeing through the ring. The idea is reminiscent of the Zen image of "far mountain-ranges without end, walls of rock, row upon row."[30]

In this kind of eternal recurrence the spirit of gravity is overcome. The frame of the self, in which all things thrown high fall back on oneself, is broken through. The world of eternal recurrence is inhabited by winged things, an emerald sky traversed by birds that are "free" and "shine in the sunlight." Nietzsche speaks of our being "fliers of the spirit," an idea echoed in the following poem dedicated to Lou Salomé:[31]

> Dear friend!—said Columbus—never
> trust a man from Genoa!
> He always stares into the blue—
> and farthest things entice him on!
> The one he loves he entices too
> far beyond in space and time—
> Above us shines star after star,
> around us roars eternity.[32]

The time that can be lived where eternity roars is at the same time a liberation from time—an "ecstaticizing" of time, as it were. It is also the self itself "ecstaticized" in the "timeless" moment. The entire world-process becomes the activity of the self's will and all worlds are embraced. This is the moment in which "the world worlds" (*die Welt weltet*).[33]

Nietzsche compares those unable to step out of the frame of the self to invalids. In the chapter of *Zarathustra* entitled "The Convalescent," he describes the recovery from such an illness.

> I, Zarathustra, the advocate of life, the advocate of suffering, the advocate of the ring—I summon you, my most abyssal thought! . . .
>
> My abyss speaks, I have turned my ultimate depths inside-out to the light! [III, 13]

Regarding the turning of one's abyss inside-out to the light, Nietzsche writes in *Beyond Good and Evil*: "When you look into the abyss for a long time, the abyss also looks into you" [BGE 146]. This means that the abyss within the self inverts itself and its depths are heaved up into the summit. Zarathustra's saying "Abyss and peak are joined" and "midnight is also midday" also refers to this phenomenon.[34] The "abyssal thought" is the idea of eternal recurrence. The inversion and turning inside-out of the abyss, and its beginning to speak, mean that the peak that is upheaved from within has broken through the frame of the ego and penetrated Zarathustra body and soul. The abyss becomes Zarathustra and Zarathustra becomes the abyss—and the eternal recurrence itself. Eternal recurrence is *ekstasis*, and this *ekstasis* is the ultimate cure of the disease.

Unlike mystics of the past, for Nietzsche the moment is not connected to an immovable eternity transcending time. The moment itself returns:

> And if everything has already existed: then what do you think, dwarf, of this moment? Must not this gate also already—have existed?
>
> And are all things not so tightly tied together that this moment pulls *all* coming things after it? And so—even it itself? [III, 2]

The moment *is* now has already *been*, thanks to the ring of time in which no point is fixed. Time is taken as something that necessarily returns eternally. "Must we not eternally return?"

6. Love of Fate and Eternal Recurrence

It should be clear by now that fate is the union of the moment with eternity. Earlier we noted the equation of *ego* and *fatum* in which the interconnections among all things are "enormously coincidental," and in which each act of the self is conditioned by all things past even as the self itself conditions all things that are to come. Zarathustra is now saying that because all things are tied together, this moment itself must recur. Since the necessity of fate governs the unity of all things and is one with freedom of will, or chance, the self is one with fate. But we must press on further to see the ultimate form of Nietzsche's so-called fatalism.

In a posthumously published note Nietzsche writes: "My consummation[35] of fatalism: (1) through eternal recurrence and pre-existence, (2) through the elimination of the concept of 'will' " (XIII, 75). In another passage he says that the idea of eternal recurrence provides "a counterweight to extreme fatalism" and involves the "elimination of the concept of necessity [*Notwendigkeit*]—elimination of the 'will'—elimination of 'knowledge as such' " [*WP* 1060]. To eliminate will and necessity from the idea of eternal recurrence in this way is to provide a counterweight to fatalism. But Nietzsche also says that eternal recurrence itself *is* fatalism. This is not the self-contradiction it appears to be at first sight.

To begin with, the elimination of "knowledge" should be clear from what has already been said. Knowledge as such means knowledge of "Being" itself, divorced from the actual reality of ephemeral becoming; in this sense it means knowledge of "truth." But what is called Being itself, or truth, is for Nietzsche actually mere appearance. It is the ephemeral world of becoming, which is usually taken to be mere appearance, that is for him reality. Moreover, in a world of becoming which eternally recurs, even the deception that there is knowledge of truth or Being is acknowledged as useful for life as it is, and is therefore affirmed. Knowledge as such is negated only to be reaffirmed as a part of illusion. All things become phenomena of the will in the form of mere appearances, without there being *anything of which* they are appearances. Nietzsche expresses this idea by saying: "Impermanence could be interpreted as the enjoyment of the creative and destructive force, as *constant creation*" [*WP* 1049]; or as "ecstatic affirmation (*Ja-sagen*) of the holistic character of life" [*WP* 1050].

Thus the world of eternal recurrence is a phenomenon of will. As Nietzsche says in the final lines of *The Will to Power*: "*This world is will to power and nothing besides!* And you also are this will to power—and nothing besides!" [*WP* 1067]. At this point not only knowledge as such but even the concept of will itself becomes useless, insofar as will is nothing more than a striving against things that resist it. But in the standpoint of eternal recurrence both the resistances and the striving against them have been overcome. As Nietzsche says, the world is "divine play" (*göttliches Spiel*). This does not mean that whatever resists or expends effort simply disappears; if it did, there would be no "play." It is rather a standpoint where resistance is resistance and yet becomes not-resistance, where striving is striving and yet becomes not-striving.[36]

To eliminate the concept of will does not mean to return to the standpoint of a bystander with respect to the world-process. To say "Well, then! Once more!" is the greatest will and resolution. But through such will time becomes an arc, and the world is understood as something that eternally recurs. That the world worlds as it does is its "play." That the self wills means that it wills really and truly, even though it is no more than the play of waves in a recurring world. Thus will in the ordinary sense is overcome, as is necessity. Necessity in its immediacy as fate is play. Necessity in the sense of something that binds disappears. This is why Nietzsche refers to eternal recurrence at some times as fatalism and at others as the counterweight to it. In contrast to traditional forms of fatalism, absolute fate comes to mean absolute freedom: "To *liberate* absolute necessity *entirely from purpose* . . . It is only the innocence of becoming that gives us the greatest courage and the greatest *freedom*" [WP 787]. This is the ultimate standpoint at which recurrence is said to be fate.

7. The Self-Overcoming of Nihilism

However abruptly the thought of eternal recurrence may have come to Nietzsche, its development is woven into the whole fabric of his ideas. At this point we may look more closely at these interconnections.

First of all, the idea of recurrence is the eternal affirmation of becoming. In a passage from the notebooks Nietzsche speaks of the idea of "*Duration [Dauer]* with an 'in vain,' without goal or purpose" as "*the most paralyzing* thought."[37] The passage continues:

[Let us think this thought in its most terrible form:] existence, just as it is, without meaning or goal, but recurring inevitably, without even a finale in nothingness: "the eternal return."

This is the most extreme form of nihilism: nothingness ("meaninglessness") eternally!

The European form of Buddhism: the energy of wisdom and force compels one to such a belief. It is the *most scientific [wissenschaftlichste]* of all possible hypotheses. [WP 55]

I shall return to Nietzsche's idea of nihilism as the European form of Buddhism later. The idea that the nihilistic formulation of eternal recurrence is the "most scientific" of all hypotheses may be understood in connection with his remark that: "the two most extreme ways of thinking—the mechanistic and the Platonic—coincide in the eternal recurrence: both as ideals" [*WP* 1061]. This seems to amount to a supersession of the extreme forms of realism and idealism. Nietzsche's standpoint was to grasp reality from the abyssal depths of the nihility that was left over after all ideals, including God, had been negated.

In *Twilight of the Idols* Nietzsche writes as follows, under the subheading "The Immoralist Speaks":

> The philosopher despises the human being who wishes, even the "desirable" human being—and, above all, all wishes, all human *ideals*. If a philosopher could be a nihilist, he would be so because he finds Nothing behind all human ideals. . . . How is it that human beings, who as a reality are so worthy of reverence, deserve no respect insofar as they wish? . . . What justifies human beings is their reality—which will justify them eternally. How much more worthy is the actual human being in comparison with some merely wished-for, dreamed up, faked and bogus human? with some *ideal* human being? And it is only the ideal human being that is distasteful to the philosopher. ["Skirmishes of an Untimely Man," §32]

This is an anti-metaphysical standpoint that negates all idealisms and renaturalizes everything that has been denaturalized. What distinguishes Nietzsche from the usual naturalism of the period is that he understands naturalism at the same depth as the most extreme idealism, and from there its negation is transformed into an affirmation. In this sense one might call it the most metaphysical of anti-metaphysics. Reality and becoming are understood as the eternal recurrence of "the meaningless" from a standpoint taken up in the very midst of the real world of becoming, in order thoroughly to excavate the ground of that world. Unlike a simply mechanistic view, however, the world is affirmed abyssally as being inevitable. This is the standpoint of will that can hardly be called will any more, the standpoint of will to power where the world is understood as the "historical" world of value-establishment and value-interpretation seen perspectivally. Something like this seems to be behind Nietzsche's talk of the coming together of the mechanistic and Platonic views. Although influenced by the positivism of his age, he went through and beyond it. By living through nihilism, he arrived at the idea of eternal recurrence as "the most scientific of all hypotheses"; indeed, we might say that this was his way of resolving the problem of science and religion.

Nietzsche refers to the thought of eternal recurrence as "a *hammer* in the hand of the most powerful human," and as "the disciplining thought."[38] The reason he liked to speak of the thought as a hammer is that eternal recurrence means "nothingness (meaninglessness) eternally", and thereby constitutes "the extreme form of nihilism." It is "the *most difficult* thought"[39] because it radically negates the gods along with all the ideals and values that had previously constituted the ground of existence. Nietzsche believed that only those who could bear the thought courageously and without deception in order to consummate their nihilism would be able to attain the will to the transvaluation of value and absolute affirmation. This is why the thought of eternal recurrence is said to be "the consummation and *crisis* of nihilism" or "*the self-overcoming of nihilism* (the attempt to say Yes to everything that has hitherto been negated)" (XVI, 422). Because such nihilism is the end toward which the history of modern Europe is heading, the consummation of nihilism—the idea of "meaninglessness eternally"—is at once a crisis that has befallen history and a turning point within history. Nietzsche himself says that "the doctrine of eternal recurrence is the turning point of history" (XIV, 364). It must also be the turning point reached internally by one who reflects on himself within history. In other words, it must be a consummation of nihilism within the self and at the same time an overcoming of nihilism. This is why Nietzsche thinks of the thought of eternal recurrence as a hammer that disciplines.[40]

> Friend *Zarathustra* has come, the guest of guests.
> Now the world laughs, the great curtain is rent.
> The wedding day has come for light and darkness . . .[41]

This offspring of the marriage of light and darkness Nietzsche calls Dionysus. Reference was made earlier to Nietzsche's "experimental philosophy," a philosophy lived so as to "preempt the possibilities of fundamental nihilism" and say "yes" to the world:

> Such an *experimental philosophy* . . . wants to break through to the opposite [of negation]—to the point of a *Dionysian affirmation* of the world as it is, from which nothing has been subtracted, eliminated, or selected—it wants eternal circular

process. . . . The highest state that a philosopher can reach: to adopt a Dionysian stance toward existence—my formula for this is *amor fati*. (*WP* 1041)

Here we see the interrelationships among such basic ideas of Nietzsche's as nihilism, eternal recurrence, *amor fati*, and Dionysus.[42] From the Dionysian perspective the impermanence in which everything arises and perishes can be interpreted as a kind of "ceaseless creation." Nietzsche also speaks of "the great pantheistic sharing of joy and suffering," and "the ecstatic affirmation of the total character of life" [*WP* 1050]. He means to include in this affirmation the joys and sufferings of life as well as an ecstatic and self-oblivious co-rejoicing and co-suffering. His use of the term "pantheistic" is not unimportant, for what is overcome by eternal recurrence is only "the God of morality," and belief in the recurrence opens one to a pantheistic affirmative attitude toward everything. He asks himself, and then answers, the question of whether it is possible to think of a God not in moral terms but "beyond good and evil":

Could pantheism in *this* sense be possible? Can we eliminate the idea of purpose from the [world-]process and *nevertheless* affirm the process?—This would be the case if something within the process were attained at each moment of it—and always the same thing. [*WP* 55]

Similarly, in the section mentioned previously he speaks of "the total character of life as something always the same throughout all possible change, something equally powerful, and equally blissful . . ." For Nietzsche, what remains the same throughout the process, never departing from ever-changing arising and perishing, is the will that affirms eternal recurrence. This is the perspective of the new "pantheism"—qualitatively different from previous and subsequent pantheistic ideas—and Dionysus is the god who embodies it.

The idea that the same thing is attained at every moment within the process is reminiscent of Kierkegaard's talk of the moment as an "atom of eternity within time" and of "repetition" in every moment.[43] Nietzsche, too, enjoins us to "impress the image of eternity upon *our* lives."[44] The difference is that while Kierkegaard ends up in a Christian theism, Nietzsche ends up in a unique anti-Christian pantheism, which is to be a "religion of the most free, most cheerful and most noble souls." These souls must be able to improvise life's verses, like free birds that shine in the sunlight.

Dionysus is a "religious affirmation of life." Here we may recall that Nietzsche speaks of "the two types: Dionysus and the Crucified" (*WP* 1052), and of the difference between two views of the meaning of suffering, which was equally important for him and for Kierkegaard. On the Christian view, suffering is a way to a kind of sacred existence, and on the Dionysian view, existence in this world is already sacred enough for us to affirm[45] enormous suffering.

The most remarkable feature of Nietzsche's "religion" may be the sound of *laughter* that echoes through it. He teaches that one can laugh from the ground of the soul, or rather that the soul's "groundless ground" is laughter itself. "What has been the greatest sin on earth so far? Was it not the words of the one who said 'Woe to those who laugh here!'," says Zarathustra [IV, 13]. The text of *Zarathustra* alone is studded with various kinds of laughter. For example:

> "Courage which scares away ghosts creates demons (*Kobolde*) for itself—courage wants to laugh."

> ". . . *laughing lions* must come!"

> "So *learn* to laugh over and beyond yourselves! . . . you higher men, please *learn*—to laugh."

> ". . . I myself pronounced my laughter holy."

There is also a striking, extremely mystical smile:

> Oh heaven above me, you pure and deep thing! You abyss of
>   light! Looking at you I shudder with divine desire.
> To throw myself into your height—that is *my* depth! To hide
>   myself in your purity—that is *my* innocence! . . .
> Together we learned everything; together we learned to climb up
>   to ourselves and beyond and to smile cloudlessly.[46]

A paradigmatic example of a religion that has attained the stage of being able to laugh is Zen Buddhism, the history of which also reverberates with laughter of various kinds. For example: Yakusan climbed a mountain one night and, on seeing the clouds suddenly part to reveal the moon, he let forth an enormous burst of laughter. It is said that his laughter resounded over a distance of more than ninety leagues. A poet of that period commemorated the event with the following lines: "Once, directly above a lonely mountain peak, the clouds parted: the moon. There was laughter from the entire soul."[47] Or again, it is said that Hyakujō was beaten by Ōbaku and thereupon burst out laughing: "He shook with laughter and went straight back to his room."[48] Of Gyōzan's sonorous laughter Setchō said in admiration: "Now his laughter has died away. Where will he have gone? It is appropriate for stirring up the lamenting wind."[49] What Nietzsche calls "laughing malice" (*lachende Bosheit*) corresponds to the Zen saying: "In laughter there is a blade." Other such instances of laughter are too numerous to mention.

Along with laughter, *folly* is also a characteristic of Nietzsche's new "religion." Madness and folly have often appeared at the heights of religious experience. In Nietzsche's case it is connected with his insight into eternal recurrence. As an example, consider the poem entitled "To Goethe," in which he tried to show Goethe's true spirit by turning inside-out his idea that "the transitory is merely a metaphor."

> The imperishable is merely your metaphor!
> God the ineluctable just a poet's deception.
> World-wheel, rolling on, skims goal on goal:
> Fate, says the grumbler, the fool calls it—play
> World-play, imperious, blends being and appearance:
> The eternally fooling force blends *us* in too![50]

To immerse oneself in the "play" of the samsaric world and its groundless activity, and to live it to the utmost, is the "pantheistic" life discussed earlier; and this is what is common to both of "us" (namely, Nietzsche and Goethe). What Nietzsche means in speaking of becoming a "child," and what he calls "*my*" innocence (being without guilt), is participation in the world-play which is at once laughter and "folly." When the world and its eternal recurrence become the laughter of the soul, not only the spirit of gravity but also the nihilism of "nothingness (meaninglessness) eternally" is for the first time eradicated from the ground of the soul. In the section entitled "On the Vision and Enigma" we find Zarathustra walking alone, the dwarf having disappeared, and coming upon a young shepherd writhing on the ground in the desolate moonlight with the head of a snake in his mouth. Zarathustra shouts to him to bite it off. The young man does, and springs up to laugh "a laughter that [was] no human laughter."

No longer a shepherd nor a human being—one transformed, radiant, who *laughed!* Never yet on this earth has a person laughed as *he* laughed!

Zarathustra's soul thirsts with yearning for this laughter; it is his yearning for the *Übermensch*. This is the self-overcoming of nihilism itself in Nietzsche.

Chapter Five

Nihilism and Existence in Nietzsche

1. "God is Dead"

When he published a new edition of *The Gay Science* in 1886, Nietzsche added a fifth book entitled "We Fearless Ones," in the first aphorism of which he writes as follows:

> *The meaning of our cheerfulness.* The greatest recent event—that "God is dead," that belief in the Christian God has become unbelievable—is already beginning to cast its first shadow over Europe. For the few at least, whose eyes, the *suspicion* in whose eyes is strong and sharp enough for this spectacle, some sun seems to have set, some ancient and deep trust to have turned into doubt: to them our old world must seem daily more like evening, more suspicious, stranger, "older." [*GS* 343]

Ordinary people do not understand the implications of this event. They do not understand "how much must collapse, now that this belief has been undermined, because it had been built upon it, supported by it, and had grown into it: for example, the whole of European morality." However, Nietzsche presses those who are supposed to have already clearly seen the shadow that was soon to cover Europe: "What is the matter that even we look forward to this approaching gloom without any sense of participation, and above all without any worry or fear for *ourselves?*" The upshot of this event is not necessarily sad and gloomy; it is rather something like a new kind of "illumination, happiness, relief, serenity":

> In fact, we philosophers and "free spirits" feel as if we are illumined by a new dawn, on receiving the news that "the old God is dead"; our hearts overflow with gratitude, wonder,

premonition, anticipation. At last the horizon seems to us open again, even if it isn't bright; at last our ships may venture out again, venture out in the face of whatever danger; all the daring of the searcher after knowledge is again permitted; the sea, *our* sea again lies open before us; perhaps there has never yet been such an "open sea."

The passage exemplifies the structure of Nietzsche's nihilism and existential attitude perfectly. His nihilism emerged with the death of the Christian God, and his existential attitude is that of a sea-farer departing on a voyage of dangerous exploration into the vast ocean of life that had opened up as never before through the death of God.

For Heidegger, Nietzsche's statement that "God is dead" means that "the suprasensible world is not an effectual force. It affords no kind of life. Metaphysics, which is for Nietzsche western philosophy understood as Platonism, is over" (*Holzwege* 200).[1] It means further that that "the sphere for the essential being and appropriative event [*Ereignis*] of nihilism is metaphysics itself." I would add emphatically that Nietzsche extended the sphere of nihilism not only to metaphysics but even more so to the field of ethics. At any rate, Platonic/Christian metaphysics and its entire system of ethics have become problematic. In that sense: "Nietzsche's phrase gives a name to the destiny of two thousand years of western history." How, then, did Nietzsche himself take the fact that the entire Platonic/Christian system had lost its historical influence?

It is clear that the rise of the natural sciences in the modern era struck a forceful blow to that system. Nietzsche speaks of this in *On the Genealogy of Morals*:

Has the self-diminution of the human being, its *will* to self-diminution, not progressed inexorably since Copernicus? Alas, the faith in human worth, its uniqueness and indispensibility in the rank-order of creation has gone—the human has become an *animal*, literally an animal, without reservation or qualification; the human, who formerly believed itself to be almost divine ("child of god," "God-man"). Since Copernicus, humanity seems to have got itself on to a sloping plane—already sliding faster and faster away from the center—into what? into nothingness? into the *"piercing* feeling of its own nothingness"? That's fine! this would be just the right way—into the *old* ideal? (*GM* III, 25)

In fact, when Copernicus unhinged the earth from its central position in the heavens, he also banished human being from its central position in the spiritual world, the world of morals in the broad sense. As the external world gradually ceased to be "God's creation," so too did "the relation to God" gradually disappear from the inner world. Human beings, whose relation to God was lost, now began to appear to be related to animals. With the Enlightenment of the eighteenth century, a new atheism took form with social-scientific consequences. After going through Rousseau, Kant, and Hegel, this atheism reappeared in a still deeper form. Eighteenth century atheism, the "first wave" of atheism in the modern era, merely denied the existence of God from the standpoint of a mechanistic view of nature; the second wave, nineteenth century atheism as represented by Feuerbach, tried to radicalize the denial by forging ahead to a point of paradox or irony.

In this later development, atheism arrived at the position that the concept of a God who created human beings is merely a fiction created by human beings, and in the process tried to elucidate the psychological process by which this fabrication came to be. The fact that the origin of "God" is located within consciousness and that it involves a self-deception meant that atheism was no longer an idea that assaults us from without, but one that strikes to the very roots of subjectivity. Besides its psychological (or, as it would later be called, "psychoanalytical") explanations of how the concept of God arises within human consciousness, this deeper atheism also projected the model on to history, in an effort to explain the origins of religion in human history. These two approaches, like the blades of a scissors, cut the concept of "God" off at the roots. Nietzsche appears to have been aware of this phenomenon:

> *Historical refutation as the ultimate refutation.* Formerly one sought to prove that there is no God—nowadays one demonstrates how the belief that there is a God could *arise* and how it gained such weight and importance: with that, the counter-proof, that God doesn't exist, becomes superfluous. When one formerly refuted the "proofs of the existence of God" that were put forward, there always remained the doubt whether better proofs could be found than those just refuted: in those days atheists did not know how to make a clean sweep. (*Dawn* 95)

This deeper atheism does not simply stop with a shaking of the foundations of religious consciousness; it also confounds human self-consciousness and forces one to a new self-understanding. Feuerbach must have made his contemporaries feel as if the ground had been dug out from under their feet. While for some it must have caused severe torment, for others it must have instilled a strong feeling of liberation. Nietzsche places the "young Germans" of the 1830s and 1840s in this latter group (*GM* III, 4).

2. Critique of Religion

Nietzsche also tried to explain the origin of "God" from a variety of perspectives, using an ironical method similar to Feuerbach's. The idea begins, he says, in fear. Members of ancient tribes, indebted to the founder of the tribe for their existence, felt a responsibility to offer sacrifices to the first ancestor. Their fear of the ancestor was like a debtor's fear of a creditor. The sense of indebtedness increased as the tribe grew larger and stronger, until finally the ancestor of the tribe, whose power was always greater still, was transformed into "God" by the inventive power of ever-increasing fear. When various tribal societies were then integrated into a large, universal kingdom, "God" became a universal God, until finally, as in Christianity, there appears the greatest God and the greatest feeling of debt (*GM* II, 20). This accounts for moralistic ideas of God, such as "God the judge" and the "God of justice."

Nietzsche's critique touches not only the "God of justice" and supreme goodness, but also "God as creator" and supreme being. Behind his critique lies a denial of the notion of "being" and of the will as "cause." In *Twilight of the Idols*, for example, he argues that we observe the world of so-called "inner facts" and think that a certain thing is caused by an act of will. We understand the "motive" of the act as proceeding from consciousness or "spirit" in the form of an antecedent cause. Finally, we suppose that a certain idea, which determines the motive, is being generated by the "ego" or "subject."[2] In other words, in the "inner world" three things— will, spirit, and ego—are said to work as "causes." For Nietzsche, however, these concepts are pure fictions. That the ego generates something of its own free will, according to certain motives, is merely a superficial interpretation of an essentially elemental event—what Nietzsche calls the process of life, whose essence is "will to power."

Nietzsche goes on to show how we project these three fictions on to the external world. First, the concept of the ego is projected and generates the concept of "being"; the concept of a "thing" that exists is merely a reflection of the ego understood as a cause. Next, "spirit" projects the "thing-in-itself"—a world of suprasensible being (Nietzsche's "*Hinterwelt*")—behind the "thing." This projection of "spirit" culminates in the idea of "God" as the supreme suprasensible being. "The error of the spirit as cause is mistaken for reality! And made the measure of reality! And called *God!*" This psychological process, at work since time immemorial, sees all events as one activity, all activity as the result of will, and all will as belonging to a single actor or "subject." With this idea in hand, Nietzsche set out coolly to pursue the post-Copernican view to its ultimate consequences. The anthropomorphic view of the world, according to which the intention or will of someone lies behind events in the external world, was totally refuted by science. Nietzsche wanted to erase the last vestiges of this anthropomorphism by applying the critique to the inner world as well. From the most human world, the inner world that one believes belongs to oneself, he drove out entirely the "human, all-too-human" way of seeing.

Nietzsche also wielded his critical irony against the morality of pity with its belief in the "God of love" and the "God of redemption." Here we see the incisiveness and depth of his critique of religion at its best. All the great religions are concerned with saving the suffering who are unable to endure the burden of life, those grown weary to the point of exhaustion and sick of life. Religion transforms suffering, weariness, and sickness into a self-conscious denial of life that positively wills the denial of life and seeks redemption in "life against life" [*GM* III, 13]. Suffering and weariness with life are signs of the weakening of the will to live; they generate a non-will, a "not wanting to will" that leads to the degeneration of life. Religion changes this direction around by deliberately, intentionally, and willfully making life degenerate—in other words, by restoring will but perverting it to the negation of life. Religion is thus a schizophrenia of the will, a case of "life against life." This is what Nietzsche means when he says that "[human beings] would sooner even will *nothing* (*das* Nichts *wollen*) than *not* will" (*GM* III, 1). The will to deny life is "will to nothingness," "nihilism," and "the last will" (*GM* III, 13). It draws the outer borderlines of will, at which religion then establishes itself. This is the sense in which Nietzsche finds nihilism at the basis of religion and sees redemption as a condition of absence of suffering (*Leidlosigkeit*), "a hypnotic feeling of nothingness (*Nichts-Gefühl*)" [*GM* III, 17]. For the weary and suffering of the earth, this "nothingness" takes on a positive value as the highest good that can be desired. This is a psychological inevitability. Nietzsche says that in religion the highest good is called

"God," but that the true nature of "God" is actually "nothing": "According to the logic of emotion in all pessimistic religions, nothingness is called God." Peace in "God" is rest in nothingness (*GM* III, 1).

Nietzsche argues further that this religious "redemption" merely tries to eliminate suffering and the discomfort of the sufferer without trying to eliminate their cause or combat the disease itself. This is his "most basic" objection to the remedy that religion offers (*GM* III, 17). The root of the disease is the negative direction of life manifest in suffering; it consists in "the non-will of the sufferer." This is why one is dissatisfied with oneself, weary of humanity, and tired of living. Religion simply converts this "non-will" into the "will to nothing." In other words, it consummates one's dissatisfaction with oneself, and at that extreme point gives one satisfaction in "God." It pushes weariness with humanity to the limit, and offers instead the image of a divine savior; it takes away one's taste for life on earth entirely, and promotes the quest for a "higher world." While suffering may be anesthetized through this process, the roots of the disease have not been touched. If anything, they grow stronger and more tenacious.

The religious attitude that stops at sympathy is inadequate insofar as "pity" merely tries to transcend or alleviate suffering. The healthy growth of life after the disease has been eradicated and the patient healed, together with the power to create the future of humanity, is absent. If anything, pity works to close off these possibilities. Nietzsche takes every possible opportunity to criticize the morality of pity, the core of his critique being that Christian pity is simply nihilism put into practice.[3]

The same formidable critique of "God" and the "higher world" resounds throughout *Zarathustra*. In the speech "On the Dwellers in the World Beyond" echoes of "God is dead" reverberate in the background, giving the feeling of awakening from a dream to face the fact that "God" was really nothing but a projection of the self.

Once [Zarathustra], too, projected his madness beyond human beings, like all who believe in other worlds. But was it in truth beyond the human?

Ah, brothers, this God I created was the work and madness of men, like all Gods!

He was a man, and only a poor piece of man and ego: from its own ashes and fire this ghost came to me, and truly! It did not come to me from the beyond!

What happened, my brothers? I overcame myself, a sufferer,
I carried my own ashes to the mountain, a brighter flame I
invented for myself. And see! then the ghost *fled* from me!

It would be a suffering for me now and torment for the convalescent, to believe in such ghosts: suffering it would be for
me now and degradation. Thus I speak to those who believe in
other worlds.

Suffering it was and inability—that created all other worlds;
and that short madness of happiness experienced only by the
one who suffers most. (*Za* I, 3)

The speech continues with Nietzsche's remarking that such
ideas as "God," the other world, and so on all stem from the activity of the "body"—a topic I shall touch upon later. One gets from
this passage the sense of a "leap of death" in which the ego, which
tries to escape to a life beyond life and thus seeks to cast itself into
nothingness, mistakes the projection of its own shadow on to the
beyond as "God" or "the other world." This is what Nietzsche
means in speaking of the true form of "God" as "Nothing." Indeed
Zarathustra goes on to say explicitly that the world beyond, "the
inhuman world from which man has been eliminated," is "a heavenly nothing."

Nietzsche's atheism shares a common motivation with Feuerbach's insofar as they both seek to gouge into the foundations of
religion—though there is a difference in the depth to which they
cut. While Feuerbach sees the concept of "God" as deriving simply from the human drive for happiness, Nietzsche sees it as coming from the self-splitting of life, the will to deny life, and the will
to Nothing, or nihilism. His is a negation of religion at the level of
the very experience of religious life, and a negation of metaphysics
at a depth equal to that of the metaphysical understanding of existence. Feuerbach had no trouble floating back up to the social surface of life after undertaking his critique of religion, there to preach
a love of humanity. For this, Nietzsche wrote in his posthumously
published notebooks that there is still the odor of theology in Feuerbach.[4] He himself drove the blade of paradox deeper into the heart
of religion and metaphysics, deepening the nihilism already inherent in them, until he achieved a standpoint of absolute affirmation
at the ultimate source of life. Nietzsche's comparison of religious
redemption to hypnosis is similar to Marxism's calling it opium,
though the perspectives from which their criticisms were made are
entirely opposite. It is easier to find similarities to Nietzsche in
Stirner, who discerned the ghost of theology in Feuerbach's "hu-

manity" and in Marxism's communist society, and who advocated the "autonomous"[5] ego that does not depend on anything else. Of this we shall have more to say in the next chapter.

3. The Stages of Nihilism

Nietzsche regards all the great religions as concealing nihilism at the core, but he also understands them as having in a sense outgrown the urge to overcome nihilism. It is important to realize this so as to appreciate how the thread of nihilism and its overcoming runs through the whole of Nietzsche's philosophy in a variety of forms and stages.

In the first place, we see a residual instinct for affirming life in the illusion of an "other world." Life that is self-affirming—will to power—continues to work through the people who invented such ideas. In this sense there is a kind of overcoming of nihilism even in religion. In the non-will which "does not want to will" (*der nicht wollen will*), Nietzsche already finds what we might call a "natural" nihilism, or nihilism "in-itself" [*an sich*]. A desperate individual who has lost all purpose in life is able, by conceptualizing a "God" beyond this life, to regain the strength and will to live, to find meaning in life—even in its sufferings and misfortunes—and thus to overcome natural nihilism. In this sense, Christian morality was "the great *countermeasure* against practical and theoretical *nihilism*" (*WP* 4; cf. also chapter two, sec. 3, above).

However, on Nietzsche's view the natural nihilism that was believed to have been overcome only sank further beneath the surface of consciousness. By operating covertly within the foundation of religion which overcomes nihilism, nihilism was raised to the level of self-reflection [*für sich*]. When the will not to want to will bends back on itself, pursues itself, and becomes the will to will nothing—that is, when mere negativity in will becomes a negativity that positively affirms negativity itself—nihilism becomes self-reflective. On this view, religion involves both the overcoming of nihilism and its deepening toward self-reflectiveness, even though religion has not yet awakened to this. Its nihilism remains, as it were, unconsciously self-reflective.

This failure of insight into the nihilism within religion has been endemic to the long history of humanity. It was thanks to the diphasic wave of atheism referred to earlier that this nihilism gradually came to awareness. In the first phase the existence of God was put into question and was denied by the worldview of the natural sciences; and in the second, the concept of God was explained psychologically and historically, and an ironical way of thinking emerged which cut it off at the roots. The spiritual basis of Christianity was for the first time undermined, and the mood of "the death of God" emerged. This marks the advent of "true nihilism," the self-conscious nihilism that Nietzsche calls "European nihilism."

In European nihilism, "will to nothing" began to be something that affirmed the will to negate, not in a self-deceptive manner but as a conscious decision to demolish what had become hollow inside and turned into a false facade. In Nietzsche's words, it is a turn from a pessimism of weakness to a pessimism of strength whereby nihilism takes on a new character and quality. This turn is at once a necessity and a resolution. There is a necessity that governs the entire transition from the natural nihilism of those who wander and suffer throughout infinite time to religion and its morality, and then from religion to true nihilism. Far from being a merely external necessity, it is one in which life and will are woven in as its warp. Accordingly it is also influenced by the will's finding a way of resolution through crisis, deadlock, disorientation and aporia. According to Nietzsche, when true nihilism breaks through the shell of religion and sloughs it off,[6] it does so as positive will to negate, as strength of will, as genuine conscience and purity of heart.

The nihilist has thus taken a step toward the fundamental overcoming of nihilism. He has attained the standpoint where he has put nihilism "behind him, beneath and outside him"—the standpoint of "the consummate nihilist." To appreciate what this means we must discuss Nietzsche's conception of Existence in greater detail.

4. Nihilism as Existence

Formerly, human existence, morality, and so forth were understood in relation to otherworldly things such as "God" and "the world beyond." Human being and the being of all other things were conceived of in "substantial" and "ontological" relation to the supreme being. The order of relationships among human beings and other things was also considered to have its ground in the other world. Human reason, whose *idea, logos,* and *ratio* clarified the meaning of the whole order, was considered to have been modeled on the divine reason of the world beyond; hence the correct way of existing and ordering human relations was thought to consist in a conformity of human will with the divine will. Greek philosophy and

Christianity rationalized these relations differently, but they shared a common supposition of an objective and transcendent system in a world beyond which reached down to encompass human existence and morality. On this view, the human self could be itself only in relation to others and to otherworldly things, and human subjectivity could be established only in its dependence on otherworldly "objective" things. The standpoint of Existence as a relation in which the self relates to itself—that is, as subjective in the true sense—could not fully take form. The self always had something above it that ruled it; subjectivity had to crash against the wall of objectivity that marked off the realm of the beyond. Now, that huge transcendent system has collapsed, leaving in its place an infinite void. The world beyond has disappeared, and instead this world has gradually disclosed itself as resting perilously upon an eerie abyss. Our very existence, as well as our morality, has turned into an enigma. But the fact that nihilism has arrived and human beings have become a problem for themselves from the ground up has made the standpoint of Existence possible. In orienting themselves to the abyss within, people can now fully extend the horizon of their relationship to themselves.

The standpoint of Existence is a necessity of human history. The development from natural nihilism through unconscious nihilism in religion to true, conscious nihilism is seen by Nietzsche as unfolding out of dialectical necessity. Still, the resolve to take a stand consciously on nihilism requires "strength" and the courage of decision. One must "internalize" (*erinnern*) necessity,[7] shoulder it as one's fate, and make oneself into fate—*ego fatum* (see chapter four, sec. 2, 3, and 6 above). This resolution involves an overcoming of self-deception and is a radical confrontation with the faith that has dominated human beings from the distant past up to the present and provided their existence and morality with its foundations.

Nietzsche had the clarity of insight to recognize that it is our destiny to live through one of the greatest turning points in human history. Confrontation with established otherworldly religion and metaphysics, which had held sway for thousands of years, means identifying with the greater destiny of humankind, now in the process of evolving toward a totally new and unknown sphere. In this process, the self becomes the arena of destiny's unfolding, its groping tentacle. This in turn entails an entirely different (and perhaps totally opposite) view from the one that had hitherto prevailed, a totally new interpretation of life and the world—in short, an experiment in the "revaluation of all values." Nietzsche compares the change to a departure for a voyage into a vast and uncharted ocean.

His entire thought is permeated by this kind of deep consciousness of his own historical situation.

The self's identity with fate consists in the realization that the self is the manifestation of the fate of the human race and is, so to speak, its self-expression. Nietzsche's ideas about the self and destiny are illustrated in his confrontation with Jesus as the Antichrist. Because of the violence of his language on this issue, he was suspected of being a megalomaniac or a madman, but this suspicion stemmed from an inability to understand what he meant and to assess the depth and breadth of his vision fairly. In describing himself as "the first consummate nihilist," Nietzsche refers to his having discerned the signs of the incipient, radical turning of human destiny—a fate he shoulders resolutely. Nihilism meant that an unknown ocean was opening up and its horizon beginning to brighten, and that only those prepared to set sail and encounter every possible danger are Existence.

Nietzsche expresses the same idea in the posthumously published notes through a related metaphor. The challenge of dry land to creatures used to living in the sea meant a completely unprecedented transformation of their lives, bodies, and habits. What is happening now to human beings is the opposite: the dry land is being washed away and everything is returning to the sea. "I wanted to say: I was born as a land-animal like everyone else, and now in spite of that I must be a sea-animal!"[8] For the nihilist Existence means the forced resolve to a fundamental change, driven by the inner necessity of fate.

5. The First Stage of Existence

In the well known opening speech of *Thus Spoke Zarathustra*, Nietzsche explains the three transformations of the spirit. The spirit first of all has to become a camel, then the camel a lion, and finally the lion a child. The spirit that becomes a camel is the spirit of reverence. It kneels down, wanting to be loaded with heavy burdens, and by bearing the heaviest things it is able to enjoy its own strength. In order to break its pride, it demeans itself, lets its own folly shine forth, takes leave of what it has conquered, refuses to be consoled when sick, steps into the waters of truth even when they are dirty, loves those who despise it, and extends its hands to frightening ghosts. Such is the spirit of the camel, which hurries into the desert. But when it has entered into the deepest solitude of the desert, the spirit changes into a lion. The spirit wants to seize

its freedom and become master in its own desert; it wants to overcome the great dragon, which up until now it had been calling Lord
and God—the "Thou shalt." On the scales of this dragon shine various values, thousands of years old.

"All value has already been created, and all created value—
is me. Truly, there shall be no more 'I will!' " Thus speaks the
dragon.

Nevertheless the spirit of the lion dares to say "I will." The creation
of new values is something of which the lion itself is not yet capable; but it can create freedom for new creation. To brandish a holy
No in the face of duty and to take for itself the right to new values,
that only the spirit of the beast of prey is capable of. But what even
the lion was unable to do, the child can achieve.

Innocence, the child is, and forgetting; a new beginning, a
play, a self-propelling wheel, a first moving, a holy Yes-saying.
Yes, for the play of creation . . . one needs a holy Yes-
saying: the spirit now wants *its* will, the one who had lost the
world now wins *its* world.

This was the speech Zarathustra made while he was in the town
called "The Motley Cow."
A similar passage appears in the unpublished notebooks. It
bears the title: "*The Way to Wisdom.* Pointers to the Overcoming of
Morality," and speaks of "three stages."[9] The first stage:

To revere better (and obey and *learn*) than anyone else. To
gather all things worthy of reverence into oneself and have
them fight each other. To bear all things that are heavy and difficult. Ascetiscm of the spirit—boldness. Time of community.

The second stage:

To break the revering heart, when one is *bound tightest*. The
free spirit. Independence. Time of the desert. Critique of everything that is revered (idealization of everything that is not
revered), attempt at reversed valuations.

And finally, the third stage:

The great decision to affirm, irrespective of whether one is capable of a positive attitude. No longer any God or human being *above* me! The instinct of the creative one, who knows *what* he is putting his hand to. Great responsibility and innocence. (In order to take joy in anything one must call *everything* good.) To give oneself the right to action.

To this last Nietzsche adds the noteworthy remark: "Beyond good and evil. He takes on the mechanistic worldview and does not feel himself humbled before fate: he *is* fate. He holds the lot of humankind in his hands." The meaning of the words "he is fate" should be clear from our earlier treatment; its relationship to the posture of beyond good and evil, and to the mechanistic worldview, will be taken up later.

Combining the passage from the notebooks with that from *Zarathustra*, it becomes clear that the new path of wisdom which Nietzsche thinks moderns should strive for differs from the ancient path of the "sage," whose paradigm is Socrates, as well as from the path of the medieval "saint" who sought to imitate Christ. This new stage in the development of spirit—"a way to wisdom and pointers to the overcoming of morality"—leads into the desert of nihilism and thereby enables one to create in oneself a "holy No" and "freedom." It shows a way to overcome nihilism through this new-found freedom, and ultimately to come to a reaffirmation of the world and a re-creation of values. Unlike former paths of wisdom, this new path must pass through the desert of nihilism; indeed, it demands the negation of the earlier paths. Nihilism opens up before us moderns, who have become unable to believe in either Socratic-Platonic metaphysics or Christian religion, as an immense and eerie expanse. (In comparison with Nietzsche's three-stage path, the "three stages on life's way" in Kierkegaard remain, in spite of their modernness, essentially medieval.)

The town called "The Motley Cow" is no doubt a metaphor for the contemporary world, abustle with colorful assertions, ideas, and the like—none of which could endure the crossing of the desert. The spirit of the camel—reverence, obedience, learning, kneeling down before all honorable things of value, and bearing all burdens—is meant to include the true religious life, which is always digging down into the being of the self and morality through to the most extreme situations of this life, by relating itself to a "God" and "world beyond" projected as the far side of this world. Nietzsche recognized the extent to which life first acquired "depth" through

metaphysics, religion, and their moralities. Contemplative knowledge, which bores beneath the surface of the things of life to return
to the fundamentals, the keen sensitivity that discerns the subtle
colorings of human character, feelings and so on, and above all
"truthfulness" (*Wahrhaftigkeit*), or "honesty" (*Redlichkeit*), which cannot suffer subtle deceptions or self-deceptions with indifference but
ceaselessly tries to break them down—all these and more indicate
the depth that religion and metaphysics gave to life.

While Nietzsche surely had Christianity in mind, the first
stage appears to have a broader compass. One finds in it elements
different from, and at times opposed to, Christianity, which probably derive from the philosophical life. Rejecting those who offer
consolation, leaving one's cause when it celebrates its victory, and
stepping into the waters of truth even when they are dirty probably
allude to the philosophers of ancient paganism. At any rate Nietzsche demands that one "gather all things worthy of reverence into
oneself and have them fight each other." What is common to all the
features mentioned is "asceticism of spirit" and courage to renounce
the ordinary life of the "motley cow." This path has been taken by
many great people—whom Nietzsche calls the "higher humans"—
from antiquity until the present day. The spirit's becoming a camel
involves living according to the aims of these "higher humans,"
loading oneself with everything of value from the historical tradition. This is perhaps why the first stage is said to be the "time of
community," even though the spirit thus laden will soon leave the
streets of "The Motley Cow" and head for the desert.

From this point on, Existence as nihilism begins. The bearing
of burdens, reverence, and cultivation through the religious or
philosophical life represent a preparatory stage. The transformation
into the camel, the first stage on the path to wisdom, involves both
immersing oneself in the teachings of traditional religion and metaphysics as well as a turn to nihilism which breaks through them. It
involves what was spoken of earlier as a turn to the unconscious
nihilism at the core of religion and metaphysics, and from there to
true, conscious nihilism. The stimulus for this turn, that which
drives the camel into the desert, is provided by the virtues of honesty and truthfulness cultivated by the morality of religion.

When religion brought the individual before God, a mirror
was set up at a far distance, beyond the reach of all the desires and
drives that conceal one from oneself and confine one within oneself.
This pristine glass[10] offered an ironical perspective on the multitude
of vanity-mirrors in which human beings titivate themselves. This is
a new optics of the spirit that tries to reflect the self's transcending

itself. The power of this kind of self-reflectiveness or self-criticism, which comes refracted from the far side of the self, is the "honesty" that tries its utmost not to deceive itself or others. What is more, this power now turns the point of its spear against the religious morality that was its womb. Even after such otherworldly ideas as "God" and the "true world" are recognized as groundless, the moralities supported by them continue to live on. Human beings cannot help leaning on them, even though they have become essentially false and void. According to Nietzsche, the shadow of God lingers on in the present age even after God has died [*GS* 108], and therefore the most necessary virtue is the honesty to "shatter morality itself" (XIII, 101). In this sense he also calls it "a virtue in the process of becoming" [*eine werdende Tugend*].

> Many worthy people still stand at this *level of truthfulness* [*Wahrhaftigkeit*] . . . However, one should note that honesty [*Redlichkeit*] is found among neither the Socratic nor the Christian virtues: it is one of the youngest virtues, not yet properly ripened, still often misjudged and mistaken for something else, still hardly aware of itself—something in the process of becoming [that we can further or obstruct as we see fit]. (*Dawn* 456)

Here Nietzsche distinguishes "truthfulness" in religion and morality from the "honesty" that emerges from that perspective in a self-critical manner. What is common to both is that the self will not deceive itself and has the courage to say, "This is the way I am." A life reverently immersed in the world of religion, metaphysics, and morality, and turning to nihilism—the Existence of the spirit which readies itself and departs as "a camel"—represents living in this kind of truthfulness and honesty.

6. The Second Stage of Existence

The second stage of Existence as nihilism is the turn from the preliminary stage of nihilism to Existence as nihilism itself. It is the transition from *masked* nihilism, which negates this world through affirming the beyond, to *true* nihilism, which makes this world into a problematic "X" by negating the beyond. The motive force of this turn, as we just saw, is the virtue of honesty. What, then, is the nature of the second stage on the way, the transformation of the spirit into a lion? It is the transition from the utter depths of atheism which killed the great dragon "Thou shalt" to the birth of the profound freedom of "I will." It throws off the feeling of reverence and lets the spirit become free and independent, critical of everything hitherto held in esteem and intent on a revaluation of values. In short, it is the shift toward the consummation of nihilism and, through nihilism's own strength, to its self-overcoming.

After the announcement of the death of God, we find ourselves pushed back to this life of "illusory appearance" (*Schein*) and the perpetual flux of becoming, a life now devoid of all aim or purpose. All processes in this world, if their goals are pursued to the extreme, end up in a terrifyingly deep void. Seen from this basic standpoint, all things appear to end in "trouble in vain," and to be futile and meaningless. They are, in a phrase from *The Will to Power*, "heading toward a state of universal nothingness (*Nichts-Zustand*) . . . Disappointment concerning *the purpose of becoming* [is] the cause of nihilism" (*WP* 12A). Elsewhere Nietzsche explains:

> The great danger is not pessimism . . . but the *meaningless-ness* of everything that happens! The moral interpretation has reached the verge of collapse simultaneously with the religious interpretation . . . The real great anxiety is that *the world no longer has any meaning.* . . . Now I am proposing a new interpretation, an "immoral" one, in relation to which our morality up till now appears as a special case. (XIII, 90–91).

"Immoral" here is, of course, intended in the sense of "beyond good and evil." The meaninglessness of every possible event—the fundamental anxiety of the modern age, or the "state of universal nothingness"—is closely connected with the rise of modern science. In fact one of the essential driving forces of Nietzsche's nihilism is his radical and fearless pursuit of the scientific spirit. In *On the Genealogy of Morals*, we read:

> Just *what* was it, in all strictness, that *triumphed* over the Christian God? The answer is in my *Gay Science* (aph. 357): "Christian morality itself, the concept of truthfulness taken ever more strictly, the father-confessor subtlety of Christian conscience, translated and sublimated into scientific conscience, into intellectual cleanliness at any price." (*GM* III, 27)

How did Nietzsche himself understand the "scientific conscience"? Is his notion of "scientific" the same as what many scientists, scientific philosophers, and others in the fields of politics, economics, sociology, and psychology understand by the term? Or, if not, what then? It is important to be completely clear on this question if we are to understand Nietzsche's nihilism and its unique position in modern thought.

The stage of the lion in the desert began with the breakdown of the feeling of respect. It was also said to involve an acceptance of the mechanistic worldview and a refusal to submit to the necessity of fate; in fact, the two are intimately connected. Nietzsche writes in another context:

> The self-overcoming that the researcher in the field of morality demands of himself requires not being prejudiced with respect to circumstances and actions which he has learned to revere. He must, as long as he is a researcher, "have broken his revering heart." (XIII, 120)

In other words, the self-overcoming that dissolves the feeling of reverence entails adopting the standpoint of a researcher, and vice-versa. Scientific research is a unitary Existence that from the beginning engages the being of the one doing the research. To strive scientifically for full understanding of all phenomena of the world—including the world within—is the very mode of existence in which one relates to and overcomes oneself. Nietzsche appropriates the spirit of science by apprehending as deeply as he can the spirit of the scientist. This is also clear from his saying that the mechanistic worldview constitutes a particular kind of training and discipline: "To promote the mechanistic view to a regulative principle of method. Not as the worldview that has been best proven, but as the one that requires the greatest rigor and discipline and that most throws all sentimentality aside" (XIII, 82). He also calls the methodology of the mechanistic worldview "the most excellent and most honest (*die redlichste*) by far" (XIII, 83).

This shows us how Nietzsche understood the scientific (and in particular the mechanistic) view underlying every problem in the modern age as a problem of the honesty and conscience of the self, and in this form incorporated it into his own Existence. The religious (Christian) view of nature, history, and human experience has, he says, become outmoded; it represents and "something that is *over*, with conscience *against* it, and that seems to all more sensitive consciences something indecent, dishonest, lying . . ." (*GM* III,

27). This appropriation of the scientific spirit was the most painful and thorny path Nietzsche had walked since the time of *Human, All-Too-Human*.

7. Nihilism as Scientific Conscience

The distinguishing mark of Nietzsche's view of science is that the scientific worldview "scientific" thinkers consider to be the "best proven" one is precisely the problem for him. By viewing science as incorporating the perspective of the way of being of the person who practises it, he relates the question deeply to his nihilism, as is suggested by a passage in *The Gay Science*. The aphorism after the opening section of Book V, in which it was said that God has died and the ocean of life opened up, is entitled "The Extent to Which We, Too, Are Still Pious," and reads as follows:

> In science convictions have no citizens' rights, and with good reason: only when they decide to descend to the modesty of an hypothesis, of a provisional experimental standpoint, [of a regulative fiction] may they be granted admission and even a certain value within the realm of knowledge. . . . Wouldn't the disciplined training [*Zucht*] of the scientific spirit begin with one's denying oneself any more convictions? . . . or, *in order that this training might begin*, wouldn't there have to be a conviction there, one that is so domineering and unconditional that it sacrifices all other convictions to itself? . . . [the conviction that] *"nothing* is needed *more* than truth, and in comparison with truth everything else has only secondary value."*—What is this unconditional will to truth? Is it the will *not to let oneself be deceived?* Is it the will *not to deceive? . . .* "Will to truth" means . . . "I will not deceive, not even myself"*—and with this we are on moral ground. . . .* The question: why science? leads back to the moral problem: *why morality at all*, if life, nature, and history are "immoral"? There is no doubt that one who is truthful (*der Wahrhaftige*) in that daring and ultimate sense that is presupposed by the belief in science *thereby affirms another world* than that of life, nature, and history; and as long as he affirms this "other world" must he not thereby deny its opposite, this world, *our* world? . . . in other words our belief in science rests on what is still a *metaphysical belief*—even we contemporary seekers after knowledge, we godless antimetaphysicians, take *our* fire from the flame lit by

a faith thousands of years old, from that Christian faith, which was also the faith of Plato, that God is truth, that truth is divine. But how would it be if precisely this should become more and more incredible, and if nothing should prove to be divine any more [unless it were error, blindness, lies—if God himself should prove to be our longest lie?] (*GS* 344)

As long as those who try to be "scientific" in the modern age— whether as scientists or as philosophers who adopt an atheistic or anti-metaphysical standpoint in advocating scientific method—hold to an absolute "truth" as "men of truth" dependent on an unconditional "will to truth" that advocates pursuing this "truth" to the end, they have not stepped out of the shadows of metaphysics and of quasi-Christian faith and its morality. In this sense even we in the present age remain pious and show traces of a negative attitude to this life.

In the same aphorism Nietzsche also says: "Will to truth, that may perhaps be a concealed will to death." Within this phenomenon, no less than within religion and metaphysics, he finds a latent nihilism. This helps explain the rigorous demand he makes on science and the scientific spirit: to question the morality of "will to truth" buried in the foundations of science itself. Even after the death of God and Christian morality as a target of confrontation, the standpoint of the scientific spirit, positivism, anti-metaphysics, or atheism remains grounded in morality and dependent on "will to truth." Nietzsche's anti-metaphysics and atheism sought to get at these standpoints from behind. His is a higher-level atheism in virtue of his having moved from a masked, unconscious nihilism to an explicit and self-conscious nihilism. For him the radicalization of the scientific conscience was inseparable from a commitment to this kind of nihilism.

In discussing "the whole of our modern science" Nietzsche writes: "the voices [of the trumpeters of reality] do not come from the depths, it is *not* the abyss of the scientific conscience that speaks through them—for the scientific conscience of today is an abyss . . ." (*GM* III, 23). As far as scientists and other scientific thinkers are concerned, even the atheists among them base themselves on morality:

> Clearly morality has never been a problem; it was rather precisely where people, after all kinds of mistrust, discord, and disagreement came together, the hallowed place of peace

where thinkers took a rest even from themselves, where they caught their breath and regained their vigor. (*GS* 345)

Nihilism appears when the consummate radicalization of the scientific spirit focuses on the morality at the basis of science itself.

The question of the nihilism of the consummate scientific conscience is discussed in the next aphorism, "Morality as a Problem":

the great problems all demand *great love* . . . It makes the most telling difference whether a thinker faces his problems personally (*persönlich*), so that he has in them his fate, his distress, and also his best happiness, or rather "impersonally" (*unpersönlich*) [objectively and selflessly] . . . How is it then that I have never met anyone, not even in books, who approached morality in this *personal* way (*als Person*), who knew morality as a problem and this problem as *his* personal distress, torment, voluptuousness and passion? . . . I do not see anybody who has dared to give a *critique* of moral value judgements; I fail to see the slightest attempt at scientific curiosity toward them . . .

What Nietzsche calls *persönlich*, we would today call *existential*. Ordinarily, the existential and scientific attitudes are regarded as polar opposites, in that the latter is considered impersonal, non-individual, and objective. Nietzsche, however, calls for a union of the existential and the scientific such that what is scientific is scientific in virtue of being existential, and vice-versa. Everything depends on how a problem becomes a problem and where it is articulated from. Great problems, he says, demand great love, and those who are capable of great love are strong, fulfilled, and dependable spirits, spirits firmly grounded in themselves. Great problems cannot be *borne* by frogs or weaklings. Only those able to make great problems their own, only those who have invested their fate, distress, and happiness in them, can endure the great problems that have emerged in the human world through the rise of science, and thereby draw the ultimate consequences from the scientific viewpoint. The Existence of such strong, fulfilled, and dependable spirits partakes of the spirit of the lion.

Nietzsche explicates the scientific-existential spirit in an aphorism entitled "Our Question Mark":

Who in the world are we then? If we simply called ourselves—using an older expression—godless ones or unbelievers, or even immoralists, we wouldn't believe that this would come close to designating us. [*GS* 346]

He is speaking here of a stage beyond that of trying to convert a lack of faith into a kind of faith or goal, or even martyrdom, as atheists in the past have done. He continues:

> We have been boiled down and become cold and hard in the insight that the world proceeds in a manner that is not at all divine, that even by human standards it is by no means rational, merciful, or just: we know that the world in which we live is ungodly, immoral, "inhuman."

Such understanding and insight is equivalent to the "fate, distress, and happiness" of the scientific-existential spirit. Nietzsche goes on to say that those who have adopted such a standpoint are seized by a profound suspicion—the suspicion

> that there is an opposition between the world in which we have up till now been at home with our venerations—for whose sake we perhaps *endured* living—and another world, *which we ourselves are*: a merciless, fundamental, deepest suspicion about ourselves that is more and more attaining worse and worse power over us Europeans and could easily confront the coming generations with the terrifying Either/Or: "either abandon your venerations or—abandon yourselves!" The latter would be nihilism; but wouldn't the former also be—nihilism? This is *our* question mark.

God, morality, will to truth, humanity, the world established by our "will to veneration"—if we abandon these, life becomes unbearable. The real world, and our survival in it, would lose all meaning, value, and purpose. But this is the very commitment that science asks of us, having transformed the world in which our lives had meaning into an unbelievable figment and opened up a purposeless and meaningless world as the real world. This is where nihilism as the threat of "the universal state of nothingness" appears. Here is the dilemma: one can no longer remain with the traditional world, and yet one cannot take a stand on the new worldview. Whichever way one turns leads to nihilism. Here is our "distress and torment" and the deepest anxiety of our being.

Nietzsche describes this dilemma in *The Will to Power* as a conflict in which "that which we recognize we do *not* value, and that which we should like to deceive ourselves about we *may* no longer value" (*WP* 5). Or again:

> From this standpoint one recognizes the reality of becoming as the *only* reality, forbids oneself any kind of escape to other worlds and false divinities—*yet one cannot endure this world even though one doesn't want to negate it.* (*WP* 12)

That the world is in this sense "ungodly, immoral, and inhuman" is the expression of an atheism, lack of faith, and amoralism at a stage far beyond the traditional forms of non-belief. The difference from the atheism of Feuerbach and Marx, who advocated a morality of human nature, and an atheism for the sake of a society that is to realize such a morality, is patent. (This is the source of Nietzsche's severe criticisms of democracy and socialism.) For him, the nihilistic consequences of atheism put morality and human nature in doubt. Such radical thoroughness was possible only because he had first opened up in his own person the scientific-existential standpoint. And this in turn required a strong spirit that rests firmly in itself in the midst of profound distress and anxiety—the spirit of the lion in the desert.

8. Science and History as Existence

I have dwelled on the relation between nihilism and the scientific spirit in Nietzsche because I consider it a matter of some moment. In transforming the scientific spirit into Existence truly, honestly, and with conscience, we cannot but expose the world that gives meaning to life as a lie. This nihilistic dilemma is the destiny of the modern period which has been taking shape for thousands of years. The problem is not something that can be solved by the methods of economics, politics, culture, or what have you. Nihilism can be overcome only through nihilism itself.

What Nietzsche calls the *Wende der Not*, the "turn of need," can take place only from within distress itself. The severest distress is at the same the greatest possibility of freedom—a freedom which exposes anything that controls the self from above as a lie, a spirit in which "there is no God or human being above the self." The spirit of the lion is not itself the creation of new values, but is said to provide the freedom for such creation. In the midst of the great problems it knows the happiness of one who has won the freedom for a new and unknown world. Both the distress and the freedom and happiness into which it turns are grounded in the equation of the self with fate. The distress that is at the same time the conversion of distress is the Existence in which the necessary outcome of several thousand years of history comes to consciousness in the self, and is borne resolutely in such a way that the self becomes a manifestation of this outcome.

In this process the self becomes a true self. It is not the product of learning or instruction but a self come to light through itself. The spirit as camel was the spirit of reverence and learning. But the self that has grown strong under the bonds of all that has been learned eventually "breaks the revering heart" and sheds everything that had been acquired through reverent learning as an outer husk, casting it aside to make way for the true self. An aphorism in *Beyond Good and Evil* expresses the point well:

> Learning transforms us, it does what all nourishment does that also does not simply "maintain"—as the physiologist knows. But in our ground, deep "down below," there is surely something unteachable, a granite of spiritual fate [*Fatum*], of predetermined decisions and answers to predetermined and selected questions. With every cardinal problem there speaks an unchangeable "that is me": about man and woman, for example, a thinker cannot learn but only finish learning—only finish discovering how things "stand firm" in him on that topic. One finds at times certain solutions to problems which make for strong belief just in *us*; perhaps one calls these henceforth one's "convictions." Later, one sees in them only steps toward self-knowledge, signposts to the problem that we *are*—or, more correctly, to the great stupidity that we are, to our spiritual fate, to the unteachability deep "down there." (*BGE* 231)

Nietzsche's talk of the "granite of fate" that we are is reminiscent of Goethe's short essay entitled "On Granite."[11] Sitting atop a mountain on an exposed piece of granite, overlooking a vast vista stretching out from beneath him, Goethe immersed himself in the thought that the vista had undergone numerous changes in the long history of the earth; that the granite on which he was sitting extended down deep into the earth's strata to form the backbone of the earth's crust throughout all its changes and movements. The image illustrates the idea of the self as a fate deep within our foundations: fate as self—"that is me." This level is unreachable by teaching or learning; it is the true self that does not change. Since this is something unteachable, it may equally well be called "the great folly." That very folly is the object of our self-knowledge, our "self is this," and all convictions acquired through learning are no more than tracks leading toward it.

This idea is reminiscent of those Zen masters who advocated a transmission of teachings without dependence on scriptures, by pointing directly to the human heart, and whose ideal was to be "concentrated and immovable as a fool, like an idiot."[12] For Nietzsche, the ideal was to be "free as a bird" (*vogelfrei*), in much the same way as the Zen masters who taught "the way of the bird." Dozan, who taught the way of the bird, speaks of "not going the way of the bird."[13] Another Zen master says: "A hidden bird sings volubly and flies out of the clouds into the distance of mountain peak upon mountain peak."[14] This kind of great affirmation took the form of "love of fate" in Nietzsche, insofar as for him the self coalesced with problems that had unfolded through history. In the great confrontation—or rather the great experiment—with history, the deeper the problems, the more deeply the self becomes itself. (This is the difference between the existential character of this "experiment" and experiments in the natural sciences.) In the end, "deep down below" a problem emerges of which one can say only that the self *is* the problem, or that the self itself turns into *its* problem. There the ground and innermost nature of the self is reached, that is, the soul of the self as love of fate (see above, chapter four, sec. 3). In this the self is realized as the necessary consequence of past history and the necessary beginning of history to come. This is why Nietzsche uses an expression reminiscent of the Christian doctrines of election and predestination: "predetermined decision and answer to questions chosen in advance." This means self = *fate*. The great history of humanity has turned into the Existence of the self, so that one stands in the spirit of history = Existence.

The spirit of science = Existence is need and at the same time the turn of need, aporia and at the same time the breaking through of aporia. It signals the beginning of the progress of historical necessity, a setting out toward the creation of new values and the beginning of revaluation. To be compelled to the overturning (*Umwendung*) of all values means that the existential turning of need (*Wende der Not*) presses from within the self as necessity, and that history actualizes the necessity (*Notwendigkeit*) of history itself through the fate of humanity as the elect chosen by history itself. In this, the spirits of science = Existence and history = Existence are fused. Cosmology and the historical view, the interpretation of human being in the world and the critique of morality in history, converge in Existence. This was Nietzsche's method: to confront through science the great problems that arose from the depths of history. Existence for him means the endeavor to "discipline" oneself in the confrontation with great problems, and thereby to reach the self-realization of "the unteachable," the ground of the self; or, through the disciplining of the self and human transformation, to become one who can endure the great problems, and to improve oneself to the point that one is chosen by history.

9. "Living Dangerously" and "Experimentation"

As mentioned above, the image of Existence is that of a seafarer setting sail into a vast ocean against a bright horizon in search of an unknown land. Nietzsche notes in several places that Existence is something dangerous. For example, in *The Gay Science* he speaks of the courage to understand:

> The secret for harvesting the greatest fruitfulness and the greatest enjoyment from existence is *to live dangerously (gefähr-lich leben)!* Build your cities on the slopes of Vesuvius! Send your ships into unexplored seas! Live at war with your equals and with yourselves! (*GS* 283)

Nietzsche often spoke of the necessity for courage in pursuing thoughts and their consequences. A note from the unpublished manuscripts reads: "My task is to prove that the consequences of science are *dangerous*. It is all over with 'good' and 'evil' . . . and so we love adventure and embark upon the ocean" (XIII, 53). Earlier we heard him speak of the contemporary scientific conscience as an "abyss." Throughout modern science and scientific ideas there is no sound of the scientific conscience's talking, he says, and this means that the voice of those who are "scientific" is not sufficiently coming "out of the depths." People are unconsciously avoiding the scientific-existential consequences of science, and science has thus become "a means of self-anaesthesia" (see *GM* III, 23). The courage honestly to take upon oneself the danger of such consequences is lacking.

In this connection Nietzsche tries to show, as he puts it in *Ecce homo*, "from what depths . . . 'science' has become *gay*" [*EH* III, *"The Gay Science"*]. In his "Hymn to January," he says that the ice of his soul has been pierced by a spear of flame and now rushes roaring to the sea of its greatest hope, ever brighter, ever healthier, and freer in loving and fateful necessity.[15] This kind of "gay science," where one throws oneself into the abyss of scientific conscience, when the soul becomes *amor fati* and the self becomes fate, yields the richest harvest and also the greatest enjoyment of existence. To do this, Nietzsche says, one needs the courage to live dangerously, beyond the morality of "good and evil."

His frequent talk of *experiment* and references to his own method as "experimental philosophy" [*WP* 1041] illustrates his standpoint of science = Existence and history = Existence. Earlier we heard him call himself a "daring and researching spirit who has already lost his way once in every labyrinth of the future" [*WP*, Preface §3]. Here he adopts a standpoint of scientific and historical Existence. Or again: "One kind of honesty [*Redlichkeit*] has been alien to all founders of religion and similar people—they have never made their experiences a matter of conscience for knowledge" (*GS* 319). Even today religious people are this way: they have a thirst for things that are *against reason*:

> But we others, we thirsters after reason, want to look our experiences straight in the eye, as we would scrutinize a scientific experiment, hour by hour, day by day! We ourselves want to be our own experiments and experimental animals.

Here his standpoint unites the historical critique of religion and morality with the spirit of scientific inquiry in Existence.

10. The Third Stage—Existence as Body

It is in the third stage, with the transformation of the spirit of the lion into that of the child, that we reach Nietzsche's philosophy of affirmation, where ideas such as love of fate, eternal recurrence, Dionysus, will to power, and the underlying perspectival interpretation of the world play an essential role. It is in this stage that nihilism is split asunder and the ice of the soul melted by the flaming spear of Dionysian affirmation. Having dealt with this topic already, I shall restrict myself here to a treatment of "the body" in Nietzsche, a theme that received only cursory mention earlier.

In the speech "On the Dwellers in the World Beyond" in Part One of *Zarathustra*, we are told that what made people imagine gods and a world beyond was weariness with life. Nietzsche says that it was not "soul" or "spirit" that made people invent a world beyond, or a God behind this world and beyond the world inhabited by the body, but rather the sick and exhausted "body" itself.

> Sick and moribund were those who despised the body and the earth and invented the heavenly realm . . .
>
> A sickly thing is their body for them, and they would gladly get out of their skins. Therefore they listen to preachers of death, and themselves preach worlds beyond. [*Za* I, 3]

We should not take this talk of the sick and exhausted body, nor the opposite expressions of curing and health, in a merely physiological sense, at least not in the ordinary sense of the term. In the same speech we read:

> This creating, willing and valuing I . . .
>
> This most honest being, the I—speaks of the body, and it still wants the body even when it poetizes and raves and flutters with broken wings . . .
>
> My I taught me a new pride, and I teach it to human beings: no longer to bury their heads in the sand of heavenly things, but to bear them freely, heads of the earth, which create a sense of the earth!

Nietzsche also speaks of "the voice of the healthy body [as] a more honest and purer voice." Therefore the healthy "body" is the standpoint of the creating, willing, and valuing "I" itself, and a standpoint that creates a meaning for the earth.

The standpoint of the "I" who creates and wills is one that has endured through the northernmost zone of nihilism. "Soul," "spirit," and "the world beyond" were set up as denials of the body and the earthly world; next, nihilism appeared as the denial of this standpoint; and finally, in the overcoming of this nihilism the body is restored as the standpoint of the creating and willing "I." This is not—as it is often taken to be—a case of simple body worship. Creating and willing begin to flow like a mountain stream when "the ice of the soul" (nihilism) has been broken through and melted by the flame of affirmative life (will to power). It is a question here not only of various processes of "somatic" life, but also various processes of "consciousness" (such as reason, will, and so on) which are being understood from the "physiological" standpoint. (It is particularly in the unpublished notes that we find traces of Nietzsche's attempts at a "physiological" understanding of consciousness.[16]) At any rate, when nihilism is overcome through nihilism in the standpoint of science = Existence mentioned earlier, and when nihilism is transformed from negation to affirmation, the result appears in the form of *Existence as "body."*

In his speech "On the Despisers of the Body," Zarathustra says:

> "Body am I and soul"—thus speaks the child. And why shouldn't one speak like children?
> But the awakened one, who knows, says: Body am I entirely, and nothing more: and soul is only a word for something about the body.
> The body is a great reason[17] . . .
> Your small reason, my brother, which you call "spirit," is only a tool of your body, a small tool and toy of your great reason. . . .
> Behind your thoughts and feelings, my brother, stands a powerful commander, an unknown director[18]—who is called Self. He lives in your body, he is your body. [I, 4]

Nietzsche emphasizes that this "Self" is not the conscious self that we normally call "I," but something prior to consciousness and self-consciousness, something that "lives in the body and is the body." One might call it the self as primordial life itself. What we call consciousness or self-consciousness is merely the result of an interpretation—indeed a *false* interpretation—of the activity of this primordial life. At the same time, Nietzsche recognizes that this false interpretation arises from the demand for the self-preservation of life, and is therefore useful for life. In opposition to science based on the morality of "will to truth," which takes it as self-evident that nothing is more important than truth, he insists that: "both truth *and* untruth constantly show themselves to be useful" (*GS* 344). This idea is behind the following words which are the continuation of the previous quotation from *Zarathustra*:

> The Self says to the I: "feel pain here!" And it suffers and ponders how it might avoid further suffering—and precisely this it *should* ponder.
> The Self says to the I: "feel pleasure here!" And it is happy and ponders how it might continue to feel happy—and precisely this it *should* ponder.

This passage clarifies the meaning of Zarathustra's saying that the Self is the commander behind one's thoughts and feelings. Pleasure, suffering, thinking, and so on are normally held to take place in the conscious "I," but their source is a life deeper than and prior to the "I," a manifestation of "will to power" which constitutes the essence of life. The so-called "I," what we normally take as the self, is merely a frame of interpretation added to this life process after the fact. The true self is the source of the life process itself, the true body of will to power. It is what I have called "the self itself" or "the self as such," and not what is ordinarily called the "self." The so-called "I" is a tool of this greater self. This I take to be what Nietzsche means when he speaks of "body."

Therefore, even if this standpoint of body is one of affirmation, it is not the kind of standpoint that can be adopted simply by abandoning "spiritual" things—which in any event are not so easily abandoned—any more than it is easy to escape the conscious "I." The body in Nietzsche is the kind of self that is conceived from the side of an ultimate self-awakening beyond self-consciousness, or what I referred to previously as "Existence." The affirmation is on the same level as that of the religious believer who can affirm a God beyond death. From that same depth, affirmation is directed toward the body and the earth; only one who *can* affirm in this way can *be* body existentially.

Nietzsche shows the way of Existence by borrowing the figure of Zarathustra, but we may cite a perfect exemplification of this existential life from a different source:

> . . . we ourselves grow, we are changing constantly, we shed our bark, we slough our skins every spring, we become ever younger, more futural, taller, stronger, we strike our roots ever more powerfully into the depths—into evil—while at the same time we embrace the heavens ever more lovingly and ever more thirstily drinking its light with all our branches and leaves. We grow like trees—that is difficult to understand, as is all life—not in one place but everywhere, not in one direction but up and out as much as in and down . . . [19]

Nietzsche goes on to say, "We grow into the *heights*—that is our fate." What makes life so "difficult to understand" is that it grows in all directions at once. Religious-minded people usually set their sights exclusively on the heavens, allowing their roots in the earth to loosen, or even to be transplanted into the world beyond.[20] For Nietzsche, this is a radical perversion. In the East, too, it is said to be easy to enter the realm of buddhas but difficult to enter the realm of demons. At the other extreme, ordinary materialists and believers in the body take the easiest path of remaining on the surface of the earth. By not extending one's branches and leaves toward the heights, one is unable to strike roots probingly into the depths underground, into the innermost recesses of life—"into evil." The spiritual person moves inwards; the scientific person, outwards. The difficulty is finding a standpoint "beyond good and evil" within life itself, entering into the heavens and subterranean realms at the same time, and living in a place where inside is outside and outside is inside. But this was precisely what Nietzsche had in mind in speaking of the body as Existence that "supersedes" spirit from the ground of spirit itself. From within the *growth of this life*, a new goal emerges—the *Übermensch* who overcomes the present mode of human being and restores a sense to the "earth."

11. The Dialectical Development of Nihilism

Looking back over everything that has been said so far, it strikes me that there is a kind of dialectical process at work in Nietzsche's thinking on nihilism. On the one hand, we see a process of pushing the negation of life to the extreme; and on the other, a process in which, through that negation, will—namely, will to power as the affirmation of life—begins to assert itself as will. The two dynamics work together inextricably. I referred to "natural" nihilism as a loss of will and a weakening of life. The will to life which overcomes this by setting up a world beyond is also a "life against life," or "will to nothing," hiding behind the robes of religion and metaphysics. True nihilism, which disrobes the masquerade, is the self-conscious will to negate and is a springboard to will to power. Here life, or will, consummates its self-affirmation by pressing its self-negation to the extreme through self-criticism and self-overcoming. Life, or will, thereby returns to its own original, its most elemental and natural mode of being. It returns to itself, where the beginning is the end and the end is the beginning—in short, to the mode of being as "body."

The following passage, stressing the significance of criticism, describes this process:

> *In favor of criticism.*—Now something appears to you as an error which you formerly loved as a truth or a probability believe that your reason has thereby won a victory. But perhaps your error was at that time, when you were someone else— you are always someone different—as necessary for you as all your present "truths," just like a skin that concealed and veiled many things that you still may not see. It is your new life that has killed that opinion for you, not your reason: *you*

no longer need it, and now it collapses and the unreason crawls out of it like a worm into the light. When we practise criticism, it is nothing arbitrary and impersonal—it is, at least very often, a proof that there are driving forces alive in us which are throwing off a husk. We deny, and must deny, because something in us *will* live and affirm itself, something that we perhaps do not yet know, and do not yet see!—This is all in favor of criticism. (*GS* 307)

This unknown "something" is the growth of life, whose essence consists in a force that drives life itself on and on to ever further growth—will to power. Through this constant transformation we are "always a different person." What we previously held to be the truth is now seen to be error and "unreason." This change comes about through the self-criticism of life, not through the power of reason. In the *desire* to affirm itself, life carries on self-criticism and self-negation. Here we see Nietzsche's anti-intellectualist voluntarism, according to which all irrationality and all error—including even the self-deception of life—are but manifestations of life itself at a given stage, forms of life seen from a given perspective, useful outer skins whose purpose is the preservation of life itself. This "perspectivism" of Nietzsche's makes "will to deception" an inherent part of life.

The dialectic we have been describing in the growth of life, the will's circling back on itself, pervades Nietzsche's ideas of nihilism and Existence. It also belongs to the logic of the greater history of humanity. We have already touched on the relation between the dynamics of history and the existential self-awakening of the individual. Against that backdrop, the following passage from *The Will to Power* illustrates Nietzsche's vision of history as a whole:

> *Total insight.*—Every great growth actually brings with it a tremendous *crumbling* and *perishing*: suffering and the symptoms of decline *belong* to times of great progress; every fruitful and powerful movement of humanity has at the same time created a nihilistic movement. Under certain circumstances it would be a sign of incisive and essential growth, of transition into new conditions of existence, that the most *extreme* form of pessimism, true nihilism, would come into the world. *This much I have grasped.* (*WP* 112)

Chapter Six

Nihilism as Egoism: Max Stirner

1. Stirner's Context

While Dostoevsky and Nietzsche must be acknowledged as the thinkers who plumbed the depths of nihilism most deeply, we can see the outlines of nihilism—though not fully developed as such—in an earlier work published by Max Stirner in 1844, *The Ego and His Own*.[1] Thanks to the revival of interest in Stirner's work by J. H. Mackay (*Max Stirner, Sein Leben und Sein Werk*, 1897), attention has been drawn to various similarities between Stirner's ideas and those of Nietzsche. It is almost certain that Nietzsche did not read Stirner's work. If he was acquainted with Stirner at all, it was probably indirectly through Lange's *History of Materialism*.[2] In the absence of direct and substantive influence, the presence of such similarities raises a number of questions.

At the same time, comparisons must not be allowed to obscure the great difference in the foundations of their philosophies and in the spirit that pervades the entirety of their thought. Although Mackay regards Stirner far more highly than he does Nietzsche, there is in Stirner nothing of the great metaphysical spirit excavating the subterranean depths we find in Nietzsche. Stirner's critiques do not display the anatomical thoroughness of Nietzsche's painstaking engagement with all aspects of culture; nor does one hear in Stirner the prophetic voice of a Zarathustra resounding from the depths of the soul. The unique style of Stirner's thinking lay in a combination of a razor-sharp logic that cuts through straight to the consequences of things and an irony that radically inverts all standpoints with a lightness approaching humor. In this regard his work is not without its genius. Feuerbach, even though he was one of the primary targets of Stirner' criticisms, admired *The Ego and His*

Own greatly, referring to it in a letter addressed to his brother shortly after the book appeared as "a work of genius, filled with spirit." Feuerbach allowed that even though what Stirner had said about him was not right, he was nevertheless "the most brilliant and liberated writer I have ever known."

Stirner's book showed him at his best in his confrontation with the turbulent *Zeitgeist* of the period, set in a highly charged political atmosphere culminating in the outbreak of the February Revolution of 1848. Among the intelligentsia the radical ideas of the "Hegelian left" were in high fashion. As Nietzsche was to write later: "The whole of human *idealism* up until now is about to turn into *nihilism*" (*WP* 617); and indeed such a turn was already beginning to show signs of emerging from the intellectual turmoil of the earlier period. It was Stirner who grasped what Nietzsche was to call the "turn into nihilism" in its beginning stages, presenting it as *egoism*.

Around the beginning of the 1840s a group of people who called themselves "*Die Freien*" used to gather in Hippel's tavern on the Friedrichstrasse in Berlin. The central figure of the group was Bruno Bauer, and such people as Marx and Engels occasionally attended as well. Stirner was among these "Free Ones." The trend at that time was a sharp turn away from idealism and romanticism in favor of realism and political criticism. The criticism of the liberals was focused on overthrowing the coalition of Christian theology, Hegelian philosophy, and political conservatism. It was only natural that Feuerbach's *The Essence of Christianity* which appeared in 1841 would cause a great shock through its severe critique of religion. The current of thought broke forth into a rushing torrent. In no time Marx and others had developed Feuerbach's ideas into a materialism of praxis and history, while Bruno Bauer developed them in the opposite direction of "consciousness of self." Stirner then took the latter's ideas to the extreme to develop a standpoint of egoism. It was only three years after Feuerbach's *The Essence of Christianity* that Stirner's *The Ego and His Own* was published, which shows how rapidly ideas were changing at the time. His critique of Feuerbach is directed at his basic principle of "anthropology," the standpoint that "human being" is the supreme essence for human beings. In this sense, Stirner and Marx exemplify two entirely opposite directions of transcending the standpoint of humanity in human beings.

As mentioned earlier, Feuerbach represented a reaction against Hegel's philosophy of absolute Spirit, in much the same way as Schopenhauer had, since both criticized the idealism of the speculative thinking in Hegel and the Christian "religious nature of spirit" at its foundation. But just as Nietzsche detected a residue of the

Christian spirit in Schopenhauer's negative attitude towards "will to life," Stirner recognized vestiges of the religious spirit and idealism in the theological negation of God and Hegelian idealism in Feuerbach. Both Nietzsche and Stirner, by pushing the negation of idealism and spiritualism to the extreme, ended up at the opposite pole of their predecessors. This may account for some of the similarities between them.

2. The Meaning of Egoism

At the beginning of his major work Stirner cites the motto "*Ich hab' Mein' Sach' auf Nichts gestellt*." Translated literally, this means "I have founded my affair on nothing." Here we have Stirner's basic standpoint *in nuce:* the negation of any and all standpoints. Nothing, whether God or morality, may be set up as a ground to support the self and its activity. It is in effect a standpoint that rejects standing on anything other than the self itself, a standpoint based on "nothing." The motto is ordinarily used to express the attitude of indifference to everything, the feeling of "I don't care."[3] It means a lack of interest in anything, a loss of the passion to immerse oneself in things, and a feeling of general apathy. But it also includes a kind of negative positiveness, a nonchalant acceptance of things which appropriates them as the life-content of the self and enjoys the life of the self in all things. (There are affinities here to the idea of acting in "empty non-attachment" in Lao-tzu and Chuang-tzu.[4]) Its positiveness negates any positiveness that makes something other than the self the affair to which one devotes oneself. It is an attitude of enjoying what one has rejected from the self as the content of one's life, transforming everything into the *self's* own concern. It is, in short, the "egoistic" posture.

One normally considers the higher things to be those that relate to a universal apart from the self. One devotes oneself to such matters and makes them the concerns of the self. The religious person serves God, the socialist serves society, patriots their country, the housewife her home, as the concern (*Sache*) of the self. Each sees the meaning of life in this concern and finds his or her mission in it. To efface the self and devote oneself to one's concern is regarded as a superior way of life. By making God, country, humanity, society, and so forth one's own concern, one forgets the self and invests one's interest in something outside the self which then becomes one's own *affair*. This is one's *Sache*, the focus of ideals or values regarded as sacred. The foundation of such concern could be religion or ethics, which are standpoints in which one makes some-thing beyond oneself the self's *Sache*, in such a way that the self loses its own *Sache*. But even where religion and ethics have been shaken by some "revolution" or other, these revolutionary stand-points continue to acknowledge something other than the self as the proper object of one's devotion, thus restoring in a new guise the very religious and ethical standpoints they had negated. Stirner steps in here to advocate egoism as the utter negation of all such standpoints.

Nietzsche thought that the ideals and values that had con-trolled European history up to the present were hastening the advent of nihilism as their own logical consequence. He himself pre-empted this advent voluntarily and carried it out psychologi-cally and experientially in himself, and by living nihilism through to the end turned it into a standpoint of will to power. Though he did not use the word "nihilism," Stirner tried—as Nietzsche was to do later—to demonstrate logically that previous ideals and values undermine themselves and collapse into nothing precisely as a re-sult of the effort to make them consummate and exhaustive. He proposed his idea of egoism as the inevitable result and ultimate consequence of such a collapse. His egoism emerged from his dis-covery of the hollowness of the foundations on which previous re-ligion, philosophy, and morality had rested. As a result, it attained an ironic depth not achieved by ordinary forms of egoism.

In religion and philosophy God is "all in all," and all things other than God are to devote themselves to him. From God's point of view, everything is part of the divine *Sache*. God is One, and as a unique being does not tolerate anyone's refusing to be part of the divine economy. "His *Sache* is—a purely egoistic *Sache*."[5] It is virtu-ally the same with human beings. All sorts of people devote them-selves to the service of humanity, but for humanity the only concern is that it develop itself through such devotion. For humanity, hu-manity itself is the *Sache*. As Stirner asks: "Is the *Sache* of humanity not a purely egoistic *Sache*?" (4/4).

God and humanity have set their concern on nothing, on nothing other than themselves. I may then set my concern similarly on myself, who as much as God am the Nothing of all else (*das Nichts von allem anderen*), who am my all, who am the only individual. . . . What is divine is God's concern (*Sache*), what is human is "man's" concern. My concern is neither di-vine nor human, nor the true, the good, the just, the free, and

so on; my concern is only mine, and is not universal but is—
unique, as I am unique. (4-5/5)

This is the standpoint of "the unique one and its own," which, as
we shall see presently, is all there is.

Why does Stirner refuse to acknowledge a higher self in something universal above the self? Why can he not acknowledge a truer
life than the life of the self, for example in God or humanity, nation
or society? According to Stirner, at the basis of such religious or ethical ideas—and even of ideas opposed to them—there is a standpoint of "spirit" (*Geist*) and the "spiritual" world. Once this spirit
world has been exposed as a lie, the religious and ethical ways of
life based on it are forced into hypocrisy.

In coming to this conclusion, Stirner took a position in direct
confrontation to the ideas of his immediate milieu, principally those
of Feuerbach, Bruno Bauer, and the Communists. In a time of historical crisis such confrontations take on the quality of a face-off
with history as a whole. In Stirner's own words, the problem is that
"several thousand years of history" (as Nietzsche also realized)
come to a head in the latter half of the nineteenth century. Thus
Stirner's critique of history has a very different character from the
typical observations of the general historian. As with Nietzsche, his
philosophy confronts history existentially and sees the whole of
world history perspectivally. Marx critcizes him for numerous inac-
curacies of historical fact, but for a thinker like Stirner, what is important are not the particular data but the understanding of history
as a whole.

3. Realist, Idealist, Egoist—"Creative Nothing"

Stirner divides history into three periods, which he compares to
three stages in the development of the individual: namely, boyhood,
youth, and the prime of manhood. The boy lives only in relation to
things in this world, unable to conceive of anything like a spiritual
world beyond it. In that sense he is a realist. In general the boy is
under the control of the power of nature, and things like parental
authority confront him as natural rather than spiritual powers. Still,
from the beginning there is a drive in the boy to "strike to the
ground of things and get around behind them" (*hinter die Dinge
kommen*);[6] and through the knowledge he gains he can elude or get
the better of the powers that govern him. When the boy knows
something to be true, its truth is not some independent being

transcendent to the world; it remains a truth within things. In this sense the boy lives only in this world.

The youth, on the other hand, is an idealist. He feels the courage to resist things before which he had once felt fear and awe. He prides himself on his intelligence in seeing through such things and opposing them with something like reason or conscience. His is the "spiritual" attitude. In the young man, "truth" is something ideal that exists by itself from the beginning, independent of the things of the world; as something "heavenly" it is opposed to all despicable "earthly" things. From this standpoint thoughts are no more than disembodied abstract ideas, pure "logical" thoughts, "absolute" ideas in Hegel's sense.

Once in the prime of life, however, the youth turns into an egoist. He knows that the ideal is void. Instead of looking at the world from the standpoint of ideals, he see it as it is. He relates to the world according to his concern in the interest of the self. "The boy had only *unspiritual* interests, free of thoughts or ideas; the youth had only *spiritual* interests; but the man has bodily, personal, and egoistic (*leibhaftig, persönlich, egoistisch*) interests." Or again: "The youth found himself as *spirit* and lost himself again in *universal* spirit, in [the consummate,] holy spirit, in *the* human, in humanity, in short in all kinds of ideals; the man finds himself as *bodily* spirit" (13/14).

The growth of the individual through the stages of realist, idealist, and egoist is a process of discovering and attaining the *self*. At first the self gets behind all things and finds itself—the standpoint of spirit. The self as spirit acknowledges the world as spirit, but the self must then go behind this spirit to recover itself. This consists the realization that the self is the creator-owner of the spiritual world, spirit, thoughts, and so on. Spirit is "the *first* self-discovery" (10/10); the self as egoist is "the *second* self-discovery" (13/14), in which the self becomes truly itself. With this latter stage, the self is released from its ties to this real world and to the ideal world beyond, free to return to the vacuity at the base of those things. The vacuity of *this* world was already realized in idealism; the egoist goes on to see the vacuity of the *other* world.

The egoist bases himself on absolute "nothing," and this is neither realism nor an idealism. Where formerly "spirit" was conceived as the creator-owner of this world, the egoist's standpoint sees the self as the creator and owner of spirit and the spiritual world. This is what it means to "set one's concern on nothing"— "not in the sense of a void, but creative nothing (*das schöpferische Nichts*), the nothing out of which I myself as creator create everything."[7] At the basis of Stirner's egoism is the Hegelian idea of absolute negativity (*absolute Negativität*) in which realism and idealism are superseded.

Parallel to the development in the individual from realism to idealism and egoism, Stirner sees a similar development in world history. He distinguishes between "ancients" and "moderns," the line between them being drawn at the birth of Christianity. Among these latter he also distinguishes "free people," a general term for radical liberals of the period who criticized the Christian worldview and its morality. According to Stirner, even these "free people" had not yet escaped the foundation of the Christian morality they were busy negating and hence were not yet true egoists. In the following section we shall trace this development from paganism to Christianity, and from Christianity to the liberalism that necessarily results in egoism.

4. From Paganism to Christianity

According to Stirner, the ancient pagans and the Christians after them had completely opposite ideas of truth. For the pagans, things and relations of this world and this earth were true, whereas for Christianity truth resided in heaven. While the pagan held ties to homeland and family as sacred, to the Christians these were so many empty fictions. For the latter the earth was a foreign land, and their true home in heaven. Under the influence of Hegelian thought, Stirner viewed the development from paganism to Christianity dialectically, insofar as Christianity was the inevitable unfolding of the opposite standpoint of paganism.

> "For the ancients the world was a truth," says Feuerbach, but he forgets to add the important proviso: a truth whose untruth they sought to discover—and eventually did discover (15-16/16).

Like the young boy who naturally wants to get behind things, primitive peoples were possessed of a drive to discover the untruth of things within the very perspective that regards things as true. This dialectical irony is typical of Stirner's historical perspective.

The first signs of this dialectical progression appear, according to Stirner, with the Sophists. Realizing the power of intellectual understanding, they grew progressively critical of established authority. Socrates internalized this criticism further and brought it deep into the *heart*. In Socrates the efforts of the heart to purify itself came to term, and this purification grew more and more rigorous until nothing in this world was able to meet the standard of the heart's purity. Out of this developed the standpoint of the Skeptics, who refused to let themselves be affected by anything in this world. What began with the Sophists, Stirner said, was carried ahead by Socrates and completed by the Skeptics. With the Skeptics the human individual was liberated from the bonds of life, grew indifferent to the world, and developed a posture that refused to have to do with anything—a state of mind that did not care if the whole world were to collapse. Karl Jaspers considers the skepticism represented by Pyrrho as a kind of nihilism.[8] In any event, this mentality paved the way for Christianity, since for the first time the self had come to be experienced as "worldless" (*weltlos*), as "spirit": "That one became aware of oneself as a being that is not related to anything, a worldless being, as *spirit*, was the result of the enormous labor of the ancients" (19/20). Christianity was in this sense the "result" of the development of paganism.

For Stirner, the standpoint of spirit in the true sense is not one of passive negation and *refusing to relate* to the things of this world, but an active standpoint of *choosing to relate* to spiritual things, and to spiritual things exclusively. Initially, these spiritual things are the thoughts grasped in reflection, but the spirit goes on to create a spiritual world really existing behind things. In Stirner's view, "Spirit is spirit only when it creates spiritual things." Spirit is regarded as spirit only over against spirit; it takes shape only through continued positive interest in spiritual things. This is the difference between the worldless standpoint of the Skeptics and the standpoint of true spirit in Christianity's creation of a new spiritual world. And only in this kind of creation of a world unique to itself is spirit able to become *free*. In contrast, the pagans remained in the standpoint of being "armed against the world" (24/25).

5. From Christianity to Liberalism

When Christianity set up God in the world beyond, according to Stirner, this was the inevitable result of the notion of spirit itself. Your self is not your "spirit," he says, and your "spirit" is not your self. In spirit you split yourself into two; your spirit, which is called your true self, becomes your center, and this center of the spirit is spirit itself. Even though you are more than spirit and all spiritual things come from you, you consider yourself lower than spirit. This spirit is your ideal and as such is set up in the world beyond as something unattainable. As long as spirit is imagined to be in control, it must reside in the world beyond. This is why the Christian theological worldview eventually requires an idea of God as spirit. [See pp. 30–32/31–34.] The irony of history for Stirner is that the truth of the other world which Christianity opposed to the pagan truth of this world is something of which the Christians themselves tried "to disclose the untruth—and eventually succeeded" (24/26).

During the centuries prior to the Reformation, intellectual understanding, long shackled by dogma, showed the ardor of a Sophist-like rebellion. Only with the Reformation did the problem of the heart which Socrates had pursued come to be taken up seriously. At the same time, however, the notion of the heart became so vacuous, as in the case of the so-called liberals from Feuerbach to Bruno Bauer, that "only an empty *cordiality* (*leere Herzlichkeit*) remained, as universal love for all human beings, love of 'humanity,' consciousness of freedom, self-consciousness" (25/27). This corresponds to the posture of the ancient Skeptics, ending up in the "pure" standpoint in which the heart not only criticizes everything but also keeps the criticism entirely free of any egoistic concern of the criticizer. It is the standpoint of criticism of the critical standpoint itself, or absolute criticism. Even though this view of the heart derived originally from Christianity, the religious content able to put up with criticism from the standpoint of the heart could no longer be found there. The heart, or spirit, standing in front of itself, spontaneously sees itself as having been a fiction, and with that all things become fictions. "Driven to the extreme edge of disinterested cordiality, we must finally acknowledge that the spirit which the Christian loves is [nothing, or that the spirit is]—a lie" (26/27). This is reminiscent of Nietzsche's view that through the sincerity cultivated by Christian morality the values and ideals established by that morality itself are revealed as fictions.[9]

At this point Feuerbach's anthropology steps in to liberate people from the standpoint of Christian theology. As Stirner points out, however, the attempt itself is entirely theological. Feuerbach's anthropology internalized the divine spirit into the essence of humanity ("*unser Wesen*"). As a result, we are split into an essential self and a non-essential self, and we are thus again driven out of our selves [33/34]. As long as we are not our own essence, it is really the same whether it be seen as a transcendent "God" external to us, or as an "essence" internal to us: "I am neither God nor 'humanity,' neither the supreme *essence* nor my *essence*"[33/35]. Feuerbach's idea that my essence is "humanity" and I am supposed to

realize this essence is not really any different from the Hegelian idealism he rejected. I am a human being, to be sure, but "humanity"
is not me. Being a "human being" is an attribute or predicate of
mine, but the "humanity" that is presumed to give laws to the self
and transcend the self is a ghostly illusion for the very reasons that
Feuerbach regarded God as an illusion. This ghost drains the ego of
its content, leaving it null and void. Feuerbach preached love of humanity, where "the human is God for the human." But for an "I" to
love the "humanity" within a Thou does not indicate true love, any
more than the old religion which spoke of loving God in one's
neighbor. True love means that I as an individual love a Thou as an
individual. In this way, Stirner argues, Feuerbach merely substituted "humanity" for God. Ethical love (*sittliche Liebe*) is no more
than a modern substitute for religious love (*religiöse Liebe*), which
had become difficult to sustain. True love must be totally egoistic,
individual love, the love of a Thou as an individual.

From this perspective, Stirner would have us understand spirit
as a sort of ghost. The modern world may disclaim belief in ghosts,
but what they call spirit (*Geist*) is precisely that—a disembodied
spirit or specter. Spirit is still thought to be behind everything. The
world remains full of specters because both those who believe in
ghosts (*Spuk*) and those who believe in spirit are seeking some kind
of suprasensible world behind the sensible world. In other words,
they fabricate a kind of other world and then invest belief in it.

> There are ghosts everywhere in the world (*es spunkt in der
> ganzen Welt*). [Only *in* it?] No: rather, the world itself is a kind
> of ghost; [it is uncanny—*unheimlich*—through and through.] it
> is the wandering apparitional body [*Scheinleib*] of a spirit. . . .
> and don't be surprised if you find nothing other in yourself
> than a ghost. Does your spirit not haunt your body, and isn't
> that spirit what is true and actual, and the body only some-
> thing "ephemeral, null" or mere "appearance"? Aren't we all
> ghosts, uncanny beings awaiting "redemption"—that is,
> "spirits"? (35/37)

Spirit, it is said, is holy. God is holy, humanity is holy, and so
on. But what on earth does it mean to regard something as holy?
Here Stirner launches an attack against the subjectivity behind the
objective standpoint of spirit: "There is a ghost in your head, and
you are crazy (*du hast einen Sparren zu viel*)."[10] What is this one rafter
[*Sparren*] too many? It is nothing more than an ideal created in the
head, an ideal to which one feels called or to the actualization of

which one feels obligated to devote oneself, such as the kingdom of God, the realm of spirit, or what have you. Stirner claims that the various ideals emphasized in religion, morality, law, and so on are all *idées fixes*[11] that lead people around by the nose and make them possessed. They breathe spirit into people, inflating them with inspiration (*Begeisterung*) and enthusiasm (*Enthusiasmus*). They move people and drive them into frenzy and the *fanaticism* of a blindly unquestioning fascination with "holy" things.[12] Whether it is a matter of harboring ghosts and blind faith (*Spuk und Sparren*) or of being possessed by a certain *idée fixe*, the fanaticism is basically the same. It makes no difference whether one takes religious ideals as holy, or merely regards ethical ideals as holy out of a mistrust of religion. One can be just as fanatical in one's mistrust of religion and faith in ethics—just as possessed by an *idée fixe*—as in one's religious trust [46/49]. In both cases one remains fettered, which is the essence of "spirit." Religion means to "be tied," as indicated by its etymology in the word *re-ligare*. Religion and the holy occupy the deepest part of our inner being, where freedom of the spirit emerges. "Spirit" becomes freedom within us, but in that very fact our self becomes fettered [pp. 49–52/52–5].

Feuerbach undertook to internalize spirit as humanity and to transpose religion into ethics. According to Stirner, this means making "humanity" the lawgiver rather than God, and placing the self under the governance of ethical rules rather than God. This amounts only to a change of rulers, and does not affect the self's enslavement [p. 58/62]. In fact, those who have ruled from the standpoint of spirit have done so by means of such ideas as the state, emperor, church, God, morality, law, order, and so on, thereby establishing political, ethical, and religious hierarchies. Indeed, for Stirner, hierarchy itself *means* the rule of ideas and spirit [pp. 65–74/69–79]. Spirit constructs systems of rule and obedience by sacralizing law and duty and transforming them into matters of conscience. The only thing that can fundamentally destroy this kind of hierarchical system is the standpoint of the egoist which discloses "spirit" as a fabrication. It is not hard to see how Stirner's ideas came to provide an influential philosophical foundation for anarchism.

6. From Liberalism to Egoism

The curtain came down on ancient history when the world ceased to be seen as divine. The self as spirit became master of the world and conquered it as its own possession. There God appeared as the

Holy: "All things have been delivered to me by my Father" (Matthew 11:27) [p. 94/102]. Thus the self became master of the world but did not become master of its own ideal, since the spirit was sacralized as "Holy Spirit." A Christian "without the world" could not yet become a person "without God." If the battle during the ancient period had been waged against the world, the medieval Christian battle was fought against the self itself. The battleground shifted from outside the self to within it. The wisdom of the ancients was a wisdom of the world, a philosophy; the wisdom of the "moderns" is a knowledge of God, a theology. Just as philosophy got around behind the world, so theology tries to get around behind God. The pagans completely disposed of the world, but now the problem is to dispose of the spirit. For almost two thousand years, Stirner says, we have striven to conquer the "spirit that is holy," the "Holy Spirit." However many times its holiness has been plucked off and trampled underfoot, the gigantic enemy continues to rise up anew, changing its shape and names [94–95/103].

As a prime example of this phenomenon Stirner, like Nietzsche, cites modern liberalism. He usually refers to modern liberals as "the Free Ones" [*die Freien*] in contrast to the "ancients" and "moderns" mentioned earlier. What they have in common is that they plan the social actualization of the standpoint of humanity, and try to negate the various ideals of previous religion and metaphysics as lies. Stirner distinguishes three kinds of liberal thought: political, social, and humanitarian.

Political liberalism is the standpoint of the freedom of *citizens.* The citizen class eliminated the absolute monarch and the privileged class. No longer a class, they universalized themselves into a "nation" [98/107]. Under the constitutional state of liberalism, the people gain *political* freedom and equality as members of the state. They regard this system as an actualization of their pure humanity and see anything extraneous to it as merely private or egoistic, adventitious, and therefore inhuman. For Stirner, what has happened is that tyranny of the law has replaced tyranny of the monarch: "All states are tyrannies. . . . I am the arch-enemy of the state and am suspended in the alternative choice between the state and me." Political freedom is not my own freedom because my *own will* (*Eigenwille*) is negated. It is true that in the citizen state each citizen negates the will of the ruler, who had suppressed individual will up until then, and takes a stand on personal free will. But at the same time the citizen voluntarily suppresses individual will to seek an idealized actualization of the will and freedom of the self through the state [106–109/116–119]. This political freedom means that the *polis* becomes free and the concern (*Sache*) of the *polis* becomes my concern—but this means precisely that I am tied to the state from within myself.

In the citizen state, political equality was achieved but not equality of property. Thus in place of political liberalism, *social liberalism*—namely, communism—appears on the stage. In the same way that in political liberalism each person renounces the self's immediate right to rule and transfers it to the state, thereby indirectly regaining the right to rule, everyone now has to renounce the *property (Eigentum)* of the self and transfer everything to the society, so that the people as a whole may recover the property that belongs to them. According to communism, it is not that our dignity as human beings consists in an essential equality as children of the same state, as the bourgeoisie says; rather, our human dignity consists in our not existing for the sake of the state but for each other, so that each person exists essentially through others and for the sake of others. All of us become *workers* for the others. Only in this way are all people equal and repaid in equal compensation. This is how Stirner sees communism [117/129]. Just as his critique of democracy is directed at the state as the supreme ruler, so his critique of communism is directed at *society* as the supreme property owner.

That we become equal as members of the state and grant it the status of supreme ruler actually means that we become equal zeroes. In the same way, when society is made the supreme property owner we become equally "tramps" (*Lumpen*). In the name of the interests of "humanity," the individual is first deprived of the right to rule by the state, and then even the individual's property is taken away by society. What is more, in communism we are for the first time equal only as workers, not as human beings or individual selves [119/130].

> That the communist sees in you "humanity," or a brother, is only the "Sunday-side" of communism; from the perspective of the weekday [he] never accepts you simply as a man, but merely as a human worker or a working man. The liberal principle can be found in the first aspect, but in the second the unliberal is concealed. (122/133)

The satisfaction that communism offers the spirit it takes away from the body by compelling one to work. Communism makes workers feel this compulsion as social duty and makes them think that being a worker and abandoning egoism is the essential thing. Just as "citizens" devote themselves to the state, so do "workers" obey the rule of society and serve it. But society is a tool that should rather be serving our interests. Insofar as socialists seek a sacred society, they are as shackled to religious principle as the liberals: "Society, from which we receive everything, is the new master, a new ghost, a new 'supreme being,' which makes us bear the burden of 'devotion and duty' " (123/135). Such is Stirner's conclusion.

The third form of liberal thought is *humanitarian liberalism*, as represented by Bruno Bauer and his followers. For Stirner, this form most thoroughly pursues the standpoint of "humanity" as the principle of liberalism, and is therefore the consummate form of liberalism. With the individual as citizen in political liberalism and as worker in communism, human being is understood from the perspective of the fulfillment of desire. Even in the case of a worker who regards labor as a duty to society and works mutually for the sake of others, an egoistic interest, the fulfillment of the materialistic desire of the self, lurks beneath the surface. It is the same with the citizen who regards devotion to the state as a duty. The attack of humanitarian liberalism is directed precisely at this point. The humanitarian liberalist criticizes the socialist: "As the citizen does with the state, so the worker *makes use of* society for his own egoistic purposes. After all, don't you still have an egoistic purpose—your own welfare?" (124/136). The humanitarian demands that human action be completely free of egoistic concern. Only there is true *humanity* found and true liberalism established. "Only *humanity* is dinterested; the egoist is always concerned with interests" (125/137). Thus humanitarian liberalism tries to press the negation of private and egoistic concerns to the innermost heart. It is a critical liberalism that does not stop short with criticizing others, but goes on to criticize itself.

> While the politicians thought they had eliminated *each individual's own will*, self-will (*Eigenwille*), or willfulness, they did not realize that this *self-will* found a safe refuge through *property* (*Eigentum*).
>
> When socialists take away even property, they do not notice that ownership secures its continuation within ownness (*Eigenheit*).[13]

No matter how much property is taken away, opinion (*Meinung*) in the heart remains mine (*das Meinige*), and to that extent ownership remains.[14] Therefore, we must eliminate not only self-will or private ownership but also *private opinion*.

> Just as self-will is transferred to the state and private property to the society, private opinion also is transferred to some-

thing *universal*—namely, to 'man'—and thereby becomes general human opinion. . . . Just as self-will and property become *powerless*, so must ownness [or egoism] in general become powerless. (128–129/141)

Humane liberalism demands that we abandon welfare-ism, voluntarily criticize all egoistic and "inhuman" things and attain "consciousness of self" as "humanity." Further, with respect to labor, it demands that we understand it in a universal sense, as encompassing all of humankind in such a way that spirit reforms all material things. Labor for communism, in contrast, is merely "collective labor without spirit."

Stirner says that with this kind of humanitarian liberalism, "the circle of liberalism is completed" (127–128/140). Liberalism in general recognizes in humanity and human freedom the principle of the good, and in all egoistic and private things the principle of evil. This standpoint is taken to the extreme in humanitarian liberalism in its attempt to eliminate egoistic and private concerns from the human heart. The critique that includes this self-criticism may be the best of the critical social theories, but for Stirner, it is precisely because of this that the contradiction inherent in liberalism in general appears most clearly in humanitarian liberalism. For in spite of the elimination of self-will, private property, and private opinion, for the first time the unique individual who cannot be eliminated comes to light. "Ownness"—the selfness of the self—is revealed. Critical liberalism tries through its "criticism" to eliminate from the individual everything private and everything that would exclude all others. But the ownness of the individual is immune to this purging. Indeed, the person is an individual precisely because he or she excludes from the self everything that is not self. In this sense we might say that the most unique person is the most exclusive. This eliminates even the "criticism" that tries to exclude the very thing that excludes others (namely, one's private affairs). As Stirner says: "It is precisely the sharpest critic who is hit hardest by the curse of his own principle" (134/148).

The pursuit of freedom, once arrived at humanitarian liberalism, goes to the extreme of making humanity everything and the individual person nothing. We are deprived of everything and our *Lumpen*-condition is made complete. A radical reversal now becomes possible:

If we want to attain the nature of *ownness* we must first decline even to the most shabby, the most destitute condition—

because we must remove and discard everything that is foreign to the self. (139/153)

The utmost *Lumpen*-condition is that of a naked man, stripped even of his tatters (*Lumpen*). Therefore, when one removes and discards even one's "humanity," true nakedness—the condition (*Entblössung*) in which one is stripped of all that is alien to the self—appears.[15] The tramp escapes his condition by tearing off his rags. Such is the standpoint of Stirner's egoist. The egoist is the archenemy of all liberalism as well as of Christianity: to human beings he is inhuman; to God, a devil. Though repudiated by all forms of liberalism, the egoist goes through them one after another, eliminating from the self all ghosts and rafters of *idées fixes*. Finally, with *the turn from the absolute destitution of the self*, the egoist for the first time can truly say "I am I."

7. Ownness and Property—All and Nothing

The self as egoist was present all along as the object of the most basic negations of the God of religion or the ethical person. The self was repudiated as "sinner" and "inhuman wretch." But nothing could erase the self's being the self—this bodily self, with its inherent I-ness, its ownness (*Eigenheit*). Beaten down by God, the state, society, and humanity, it nevertheless slowly began to raise its head again. It could do this because fanatics brandishing Bibles or reason or the ideals of humanity "are unconsciously and unintentionally pursuing I-ness" (358/403). Firstly, it was revealed that "God's" true body was "man," which represented one step toward the self-discovery of the ego. The search for the self remained unconscious as the ego lost itself in fanaticism over reason or the idea of humanity. In humanism's denunciations of the egoism of the ego as inhuman and selfish, the more vigorous its efforts, the clearer it became that the ego was not something to be set aside. It was only from the depths of nihility to which the ego had been banished that it could, in a gesture of negating all negation, rise to reclaim itself.

In the first half of his work, Stirner develops this ironical dialectic; in the second half, he deals with the positive standpoint of egoism, showing how the ego claims its uniqueness and ownness, embraces within itself all other things and ideas, assimilates and appropriates them to itself as owner (*Eigner*), and thus reaches the awareness of the unique one (*Einzige*) who has appropriated everything within his own I-ness and has made the world the content of his own life.

Stirner understands the *ownness* of the self as the consummation of "freedom." "Freedom" is originally a Christian doctrine having to do with freeing the self from this world and renouncing all the things that weigh the self down. This teaching eventually led to the abandoning of Christianity and its morality in favor of a standpoint of the ego "without sin, without God, without morality, and so on" [157/173]. This "freedom," however, is merely negative and passive. The ego still had to take control of the things from which it has been released and make them its own; it must become their owner (*Eigner*). This is the standpoint of ownness (*Eigenheit*).

> What a difference there is between freedom and I-ness. . . .
> I am free from things that I have got rid of but I am the *owner*
> (*Eigner*) of things which I have within my *power* (*Macht*) and
> which I control (*mächtig*).[16]

Eigenheit is the standpoint of the *Eigene*; in this standpoint freedom itself becomes my property for the first time. Once the ego controls everything and owns it as its property, it truly possesses freedom. In other words, when it overcomes even the "form of freedom," freedom becomes its property. Stirner says that "the *individual* (*der Eigene*) is one who is born free; but the liberal is one who seeks freedom, as a dreamer and fanatic" (164/181). And again: "Ownness has *created* a new *freedom*, insofar as it is the creator of everything" (163/179). This ownness is I myself, and "my entire essence and existence." Stirner calls the essential being of this kind of ownness "unnameable," "conceptually unthinkable," and "unsayable" (148/164, 183/201). The ego thinks and is the controller and owner of all thinking, but it cannot itself be grasped through thought. In this sense it is even said to be "a state of *thoughtlessness* (*Gedankenlosigkeit*)" (148/164). In contrast to Feuerbach, who considers "humanity" as the essence of human being and the egoist who violates humanity as "an inhuman wretch," Stirner claims that there is no way to separate the notion of a human being from its existence (178/195). If anything, Stirner's existentialism dissolves the essence of human being into its unnameable Existence.

From everything that has been said, Stirner's deep affinity with Nietzsche should be clear. His standpoint of the "power" to assimilate everything in the world into the self is reminiscent of Nietzsche's idea of will to power. In Nietzsche it is folly as the culmination of knowledge, and in Stirner it is "thoughtlessness" that makes all thinking my property. The ego in Nietzsche is also ultimately nameless, or at most symbolically called Dionysus. In

Stirner's case we also find the element of "creative nothing," a creative nihilism. This latter point merits closer examination.

In a remarkable passage, Stirner confronts the "faith in truth," just as Nietzsche does, and emphasizes "faith in the self itself" as the standpoint of nihilism.

> As long as you believe in truth, you do not believe in yourself and are a —*servant*, a *religious* person. You alone are the truth, or rather, you are more than the truth, which is nothing at all before you. Of course even you inquire after the truth, of course even you "criticize," but you do not inquire after a "higher truth," which would be higher than you, and you do not criticize according to the criterion of such a truth. You engage thoughts and ideas, as you do the appearances of things, only for the purpose of making them . . . your own, you want only to master them and become their *owner*, you want to orient yourself and be at home in them, and you find them true or see them in their true light . . . when they are right for *you*, when they are your *property*. If they should later become heavier again, if they should disengage themselves again from your power, that is then precisely their untruth—namely, your powerlessness. Your powerlessness [*Ohnmacht*] is their power [*Macht*], your humility their greatness. Their truth, therefore, is you, or is the nothing[17] that you are for them, and in which they dissolve, their truth is their *nullity* (*Nichtigkeit*). (353–54/ 397–98)

Stirner's assertion here that the truth of thought is one's nihility, and the power of truth one's powerlessness, comes to the same thing as Nietzsche's assertion that "the will to truth" is the impotence of the will, that "truth" is an illusion with which the will deceives itself, and that behind a philosophy that seeks truth runs the current of nihilism. Further, Stirner's idea that when thought becomes one's property it becomes true for the first time parallels Nietzsche's saying that illusion is reaffirmed as useful for life from the standpoint of will to power. In Stirner's terms, nihility as powerlessness turns into creative nothing. This "self-overcoming of nihilism" and "faith in the self" constitute his egoism. He goes on: "All truth in itself is dead, a corpse; it is alive only in the way that my lungs are alive—namely, in proportion to my own vitality" (354/ 398). Any truth established above the ego kills the ego; and as long as it kills the ego, it is itself dead, and merely appears as a "ghost" or an *idée fixe*.

> Every truth of an era is the *idée fixe* of that era . . . one
> wanted after all to be 'inspired' (*begeistert*) by such an 'idea.'
> One wanted to be ruled by a thought—and possessed by it!
> (355/399–400)

It is thus possible to discern a clear thread of nihilism running
through the fifty years that separate Nietzsche from Stirner, each of
whom recognized his nihilism as the expression of a great revolution in the history of the European world. As Stirner says: "We are
standing at the borderline." Both were truly *thinkers of crisis* in the
most radical sense.

We saw how Feuerbach criticized Hegel's absolute spirit as an
"abstraction" and offered a posture of truly real existence in place of
it. According to Stirner, this "existence" of Feuerbach's is no less of
an abstraction.

> But *I am* not merely abstraction, *I am* all in all, and conse-
> quently myself am abstraction or nothing. I am all and noth-
> ing; [I am no mere thought, but I am at the same time full of
> thoughts, a world of thoughts.] Hegel condemns I-ness, what
> is mine (*Meinige*)—that is, "opinion" (*Meinung*). However, "ab-
> solute thinking" . . . has forgotten that it is *my* thinking, and
> that it is *I* who think (*ich denke*), that it itself exists through
> *me* . . . it is merely my *opinion*. (339/381–82)

The same can be said of Feuerbach's emphasis on sensation [*Sinnlichkeit*] in opposition to Hegel:

> But in order to think and also to feel, and so for the abstract
> as much as for the sensible, I need above all things *me* myself,
> and indeed me as this absolutely definite me, this *unique indi-
> vidual*. (340/382)

The ego, which is all and nothing, which can call even absolute thinking *my* thinking, is the ego that expels from the self all
things and ideas, reveals the nihility of the self, and at the same
time nullifies their "truth." It is the same ego that then makes them
its own flesh and blood, owning them and "enjoying" (*geniessen*)
the use of them. The ego inserts nihility behind the "essence" of all
things, behind the "truth" of all ideas, and behind "God" who is at
their ground. Within this nihility these sacred things which used to
reign over the ego are stripped of their outer coverings to reveal
their true nature. The ego takes their place and makes all things

and ideas its own, becoming one with the world in the standpoint of nihility. In other words, Stirner's egoism is based on something similar to what Kierkegaard called "the abyss of pantheistic nihility" or to what Nietzsche called "pantheistic faith" in eternal recurrence. This is why Stirner called this "ownness" the creator of all things, born free. From this standpoint he can claim that, for the individual, thinking itself becomes a mere "pastime" (*Kurzweile)* or "the equation of the thoughtless and the thoughtful I" (150/166). I have already touched on the way in which the abyss of nihility reveals the true face of life as boredom (*Langweile*) in connection with Schopenhauer and Kierkegaard. The creative nihilism which overcame this kind of nihilism appears as "play" in Nietzsche and as "pastime" in Stirner.

8. The State and the Individual

Stirner differs from Nietzsche in being primarily a social thinker. The emphasis of his major work is on a critique of various social ideas and on the advocacy of a society "without government or law." Here I forgo taking on this manifold argument in order to focus on its foundational philosophical ideas of human existence itself. Social ideas are, of course, important, but for me what makes them important would be something along the lines of Dostoevsky's understanding of socialism as atheism. It is nevertheless necessary to touch upon Stirner's social ideas to some extent in order to give a comprehensive exposition of his nihilism.

Stirner exhibits the same irony toward the *state* as he does toward "truth."

It is no longer so much a matter of the state but rather of me. With this all problems regarding sovereign power, the constitution, and so on completely sink down into their true abyss and nihility [*ihr wahres Nichts*]. I—this nihility—shall drive out my various *creations* from myself. (235/259)

Stirner means that the nihility of the ego is inserted behind the authority of the state, and that in this light the fundamental hollowness of the state's authority is revealed. At that point the human relationships that are to replace the state emerge from the "creative nothing" of the individual. The same is true of political parties and *factions*: "Precisely those who shout most loudly that the state needs an *opposition* oppose most eagerly every kind of disharmony within the party. This is proof that they, too, only want—a state" [235/260]. Neither the state nor the opposition party is able to bring about the collapse of the other; rather, both collapse when they collide with the ego. This is because the citizens and party members are more than the fact of their belonging to the nation or party. Ownness, which contains at its roots something unpolitical, cannot be extinguished, no matter how much state and party strengthen their binding power. Once the ego becomes aware of its inherently unpolitical nature and becomes egoistic, state and party collapse. It is the same way with the contradiction between the state and *humankind*.

> The nationalists are right: one cannot negate one's nationality. And the humanists are right: one should not remain in the narrowness of nationalism. The contradiction is resolved only within *unique individuality* [*Einzigkeit*]: nationality is a property [*Eigenschaft*] of mine. But I am not reducible to my properties, just as humanity is a property of mine though it is only through my individuality that "man" receives Existence. (244–45/270–71)

Proudhon and the communists say that the world belongs to everybody. They make the ghost called "everybody" holy, and set it up as a terrifying ruler over the individual. But this *everybody* is actually each individual self for itself, and it is to this self that the world belongs. Stirner says: "Just as the isolated individual (*Einzelne*) is the whole of nature, he is also the whole species"; or "I am the owner of humankind, I am humankind . . ."[18] This kind of egoistic standpoint has been recovered as creative nothing from "the abyss of nihility" after having been negated by all other standpoints and having itself broken through and negated all other standpoints. Now everything lives as my own, "like my lungs."

From Protagoras to Feuerbach it has been said that "man is the measure of all things" (352/395); but it is rather the ego that is the measure of all things. This egoistic posture allows us for the first time to "judge from the self," while other standpoints oblige us to "judge from the other." Furthermore, the dissolution of all things into the "vitality" of the self as the property and "enjoyment" of the self sets up a new mode of intercourse with the world for the individual. "My intercourse with the world . . . is enjoyment of the world (*Weltgenuss*) and belongs to my self-enjoyment" (319/358). The standpoint of enjoyment of the world as enjoyment of the self in Stirner is reminiscent of the *samādhi* of "self-enjoyment," an important state in Buddhist practice. The difference is that in Buddhism the *samādhi* of self-enjoyment cannot be separated from the *samādhi* of "the enjoyment of the other."[19] This is, I would say, the locus of the fundamental distinction between nothingness [*mu*] in Buddhism and Stirner's nothingness. Nothingness in Buddhism is "self-benefit-benefitting-others,"[20] which is a higher and more comprehensive standpoint. Stirner is thinking about an "association" (*Verein*) of individuals sharing the standpoint of the unique individual, and he imagines the citizen-state of the political liberals and the society of the communists dissolving into this kind of association.

The association of unique individuals differs from the state or society in not being master over individuals and making them its servants: "You can assert yourself as an individual only within the association" (312/349). It is a relationship of individuals without mutual domination or enslavement, mutually enjoying and making use of each other. How can we conceive of egoists uniting together? Obviously we cannot take egoism in its ordinary colloquial sense. Stirner says that the happiness or welfare of others is a genuine concern of his. In order to increase the *other*'s pleasure one is willing "to sacrifice gladly innumerable pleasures" [290/323]. I am prepared to risk "my life, my welfare, my freedom"—because to enjoy the other's happiness is my happiness. "However, I do not sacrifice *me, me myself* to the other, but remain an egoist and—enjoy him" (290/324). There should be no misunderstanding the import of these words: Stirner means that one can sacrifice one's life for the other but not one's self. To sacrifice oneself for the other is to grant the other a "ghostly" power and enslave oneself to it, the self thereby failing to be itself. This is entirely different from ordinary egoism. But can we then conceive of an association of egoists in this sense? Stirner answers this question as follows:

> If they were able to be perfect egoists, they would exclude each other *entirely* and hold together that much more strongly. Their disgrace is not that they exclude each other, but that they only *half* do this. (181/198)

In another passage Stirner pursues this issue further in suggesting, perhaps with Hegel in mind, that to try to dissolve the opposition of two things into a third thing is to understand their significance in too weak a sense. Opposition should rather be intensified. That we are not entirely *separated* from others, that we seek a certain "community" or "bond" with others and recognize a certain ideal within the community, is, according to Stirner, our weakness. From this he draws the following remarkable conclusion, which is

probably one of the clearest answers to the question of how the relationship between one human being and another should be set up
from a standpoint of affirmative nihilism.

> The final and most decisive opposition, that of the unique
> individual against the unique individual, is basically beyond
> what is called opposition, yet without sinking back into
> "unity" and unanimity. As a unique individual you no longer
> have anything in common with the others and therefore also
> nothing divisive or hostile; you do not seek your right with
> respect to him before a *third* party nor stand with him either
> on a "ground of law" [*Rechtsboden*] or on any other communal
> ground. Opposition disappears in perfect separation (*Ge-
> schiedenheit*) or uniqueness . . . here equally consists precisely
> in inequality and is itself nothing other than inequality . . .
> (208–09/229)

The passage clearly exemplifies the close connection between
Stirner's social ideas and their philosophical foundation. Individuals are individuals because they stand on "nothing." And for the
same reason "decisive opposition" and its "complete disappearance" arise simultaneously between individuals entirely separated.
This is the "association" of the egoists: because they are entirely separated, they are a firm unity. "Only with the ultimate separation
does separation itself come to an end and turn into unity" (231/254).
Moreover, there are no bonds to a third party and therefore no community existing independently of the individuals, so that relationships in terms of rights and legalities disappear. This idea of
Stirner's might seem no more than a trick of logic. But insofar as
only the "ego" has the attribute of being absolutely unique, it cannot be a specimen of something universal. For this very reason, it is
possible to conceive of "nothing" at the ground of the ego. If such
egos are, moreover, to associate with each other, there is a sense in
which Stirner's understanding of their mode of association grasps
something that even Kant and Hegel were unable to appreciate. It
would seem that he has hit on something totally familiar and yet
deeply hidden concerning our association with others.

Stirner's view appears at first glance to be close to Fichte's
standpoint of pure ego, but he repeatedly emphasizes the difference
between them. According to Stirner, Fichte's ego is the generaliza-
tion of an "I" that ultimately exists outside of me. "I am not, however, one I alongside other I's, but the one and only I . . ." (361/
406). Here, a general person in any sense, even an "I" in general,

must be negated. In spite of the abyss of nihility this leaves us with, or rather because of it, I am a bodily ego. Stirner repeatedly emphasizes the fact of embodiment: "there does not exist anything higher above the *bodily human being*" (356/400). This bodily human being, as I said earlier, is understood as something that has gone through Hegel's absolute spirit and passed beyond it. Similarly, Stirner emphasizes the self's *finitude:*

> When Fichte says, "The I is everything," this appears to be in perfect harmony with my own expositions. But it is not that the I is everything, but rather the I *destroys* everything, and only the I that dissolves itself, that never "is," the —*finite* I, is really I. Fichte speaks of the "absolute" I, whereas I speak of me, the perishing I. (182/199)

The background to the finitude of which Stirner speaks lies in the dissolution of the self and the destruction of everything. Feuerbach's "humanity" is not a "perishing and individual self," insofar as the individual is said to raise itself beyond the limit of individuality, and enter into the unity of love between one human being and another. Even here the individual is seen as unable to go beyond the various laws governing this unity, "the positive and essential determinations of the [human] species." Stirner counters:

> But the species is nothing, and if the individual raises himself beyond the boundaries of his individuality, this is rather precisely he himself as an individual; he is only insofar as he raises himself, he is only insofar as he does not remain what he is; otherwise he would be finished, dead.[21]

Stirner is saying that "the human species" is merely a conceptualized ideal. This negation of the "species" is the standpoint of nihility without any kind of general person, and in this standpoint "going beyond the boundaries of individuality" has an entirely different significance. It is not that one enters into communal relationships with others at the standpoint of the species as Feuerbach would have it, but rather that the life of the individual overflows, so to speak, the limits of the self. With this, the individual becomes for the first time the living individual. This is the meaning of the terms "dissolving the self," "perishing," or not remaining in the mode of fixed "being." On this standpoint, everything that the self touches fuses with the self. This is also, I think, what Stirner means by saying that it is not that the ego *is* everything but that it *destroys* everything. Thus what he means by the *perishing* and *finite* ego is a continual overflowing of the self, where everything is melted into the self's vitality, and "enjoyed." This flow of nihility, Stirner's *"creative nothing,"* represents a *fundamental unity of creative nihilism and finitude*.

Nietzsche, it will be recalled, also emphasized the bodily aspect of human being: "the awakened one, the one who knows, says: I am entirely body and nothing besides; and soul is only a word for something about the body. The body is a great reason . . ." (*Za* I,4). Moreover, he holds fixed "being" to be an illusion, based on the "perishing" of becoming, and affirms a Dionysian life that makes this perishing one's own "ceaseless creation." He, too, subscribed to the fundamental unity of creative nihilism and finitude, which he expressed by speaking of *"this* life—this *eternal* life." Here Stirner, breaking with Feuerbach, and Nietzsche, breaking with Schopenhauer, meet at a deep level, even though their points of departure, their concerns, their perspectives, and also the character, scale, and profundity of their philosophies are somewhat different.

Marx's satirical critique entitled "Saint Max" does not show a very profound understanding of Stirner's enterprise. It rather gives the impression that the materialistic view of history does not have the wherewithal for understanding Stirner. For example, where Stirner writes: "I am not nothing in the sense of a void but creative nothing, the nothing out of which I myself as creator create everything," Marx turns the words around by saying: "The Holy Father [Stirner] could have expressed this as follows: I am everything in the void of nonsense *but* the null creator, the all from which I myself as creator create nothing."[22] Stirner could well have responded to this as follows: "You have said something wise by mistake in saying that Stirner creates nothing from everything. My standpoint is exactly as you say, but its meaning is entirely different from what you think."

For both Stirner and Nietzsche their nihilism *was* their existence, and, as a self-interpretation of their existence, their philosophy. Philosophy in turn was a stimulus toward Existence, but not yet scientific in the original sense.[23] From the viewpoint of the human way of being, both criticized the scientific standpoint. This accounts for their negative attitude toward traditional metaphysics. But can a standpoint of the fundamental unity of creative nihilism and finitude lead to a scientific philosophy? Can the inquiry into nihilism as the self-interpretation of existence yield a thinking in the form of scientific philosophy? Or to put it the other way round, can the thinking of scientific philosophy constitute a standpoint of Existence as the self-interpretation of existence? It is not until Heidegger that we have an existential *philosophy* in this sense, where the standpoint of scientific philosophy for the first time appears on the ground of nihilism. His attempt to reconnect with the tradition of metaphysics by "destructing" it[24] opened up a new and expansive phase in the development of nihilism.

Chapter Seven

Nihilism in Russia

1. Russian Nihilism

Nihilism in Russia is said to have been deeply rooted in the radical temperament of the Russian people before it took the form of thought. One feels throughout the history of Russia a kind of religious nihilism lying dormant in the souls of the people. Berdyaev saw it as a marriage of the apocalyptic spirit with nihilism. We see it clearly in the burning of Moscow in the face of the military advance of the Napoleonic army. Napoleon himself called it a savage act of insanity; in fact, it shows a will to pursue a radical absolutism of "all or nothing" that goes beyond reason, even at the price of self-inflicted injury. Napoleon, who was above all a man of cool intelligence and calculation, was unable to understand the worldview behind the great fire of Moscow. Nonetheless, the Napoleonic War ushered in an entirely new era for Russia. A definite "Europeanism" took shape in the Russian army, whose campaigns in Europe had provided a firsthand experience of the countries to the West, and particularly among the aristocratic officers of the Imperial Guard. Previously, indeed since the time of Peter the Great, the Europeanization of Russia had always occurred from above, through Czarism itself, and had consisted in attempts of the "enlightened" rulers to force Europe on to the people. Now Europe suddenly began to thrust forceful demands on Czarism by assuming the form of "young Russia," demands that threatened the end of tyranny. This was the final and most serious consequence of the reforms of Peter the Great.

The Europe which "young Russia" adopted had been baptized by liberalism through the French Revolution. It was the Europe in which Romantic passion for the nation had burst forth in the wars of liberation against Napoleon. Although liberalism and nationalism were in many ways complete opposites, they agreed on the need to free the people from absolutist rule. Young men who returned from the front as liberals or Romantics formed secret associations and tried to reform the situation of Russia in the name of Europe. Alexander I, who had begun his rule as a reformer and a liberalist, joined the post-war reaction led by Metternich to turn back the youthful tide of reform. As a result, the movement took an even more radical and revolutionary character. Nihilism and anarchism, which for a while would completely dominate the intelligentsia and become a major factor in the history of nineteenth-century Russia, emerged in the final years of the reign of Alexander I. The "Europeanists" believed that only the imitation of Europe could save the future of Russia. It was only later that "Slavophilism"—the attribution of all Russia's misfortunes to the imitation of Europe—developed out of Russian Romanticism.

In 1825, immediately after the death of Alexander I and the succession to the throne of Nicholas I, a rebellion by the "December Party" broke out. Nicholas suppressed it by force, with the result that radicalism went underground and strengthened its nihilistic features still further. Representative of the socialism of this generation were Herzen and Bakunin. Herzen addressed the peoples of Western Europe with these words:

> Thinking Russians are the most independent men in the world. Who can withstand them? The point of departure of modern Russian history lies in their radical negation of all ideas and legends of the people. . . . The abnormal respect which you people pay to the heritage of your ancestors is something we have nothing to do with. You are always wavering from right to left and hesitantly going round and round. We do not own anything, nor are we bound by anything, because we have just now begun our new lives. . . . We have nothing to lose, nor do we have anything to bind us. Therefore we can be independent. . . . We have no legends, and it is better not to have any. Because of this, we can be superior to other people who have legends.

The true embodiment of Russian nihilism was Bakunin, for whom it was not primarily a matter of theory but of lived passion. Significantly, both of these representatives came from the aristocratic class. As is well known, in 1848 Dostoevsky was implicated in a movement of the "Petrashevsky Party" and was exiled to Siberia. In the 1860s a new generation influenced by Belinsky and others emerged, opening up an unbridgeable gap between the two generations.

There are unmistakable traces of this conflict in Turgenev's novel *Fathers and Sons*. Both its protagonist, Bazarov, and Chernyshevsky, who represented the new era in actual life, clearly have the character of nihilists. Both wanted to do away with everything idealistic, both despised the element of aestheticism or love, and professed atheism. The former represented "the victory of the common people over the aristocracy," while the latter was the son of a priest from the lower classes, synthesizing the abnormal conjunction of highly intellectual and "scientific" theory with an almost religious fanaticism.

Russian atheism always had something of an inverted religious character to it. It was from the demand for truth connected with a passion for social reform, and not out of merely theoretical doubt, that Belinsky progressed to atheism. In this regard both he and Chernyshevsky were disciples of Feuerbach. In Dobrolyubov, who came after them, the motivation for atheism was to be seen as a form of Christian pity. In all these figures the demand for scientific "truth," unadulterated by subjective ideals, is directly connected with a quasi-religious fanaticism, a fanaticism that would end in terrorism, as with the Nechayev party in 1870.

As western theory, which had been fermenting continually within the Russian intellectual class since the time of the Empress Catherine, took radical form in Western Europe itself, it also transformed the fanatical religious nihilism within the Russian soul. As a result, the radical criticism of all things religious, and of the ethical and political norms based on them, turned into a quasi-religious and fanatical nihilism in Russia. The psychology of this nihilism is thus a kind of religious psychology. As Herzen suggests, the links to tradition were severed by the invasion of Western European ideas, and within the vacuum this left, Western radicalism was pushed to the extreme of atheistic nihilism, which then became a fanatical fever of the soul. This Russian brand of nihilism despised humanistic mildness and so-called "paper reforms." It sought to solve everything all at once by destroying everything. The Russians are said to have by nature a predilection for arguing "Why shouldn't it be that way?" no matter how drastic a conclusion they may end up in, pursuing the logic of an idea to the point where it loses all contact with actual reality. This tendency is surely at work in Russian nihilism.

For Dostoevsky, life as an exile in Siberia prompted a turn away from communism. As he writes in his *Writer's Diary* in 1873, he ended up by "returning to the roots of the nation, acknowledging the Russian soul, and awakening to the national spirit." This did not happen in a day, but rather took place gradually over a long period of time. What constituted the source of this change was Dostoevsky's memory of his childhood as one who was "born to a pious Russian family"; it was a reconnection with the spiritual tradition of Russia that was still alive within the soul of the people. However, at the same time Dostoevsky did not fail to see that as time goes by such a reconnection would become more and more difficult.

> Other people may not have memories such as mine. Recently I ask myself, really putting my thinking into it, what kind of memories youths nowadays are generally bringing up from their childhood. . . . Even I experience great difficulty in finally having conviction in the falseness and incorrectness of the idea that I had previously believed to be the light of the future and the truth, and so one can easily guess how difficult it can be for others who have become totally disconnected from the people, and successively and genetically from the generations of fathers and grandfathers, and have created a further and deeper chasm.

Dostoevsky's relationship to nihilism is based on this kind of historical situation. Nihilism grew up within him together with his soul. As he writes in his diary:

> Probably I could never become a character like Nechayev, but I cannot guarantee that I could never have become a member of the Nechayev party. . . . In my youth I could easily have become a member.

And in a letter he writes: "I am a child of the times, a child of mistrust and doubt, and this will never be cured as long as I live." However, unlike the liberals of the 1840s and the nihilists of the 1860s, Dostoevsky did not espouse these ideas simply as a theory of national politics and society, nor even as a philosophical theory. He took hold of the ideas existentially and as a matter of the soul. He measured nihilism against the standard of the eternal meaning of life. For him it was a question of "to be or not to be," to be decided on the basis of whether such meaning existed or not. Dostoevsky saw that at stake in such a nihilism was the life and death of the soul. A person in the kind of socialist society this nihilism envisioned would be someone "with the smell of the dead." Such a one would be an absolute slave, one who does not even know that he is enslaved, and thus dead in the soul. The leaders would be false prophets giving the people the contentment of cattle by demeaning their freedom and equality to the level of the herd.

To make nihilism into an atheism was, for Dostoevsky, to kill one's own soul and the soul of others; it was rebellion against God and a kind of Luciferean *hubris*. The fanaticism of atheism was fueled by such a spirit of rebellion, by an unbounded desire for power that could only be described as jealousy of God. Atheists would not, of course, own up to such a description. But, as Dostoevsky points out through the words of Prince Myshkin in *The Idiot*, atheists "speak *outside the issue*" even though they deny God, and "fail to touch upon the issue at all." In other words Dostoevsky made nihilism a problem at its metaphysical ground, probing to a depth that the nihilists of the period were unable to achieve. His was "reflection upon the self" in Nietzsche's sense, a lived reflection on history from within a history that does not reflect upon itself, and a psychological experiment within the self on the logical concluslon toward which history was rushing. Dostoevsky cultivated the nihilist within himself, and in the course of fighting relentlessly against the child of mistrust he became its indomitable ally. In the letter mentioned earlier he writers further:

> How much yearning for faith has tortured me (and still even now tortures me). In the face of the proof of the denial of faith it becomes that much stronger. . . . There is nothing as profound, as compassionate, as rational and yet humane, as perfect and more to be loved than Christ. . . . If someone were to prove that Christ is outside the truth and if the truth truly closes him out, I would rather remain with Christ than with the truth.

From this standpoint, Dostoevsky recognized a ground deep beneath the nihilism of the world, and which the nihilists were unable to see. He recognized what it was in the Russian soul that was turning the incoming Western European radicalism into such fanaticism: a nihilism of religious proportions engrained in the very idea of atheism.

To express this, Dostoevsky created a collection of nihilistic figures of a stature not possessed by nihilists "out there." In contrast to the actual revolutionary nihilists who aimed at the destruction of the established order, these figures come to grips with the abyss of nihility within their own souls. They feel within themselves the terrifying abyss beyond all established norms, internal or external. In contrast to the corrupted nihilists out there, who tried to numb their nihilistic sensitivity and forget themselves through self-indulgence, Dostoevsky's figures voluntarily leap into nihilism and try to be themselves within its boundaries. The nihility expressed in "If there is no God, everything is permitted,"[1] or *"après moi le déluge,"* provides a principle whose sincerity they try to live out to the end. They search for and experiment with ways for the self to justify itself after God has disappeared. They are all made to be figures of a certain nobility, pride, and sincerity. One thinks, for example, of that giant among nihilists the princely Stavrogin in *The Possessed,* or the sage-like Ivan Karamazov, or of Raskolnikov in *Crime and Punishment,* Nastasya Philipovna in *The Idiot,* and Kirillov in *The Possessed.*

The series of experiments by which these figures try to justify themselves in the absence of faith are, of course, Dostoevsky's own self-experimentations, with every one of which the seriousness increased. Raskolnikov was still able to enter on the path of renewed life through Sonya who is an emissary from God. But in the case of Nastasya, swaying indecisively between Myshkin (who could also be seen as an emissary from God) and Ragozhin (to borrow a phrase from Middleton Murray, a man "between pure compassion and pure passion"), she runs finally into the arms of Ragozhin screaming "Help!" immediately before her wedding to Myshkin. She seeks redemption through a death-leap into passion, after which Myshkin returns to the state of an idiot. Again, Stavrogin, who has already attained a strength beyond pity, recognizes his last hope for life in the passion of his love for Lisa, but discards even this hope in order to maintain the integrity of his conscience through to the end. He commits suicide without the consolation of the pity of the "angelic" Daryia. In Stavrogin, nihilism overcomes pity, the primary Christian virtue as represented by characters such as Sonya, Myshkin, and Daryia. In *The Possessed,* we meet Stepan Trofimovich who, out of his conviction of an eternal harmony behind life and the world, screams: "If there is a God, I am immortal!" Ivan Karamazov is unable to approve of the world created by God, even while approving of God, eternal harmony, and the atonement of sins. He refuses to enter into the harmony which he believes exists, because to do so would be a betrayal of the excessively absurd suffering that exists in reality: "If one is an honest person one should return the admission ticket to God as soon as possible." This progressive deepening of nihilism exemplifies Dostoevsky's indefatigable honesty and his unwavering yearning for faith.

2. Bazarov's Nihilism—"Fathers and Sons"

The word *nihilism* comes up in the conversation of Bazarov, the protagonist of Turgenev's 1862 novel, *Fathers and Sons.*[2] As Turgenev himself was later to write of the book, he first got the idea on visiting a seaside resort in August of 1860. The character of Bazarov was modeled on the personality of a young country physician of quite unusual character who had died shortly before. It was the inchoate constellation of a number of traits in this man to which Turgenev would give the name *nihilism*. He writes;

> The impression given by this person was extraordinarily intense. At first I was unable to define him to myself clearly, but I sharpened my ears and eyes as much as possible and carefully observed everything around me. I set my mind on relying only on my own perceptions. What surprised me was that I have never encountered [in our entire literature] a figure who would have given me any hint concerning the circumstance that met my eyes from every aspect.

Turgenev takes pride in the fact that as early as 1860 he had intuited signs of nihilism which nobody noticed during that period. Turgenev's "idea for a character in whom various elements are harmonized" eventually became Bazarov, the type of an individual who was beginning to appear at the time. For Turgenev, then, nihilism was imagined as the center of a personality around which a chaotic unity of traits revolved.

Firstly, one of the most evident of Bazarov's traits is a concern with *science*—in particular, the German science of that time. This was not the science that had been subordinated to philosophy, but a science that had broken free of theology just as philosophy had at the beginning of the modern period. German science thus represented the pure and independent scientific spirit. Now the liberation of science from philosophy was a major event that affected the foundation of the spiritual history of Europe. Out of it there emerged a destructive criticism of previous religion and philosophy as well as of the social ethics, culture, and everything else that had been based on them. The scientific spirit which had become *purely* scientific began to assume a kind of philosophical authority, in effect rejecting all philosophy that was not scientific, and was on the verge of hardening into an anti-religious posture resembling nothing more than a religious fanaticism fueled by its bias toward mechanistic materialism and atheism.

Bazarov dismisses all philosophy as romanticism; his favorite catch-phrase is "reality." The trend to realism, prevalent at the time, combined in his case with a nihilistic and negative spirit. Feuerbach, the philosopher of realism, claimed that philosophy must be reconnected to the natural sciences, and vice-versa, that the unity of the two is a matter of internal necessity, and that they mutually demand one another. As we saw in chapter two, he went on to advocate a new anthropology and a society of humane love based on realism. But no sooner was the scientific spirit freed from Hegelian metaphysics by Feuerbach, than it went beyond realism to work a radical change in the idea of nature. In Feuerbach, certain features such as the love of nature or seeing nature as a living thing remained; after him, nature was transformed into a completely material and mechanical world, dragging the human nature of which Feuerbach spoke along with it. For the new scientific spirit, talk of "human nature" was mere sentimentalism. The shift from the traditional *ideal* natural science to an *analytical* natural science went beyond the idea of nature to influence the ideas of humanity and morality as well. (The reason Goethe, in his later years, engaged with his color theory in so persistent and passionate a confrontation with Newton may have been that he sensed the deep crisis coming in the shift to the scientific standpoint.)

Furthermore, Bazarov's scientific realism has nihilism at its ground. Not only did he shock the people around him by dissecting a frog in his own guest-room, but he repudiated everything "unscientific" such as poetry, art, love, love of family, the traditional social system, and so forth. His nihilism is also tied in with the *socialist* spirit, which counts as the second ingredient in his nihilism. Bazarov negates everything: religion, the morality derived from religion, and the social system based on such a morality. At the same time, he is depicted as disconnected from the common people, in spite of his attempts to make contact with the local peasants and the pride he took in being a native of a farming village. Dostoevsky says in his *Writer's Diary*, criticizing the intelligentsia of the period who advocated a love of "the people," that the people they loved were not real but only an idealized fiction, closer perhaps to the rioters in Paris in 1793. It may be too much to say this of Bazarov, but one can certainly sense the intellectual's idealization in his profession of love for the peasants.

Third, we see Bazarov's egoistic character. He despises the aristocracy and at the same time is unable to throw in his lot with the people. The only course left open to him is to assert *himself* in every situation. There is a strong element of egoism in his nihilism; and yet as a nihilist who negates everything, he still entertains possibilities and ideals. In his egoism the scientific spirit of realism is conjoined with the socialistic spirit of idealism in a chaotic blend, over which there hovers, as a fourth moment, the dark mood of fanaticism so peculiar to the Russians. These apparently contradictory features that appear in Bazarov have as the sole focus of their connection the core of nihilism in his person.

Bazarov's young friend Arcady describes a nihilist as "a person who does not take any principle for granted, however much that principle may be revered" (5). Bazarov himself says: "In these days the most useful thing we can do is to repudiate—and so we repudiate" (10). Although he speaks these words in a most unperturbed tone of voice, one can sense in Turgenev's description of Bazarov a powerful negative spirit and dark, wild force, together with a profound sense of lethargy, boredom, and restlessness somewhere deep down. Even though Bazarov becomes totally absorbed in dissecting his frog, he at the same time gives the impression of harboring the suspicion that he is after all a person who is unable to achieve anything. This has to do with something deeper than a concern over the results of his scientific research, as if the chaos within him may not be the kind of chaos that is able to create, in Nietzsche's words, "a dancing star."[3] By the same token, Bazarov's socialism is incapable of leading to action. Asked whether he and his fellows had really decided not to do anything serious about the social ills besetting the country:

> "[We] decided not to do anything serious," Bazarov repeated grimly. . . .
> "But to confine yourselves to abuse?"
> "To confine ourselves to abuse."
> "And that is called nihilism?"
> "And that is called nihilism," Bazarov repeated again, this time with marked insolence. (10)

In his socialism, too, the nihilistic strength to reject everything goes hand in hand with the sense of an indescribable void.

The egoist Bazarov is acutely aware of the distance between himself and his followers. While he and his friend Arcady are staying at the house of the beautiful widow, Madame Odintsov, the following exchange takes place between them. Arcady asks: "What the devil made that idiotic Sitnikov turn up here?" Bazarov replies: "I can see you're still a fool, my boy. The Sitnikovs of this world are essential to us. I need such louts. It is not for the gods to have to bake bricks!" On hearing this, his friend suddenly began to understand the fathomless depths of Bazarov's conceit. "So you and I are gods, are we? Or rather you are a god while I'm one of the louts, I suppose?" "Yes," repeated Bazarov gloomily, "you're still a fool" (19). Bazarov's followers, including his close friend Arcady, will bake bricks for the new palace where the new gods are to reside, while Bazarov himself is the new god, or one of the gods, who is to direct its construction and become master of the palace. Soon afterwards, as soon as his love for Madame Odintsov founders, he says self-contemptuously the following:

> "Everyone hangs by a thread, at any moment the abyss may open beneath our feet, and yet we go out of our way to invent all sorts of trouble for ourselves to spoil our lives. . . . we've both of us behaved like fools." (19)

Bazarov feels like a fool, and the distance between the gods and those who bake bricks disappears. The love in which his folly showed up was the only point at which his inner nature could have broken through his nihilism.

From a certain point of view, Bazarov's nihilism is still naive in a number of respects, a kind of nihilism "in itself." There are still things in which he can believe fanatically, such as science, socialism, or the ego, and this fanaticism conditions his nihilism. His nihilism has not yet developed to the point of negating the fanatical beliefs it harbors; it has not become a nihilism "for itself." A nihilism that supports science, socialism, or ego merely helps him to believe in these things, but has not yet become a true, self-conscious nihilism. It has yet to negate the nihilism "in itself" that grounds these things and his own belief in them. The feeling of hollowness that rings through Bazarov remains no more than a vague premonition echoing from the depths of the unconscious. In contrast, a nihilism that has become self-conscious knows itself as despair and as the spirit of radical revolt, doubt, and freedom. It is a nihilism prepared to purge the nihilism latent in science, socialism, and the ego; and then to go beyond these things deep into the interior of the soul, there desperately to confront God, ideals, morality, love of one's neighbor, and the rest. This kind of nihilism does not come about merely by opposing religion, philosophy, morality, the social system, and other things external to the self. This standpoint of the "in itself" merely negates *other* things, never touching the interior of the *self* that does the negating. The self continues to possess something that can be believed in.

A nihilism no longer able to believe in itself, an introverted nihilism that has become an X for itself, ceases to provide a source for feelings of nihility. When this happens, nihilism itself gradually turns into a kind of fanaticism. Science, socialism, and the ego lose all credibility, offering no more than temporary playthings for the desperate fanaticism of a nihilism that has become self-conscious. This is the standpoint of a nihilism that has passed from the stage of science to that of philosophy, from the realm of "understanding" [*Verstand*] to the realm of "reason" [*Vernunft*]. In Hegelian terms, when reason becomes self-conscious as "reason" that has united the inner and the outer, it becomes a new task or problem for itself, becomes an X for itself, with a dynamic of self-inquiry or self-disclosure.

In this nihilism, then, the confrontation with religion or metaphysics (with God or the world of ideals) has become an internal matter for the self. One does not simply place matters outside the self, there to negate them, but penetrates to the same depth as religion or metaphysics to confront them on their own ground. In so doing, nihilism begins to long for these things within itself, to demand new gods and new ideals. Only at this stage does the nihilism born of the modern scientific spirit come to term and begin to show signs of a change. For an author, this means fighting with both the believer and the nihilist within him, standing his ground to confront the God within himself. This applies more to Dostoevsky than to Turgenev.

Turgenev has Bazarov die from an infection contracted from a small wound inflicted by mistake while performing surgery on one of the peasants. The very scalpel of science he wielded on others proves his own undoing. But the irony in this hardly amounts to anything like a full confrontation with science and its nihilism. *Fathers and Sons* concludes by speaking of "the vast repose of 'indifferent' nature" and of "everlasting reconciliation and life which has no end"; and yet it is not clear how "indifferent nature" can provide reconciliation. In Turgenev's case, the issue of nihilism has not become a thorn in the side of the author's own soul.

Fathers and Sons apparently caused an extraordinary furor when it was first published, and Turgenev immediately lost credibility with the "progressives" with whom he had been close. The Slavophiles, on the other hand, welcomed him. Turgenev is supposed to have said: "At this point only two people have understood my intentions: Dostoevsky and Botkin." At the time, Dostoevsky had not dug down to the level of truly nihilistic nihilism. His "thoroughgoing"realism was clear from the beginning already in *Poor Folk*, not a vulgar realism, but an extraordinary world of souls and spiritual forces deep within, which vulgar realism might well call pathological or exaggerated. This realism was what he called a "higher-level" or "spiritual realism." In *Poor Folk* he tries to portray the suffering and evil of real life without describing the dream of an ideal world. His characters are helpless people who are forced down by the power of society and, lacking the strength to resist, fall into despair. Dostoevsky seems to have been venting his own rebellious spirit through the characters he created, while keeping a firm hold on his own idealism.

The subsequent experience of having been sentenced to death and then sent into exile must have worked a radical change on Dostoevsky's soul. Meantime, the trend of thought in Russia was changing rapidly. A character from the older generation who appears in Turgenev's *Fathers and Sons* says: "It used to be Hegelians, and now there are nihilists" (5). In between came Feuerbach and Proudhon, of whom Belinsky, who supported Dostoevsky before his exile, was an enthusiastic admirer. During his exile Dostoevsky planned a "great novel" which would later crystallize as *Crime and Punishment*. This leads us to suspect that already at that time he was concerned with nihilism and its overcoming. In a letter to his older brother Dostoevsky asked to be sent Kant's *Critique of Pure Reason* and also some texts by Hegel (the *History of Philosophy* in particular), remarking that his entire future depended on it. Behind this one may surmise a confrontation with nihilism going on.

In *Notes from the House of the Dead*, the issue of nihilism does not yet appear. In *The Insulted and the Injured* we find an egoist who becomes in a sense even more nihilistic than Bazarov. When criticized for his misconduct, Prince Varkovsky replies: "Don't talk nonsense. Let's speak more frankly." "Well, frankly what is there that isn't nonsense?" "The individual, the ego," is his response. "All things exist for me; the entire world was made for me. . . . I can continue to live on happily on this earth. This is the best faith. . . . Since long ago I have thrown off all shackles and all duties." Varkovsky's nihilism is not yet a nihilism that has become reflective in the sense we spoke of earlier. The egoist still behaves comfortably, following where his selfish desire leads him. He seems to have the same spirit of reliance on nihility (because there is no God or morality everything is permitted) that the Christians in the Middle Ages had toward God when they despoiled the heathens. It is a kind of faith in nihilism, not yet a form of reason. Nihilism had not yet become an X, a task for itself, a fate that would question itself.

Therefore, in this egoist there is neither a struggle against nor a yearning for God or morality; there is neither a desperate persistence in nihilism nor a drive toward a new God. There is only a cynicism of understanding that tries to enjoy life by fulfilling carnal desires to the utmost, without knowing self-splitting or torment. There is a recognition of positive evil, but no desperately affirmative will to evil. Like the characters of his novels, Dostoevsky himself is not yet possessed by nihilism. Nihilism has not entered into him. Although he pursues a reality filled with suffering and evil, and is in this sense a defiant realist, he still retains the standpoint of an idealist who opposes critically from the outside. To brand evil as evil implies a standpoint of goodness. It is not a situation in which one can speak of "beyond good and evil," and consequently the distinction between good and evil becomes ambiguous.

In the case of Dostoevsky, the embracing of nihilism as true nihilism, surpassing Turgenev and indeed himself up until then, and taking the characters in his novels beyond Bazarov or Varkovsky to make them truly nihilistic nihilists, begins from *Notes from Underground*.[4] From that point on, Dostoevsky moves in a variety of directions: toward a nihilism that stands in abyssal nihility after the negation of religion, metaphysics, and morality by science and socialism (a kind of cosmological nihilism), a demonic nihilism emerging from the excavation of the ground of socialism, and a nihilism of the egoist struggling with God. At the same time, a series of issues—among them God, Christ, the great earth, the homeland of Russia and its peasants—emerge as opposing elements to confront nihilism in its manifold of forms. In the nihilism of Ivan in *The Brothers Karamazov*, these various elements are for the first time radically integrated and profoundly pursued.

3. Nihilism as Contemplation—"Notes from Underground"

The protagonist of *Notes from Underground* takes his stand on "contemplative inertia," having reached the conclusion that the best thing to do is to sink into a state of inactivity. Contemplative inertia is the ultimate negation of the real world which has become scientific and rational, a world governed by the iron laws of nature. Science resolves everything, including all that is human, into the mechanical world. As the protagonist of the *Notes* says:

> Although I do not feel like approving natural laws and the fact that two times two makes four, what about those laws of nature and arithmetic? Of course I don't try to hit my head against a wall because I don't have the necessary strength, yet I can't feel like approving of the wall simply because it is standing in front of me and I am unable to push it down.[5]

The real world confronts us with the "stone wall" of absolute "mathematical" law, and tries to dissolve me into the world and thereby to negate me. For my part, I cannot negate the world in any way, nor can I escape from it; but neither can I approve of it. The ultimate solution, wherein I could negate the world which negates me and forces me into the corner, is contemplative inactivity. Traditional metaphysics opened up an ideal, transcendent world and the standpoint of contemplation of that world in order to escape from the real world. This is now no more than a dream, the world of ideals having since disappeared. What exists is simply a real world obediently following mathematical formulas. It is not the kind of world one can breathe in. The world imagined to lie beyond it has vanished, but, in Nietzsche's words: "one cannot endure this world, which one yet does not want to negate."[6]

Out of this situation emerges the standpoint of underground contemplation. One dives to the only place left, the underground of this world, unable to dream of going beyond the real world, but at the same time unable to tolerate life on the surface. It is neither a contemplation of the heavens nor is it a submission to being pushed about on the earth: it is rather a contemplation of the world carried out from underground. Vis-à-vis the world that negates the self, contemplation maintains the nihility of the self that has been negated, contemplating the world from this nihility and thereby trying to negate the world in turn. This is the first step of a nihilism that has become self-conscious, of truly nihilistic nihilism. It signals an outright revolt against the *scientific spirit* and its rational worldview. It negates a Bazarov-like nihilism based on faith in science and goes beyond it. We might call it a Russian-style self-deepening of "nihility."

Contemplative inertia is thus inactive but not tranquil meditation. For the standpoint that represents the backbone of Western intellectual history from the *theōria* of Greek philosophy to Hegel's speculative thinking via the *contemplatio* of the Middle Ages, tranquil meditation was able to break through the "wall" of reality in virtue of the tranquility of its intellect. Behind the "wall" lay the ideals which, as it were, made the wall transparent by illuminating it from behind. In this way the intellect was able to ascend to the ideal "higher world" on the other side of the wall. But now the wall has nothing to illuminate it from behind; it has become an "impossible matter" about which nothing can be done—nothing but knock one's head against it. And if this is not to one's liking, one can only close one's eyes—and "contemplate." *This* contemplation is a reaction against being cornered and a despair. The "inertia" of inactive calm, meantime, harbors the tendency to madness through having lost all calm and any place to settle down in. It is the state in which, even though "natural laws continue to despise [one] throughout [one's] life" as a matter of mathematical law, "[since] there is no other party to get angry at, one numbs one's senses as desired into inertia."

The underground man compares himself with the *normal man* who is vigorous, healthy, and able to act immediately upon his desires. The "straightforward activity" of the normal man is the exact opposite of the one who lives in contemplative inertia. When he runs up against a wall, he bows down with honesty in the face of the impossibility and thus is never pushed into rebellion or despair. The wall never becomes a reason to change direction or turn inward to reflect; neither contemplation nor inertia results. From the perspective of the underground man, the normal man restricts his movements to the surface of the world, not sensing the confinement of the wall within the world and the self. He does not possess the "intensified consciousness" that is refracted from the wall toward the inside, the thoroughly examined self-consciousness that is "consciousness" in the true sense. This is what keeps him "dull-witted" but healthy. For the underground man, "not only an excess of consciousness but any consciousness is a disease (VI). From his perspective, even though the normal man is obtuse, or rather precisely because of his obtuseness, he is normal. In this sense the underground man cannot help considering himself as having *deviated* from "the human." This is the antinomy in his being: he cannot help considering himself intelligent, and yet his is an intelligence beyond intelligence in the normal sense, of an entirely different nature from everyday or "scientific" intelligence.

Hegel says that the world of philosophy is an "inverted" world and that there is something esoteric in the essence of philosophy. In this sense, the intelligence of the underground man is "philosophical" in his contemplation from the underground of the world. What makes him different from Hegel and other philosophers is that in spite of his intelligence—or rather, again, because he is intelligent—he cannot help feeling that he is a "mouse." His intelligence is, after all, more like *theōria, contemplatio, Spekulation* than the objective intelligence that immerses itself in the world. The intelligence of philosophers transcends the world internally by penetrating the world and looks at it from a higher plane usually associated with God. But the underground man can neither immerse himself in the world nor break through it to another dimension. His intelligence results from his being refracted back into himself from the stone wall; it is not objective but rather subjective, existential intelligence, like Kierkegaard's "self relating itself to itself," or Zarathustra's solitary person for whom one times one is two.[7]

Normally the standpoint of "contemplation" is said to be "non-existential," but in the case of the underground man contemplation becomes Existence. This is the new direction that Dostoevsky opened up in *Notes from Underground*. In this Existence the underground intellectual, the intellectual of the "inverted world," feels ashamed before normal "men"—like a mouse. In this concurrence of rising above and sinking below other "men," he cannot help considering himself in a dual sense deviant from "man." He is "the kind of man who was born from a laboratory retort."

> I regard a direct person as the real normal man, as his tender mother nature wished to see him when she graciously brought him into being on the earth. I envy such a man until I am green in the face. He is stupid. I am not disputing that, but perhaps the normal man should be stupid, how do you know? Perhaps it is very beautiful, in fact. And I am all the more convinced of that suspicion, if one can call it so, by the fact that if for instance you take the antithesis of the normal man, that is, the hyperconscious man, who has come, of course, not out of the lap of nature but out of a retort (this is almost mysticism, gentlemen, but I suspect this, too), this retort-made man is sometimes so nonplused in the presence of his antithesis that with all his hyperconsciousness he genuinely thinks of himself as a mouse and not a man. It may be a hyperconscious mouse, yet it is a mouse, while the other is a man, and therefore, etc. And the worst is, he himself, his very own self, looks upon himself as a mouse. No one asks him to do so. And that is an important point. (III)

In this hyperconscious mouse we see a prefiguration of Raskolnikov who vacillates between being an overman and a worm; it is
also the prototype from which Stavrogin and Ivan Karamazov will
emerge. This idea of the hyperconscious individual, self-conscious
in the extreme, who necessarily goes beyond the normal individual
and cannot help stepping outside humanity, provides Dostoevsky
with the raw material for the complex web of concerns that will
occupy him in his later work. In a letter from 1869, written when he
was planning *The Eternal Husband*, he remarks that the foundations
of that work are the same as those of *Notes from Underground*, and
calls them *"my eternal ground."* This had no doubt been forming in
him from before *Notes from Underground*, but in that work it first
comes to the light of consciousness.

In his first novel, *Poor Folk*, the figure of Mikhail Devushkin is
a man who lives in a corner of the world much like the underground man. Although his ambition is to become a writer, he gives
up the idea, lamenting that his writing lacks style, and makes his
living transcribing the writing of others. He says:

> If everyone had to become a great writer there would be no
> copyists. . . . Even if I resemble a mouse, I don't care—as long
> as this mouse that I am is necessary for you and I am of any
> use in the world, and if I can receive compensation without
> losing that status. But what kind of mouse is it?

The love that impels him to save his beloved takes him beyond the
limit of his means and discloses a latent fanaticism for self-sacrifice
that violates the normal human way of being, a passion "to bear burdens" a it is called in *The Possessed*. Overwhelmed by the forces of the
world, and with his love relationship gradually turning to despair,
a certain "pleasure in self-humiliation" *(Notes from Underground)*
creeps into this love. This is not yet hyperconsciousness or rebellion,
however. One senses in both Dostoevsky and his protagonists a profound Dickensian humanism in which tears of sorrow come out in
the form of humor. Devushkin writes to the lover who is slipping
away from him: "I shall die—I shall certainly die." Had he been able
to find within himself the strength of rebellion to return to life from
this ultimate despair, a standpoint like that of the underground
man as a "retort-made man" might well have come to the fore.

The hyperconscious mouse, who deviates from "man" in the dual
sense mentioned above, symbolizes the breakdown of modern *humanism*. The normal individual functions well within humanism

owing to his "dullness of wit," and this humanism gains strength on being projected on to the ideal of a new society. But Dostoevsky's "atmospheric" genius quickly sensed the breakdown of "the human" and the advent of nihilism within the new humanism. His underground man represents a deliberate experiment with this breakdown in order to show it for what it was and to allow Dostoevsky himself to arrive at his own eternal ground. As Berdyaev says, Dostoevsky's works embrace the crisis or internal denunciation of humanism, so that humanism comes to an end with Dostoevsky and with Nietzsche. The "underground psychology within the mind" that emerged in Dostoevsky's writing opened up a realm distinct from the psychology of normal people. A change took place in psychology equivalent to the introduction of irrational or imaginary numbers into the system of rational numbers. A psychology containing incommensurabilities and antinomies that cannot be resolved by normal rationality became for him a "higher reality," where attraction and repulsion, love and hate, appear as one.

The underground man sees the sudden *spasm* of sensual desire that overtakes him as a revenge. Seizures of "the sublime and beautiful" that flash like fireworks against the dark sky of dissipation only serve to heighten the contrast. The sublimest and the basest meet at their outer limits; the ideals of Sodom and Madonna fuse as one. But above all, it is the mode of being of the very "self" made hyperconscious in the retort-made man that becomes an antinomy. The self desires to be itself and to be free: it is a path to the sublime and, eventually, to God; but at the same time it is a path away from God and toward baseness. It is a life that defies rational explanation: the closer it comes to God the more it diverges from God, and the more it diverges the closer it comes. Freedom has to be exercised to the limit, but this means freedom for evil as well as freedom for good. Because this freedom is so elemental it is compared to a kind of seizure or "spasm." The standpoint of "contemplative inertia" is the standpoint of a self which faces "the wall" in such a life.

The reason why the normal man who lives above ground, the man of "straightforward action," looks dull and superficial from the viewpoint of the contemplative inertia of the underground man is that he has some foundation on which to make a comfortable abode, and also that he "mistakes immediate and secondary causes for primary ones." In contrast, the underground man asks: "Where are the primary causes on which I am to build? Where are my bases?" and continues to inquire into ever more fundamental things. It is from this posture that the standpoint of inertia emerges, impeding action of any kind. If he is slapped, he is incapable of striking back at once. Even a slap seems to be a necessary event occurring according to natural laws, as inevitable as "Two times two is four." The one who is slapped does not know how to act in the face of the stone wall of the world of two times two is four. Instead, he is thrown back from the stone wall to within himself, where he inquires without ceasing into the ground for action (in this case the action of hitting back). Try as he may to do something, all he can do is sink down into the bottomless swamp within him, inert and powerless. As a result of this "self-discipline of cogitation," the orientation of consciousness to inertia begins to look on "the essence of such things as consciousness or thought." "But then," he asks, "if *this is already that natural law*, then what will be the end of it all? It is after all *the same thing*." In other words, contemplative inertia is the state in which one naturally ends up by strengthening consciousness; the underground man conceives of it as the result of the normal basic laws of heightened consciousness. It is no more than "the lawful result [born of] consciousness." Natural laws control even the *inner workings* of consciousness and make it inert. The underground man confronts the wall within self-consciousness as well, and rebels there too. His "nihility" does not even allow the fanaticism of a Bazarov. In this, too, we see a deepening of the self-awareness of nihility.

Take an example. In order to convince oneself that an act of revenge is pure and just, and in order to carry it out calmly, it is necessary to believe that justice is its primary cause. But what justice is cannot be established with the certainty of "two times two is four." When anger wells up, it ends up dissolving "like a chemical solution" as consciousness becomes inert. Conversely, if one yields to blind feelings, one realizes the self-deception immediately and ends up despising oneself. In the end, there is no avoiding a life of contemplative inertia as a conscious spectator who stands by with arms folded. Such a life is filled with profound *ennui*, and everything becomes the same. This is a bottomless nihility and yet not a state of stagnation in which consciousness is simply dulled; quite the contrary, a violent storm rages on in the abyss of this nihility. Feelings and aspirations, having lost a path to discharge themselves to the outside, turn inward and diffuse themselves within the confines of the self. Unable to believe in the reasons for which normal individuals rationalize their purity and righteousness, and having strayed from the middle path of humanity, consciousness intensifies to the point that one is incapable of the self-deception of the normal individual and at the same time comes to feel what amounts to an abnormal secret pleasure in base things. In these straits, life tortures one with humiliating pain until finally even despair and humiliation themselves become pleasurable.

> The more conscious I was of goodness, and of all that "sublime and beautiful," the more deeply I sank into my mire and the more capable I became of sinking into it completely. But the main thing was that all this did not seem to occur in me accidentally, but as though it had to be so. As though it were my most normal condition, and not in the least disease or depravity, so that finally I even lost the desire to struggle against this depravity. (II)

In short, the underground world is one in which the "retort-made man" who has strayed from normal humanity rediscovers himself as normal. In contrast, so-called normal men who live above ground, men of "straightforward activity," have some kind of solid ground within them. They accept some kind of goal in life, or feel some value or ideal, as an absolutely consistent basis of support of which they are readily convinced. This is why such persons are able to act—and also why they are "dull and superficial." They have mistaken the most accessible secondary causes for the primary ones. Their intelligence lacks the wherewithal to question and seek the more fundamental causes, so that even if they are thrown against the wall of "two times two is four" they do not fall into despair. It does not occur to those of weak consciousness and self-consciousness to put up a resistance; they simply surrender. They rather accept the wall as part of the foundation of their lives, and they feel a sense of relief in the face of it (much as a conquered people feels a sense of relief in the face of a declaration from the conqueror).

> For such people a wall is not an evasion, as for example for us people who think and consequently do nothing; it is not an excuse for turning aside . . . The wall has for them something tranquilizing, morally soothing, final—maybe even something mysterious . . . (III)

The stone wall, two times two is four, the laws of nature, the conclusions of natural science, mathematics—these are for normal men a kind of "tranquilizer"; they contain a kind of "magic word" which brings about peace.

> As soon as they prove to you, for instance, that you are descended from a monkey, then it is no use scowling, accept it as

a fact. When they prove to you that in reality one drop of your own fat must be dearer to you than a hundred thousand of your fellow creatures, and that this conclusion is the final solution of all so-called virtues and duties and all such raving and prejudices, then you might as well accept it, you can't do anything about it, because the two times two is a law of mathematics. Just try refuting it. (III)

As the passage just quoted makes plain, what Dostoevsky is confronting is the positivistic worldview that is the logical conclusion of mathematics and natural science, as well as the positivistic or *socialist ethic* connected with it. The motto of such an ethic is: scientific, logical, rational. The Bazarovs who proclaim this motto advocate both intellectual enlightenment and economic reform. For once the intellect is enlightened and "common sense or science completely re-educate man's original nature and guide it by means of formulas," that is, once we come to act "according to reason or science," we will understand where our real normal interests lie and what our "rational and advantageous" desires are. The control of reason makes all desires rational, preventing them from taking a blind and irrational direction that would go against the person's normal interests, the supposition being that no one wittingly acts contrary to his or her own interests. At the same time a new set of economic relations takes shape, whose guiding idea is that for any problem a ready-made solution can be found. A "crystal palace" is erected for the soul within and society without, a single transparent system from which all traces of the irrational, the unscientific, or the primitive and uncivilized have been eliminated.

As is well known, Dostoevsky vehemently opposed an intellectual-rational view of ethics and social theories of positivism and socialism, and carried on an ever deeper confrontation with them throughout his life. His opposition sprang naturally from the fact that he saw them leading to the death of the soul, the mechanization of the human spirit, the internal transformation of people into a herd, and the deprivation of true freedom. Freedom was for him the ground of the human being's humanness. It was the wellspring of personality and individuality, from which all morality and ethics drew their life. More radically, freedom opens the way to the religious problem of the end of human existence, to the problem of the immortality of the soul, to God. Freedom, immortality of the soul, and the existence of God have been life-and-death problems for human existence since ancient times, as we see, for example, in Kant's practical philosophy. As Schelling had done in his *Treatise on the Essence of Human Freedom*, Dostoevsky understood freedom as freedom for evil as well as for good. Unless one understands the self within this kind of freedom, one cannot understand the *religious* significance of things like evil, sin, punishment, love, and redemption. The problems of faith in immortality, faith in the God-man, rebellion against God, and the path to the man-God can disclose the ultimate ground of human existence. Such was Dostoevsky's consistent conviction.

Moreover, just as freedom leads to the religious world, so does religion determine freedom and its morality. If faith in immortality or in God does not hold up, this necessarily results in a demonic morality (or a morality of "the possessed") in which "one is forgiven, whatever one may do." If there is no immortal base within the soul, then the soul must be subject entirely to the laws of nature. And if this is so, to avoid self-deception one has no choice but to commit suicide. (Dostoevsky elaborates the logic of this conclusion in an essay entitled "Suicide and Immortality.")

Whether or not it is possible to believe in immortality or God determines whether human freedom orients itself to God or to the Devil, whether or not a life can be lived without self-deception, indeed whether life is worth living or desiring at all. These are religious, philosophical, and ethical problems that arise from the inner depths of one's soul or spiritual nature. Put the other way around, it is only through these kinds of problems that the inner depths of the soul or spirit, the ultimate reaches of human existence, can be disclosed. Positivism and socialism block the way for such questions to arise; there is something in them that conceals the inner depths of the soul. They deliberately deny the existence of the realm within, thus overlooking the place where true freedom (as, for example, in the "pure duration" of Bergson) comes about, and deal only with the surface layers of the psyche which can be considered mechanistically and reduced to laws of the "two times two is four" variety. They deny the immortality of the soul and the existence of God entirely, to take a stand on atheism. Dostoevsky detested this way of thinking precisely because it leads to a forgetfulness and loss of the true meaning of human existence, because it renders one oblivious to the abyss of the soul in virtue of which the soul can truly *be* soul and human beings can *not be* herd animals. In this regard, all socialistic theories come to the same thing, insofar as they are based on scientific rationalism.

Dostoevsky did not live to experience the rise of Marxism in Russia. What he did know was the socialism of Fourier, the positivism of Comte and others, and the social movements and nihilism in Russia which were influenced by them. The first part of *Notes from Underground*, the philosophical section of the book, is said to be an argument against Chernyshevsky's recently published novel *What Is to Be Done?* The "crystal palace" alluded to earlier is meant to be a caricature of the *phalanx*, the cooperative commune advocated by Fourier-ism on which Chernyshevsky's novel is based. The Russian socialist movement did, of course, go beyond Fourier and, after Dostoevsky's death, it progressed to Marxism. Among the various socialist theories, including those of Fourier and Marx, there are differences in substance and quality, including a progression from the "imaginative" to the "scientific." But what Dostoevsky opposed was the tendency common to all of them *at their foundations*, the set of principles governing their approach to the understanding of the human being. This is the reason for the intensity, persistence, and seriousness of his opposition to them. It was his genius to fix on the core issue immediately and pursue it through to its ultimate conclusions.

After Dostoevsky, Nietzsche was to conduct a further and more severe critique of modern democracy and socialism for their tendency to transform people into the docile herd of "the average man." He singled out Rousseau in particular as the source of such ideas. Dostoevsky, too, ridicules Rousseau in his *Notes from Underground* for having exalted *l'homme de la nature et de la vérité*, noting that because the "man of nature and truth" is generally stupid from birth anyway, he feels justified in taking revenge against him. He also finds Rousseau's constant self-defamation in the *Confessions*, a deliberate lie spread in the service of his vanity. In other words, the man of nature and truth becomes an unnatural man of lies when it is a matter of himself. The underground man says that, unlike Rousseau, he is writing his notes "because I want to try the experiment whether one can be perfectly frank, even with oneself, and not take fright at the whole truth" (XI). He has gone beyond "the normal man who came out of the lap of nature"; this is the difference between the "truth" sought by Rousseau and by Dostoevsky, between one who sees "nature" and health as normal, and the retort-made man who considers it normal to say that "all consciousness is a disease." Herein lies the schism between the standpoints of Rousseau as the source of socialism and Dostoevsky who opposed him as a mouse in the underground basement. In the words of the underground man: "There may even be within the mouse a greater accumulation of spite and base and nasty desires than in *l'homme de la nature et de la vérité*." For Rousseau the abyss of the soul in which God and the Devil do battle was covered over. In *Notes from Underground*, however, this kind of theological—or perhaps we should say, theosophical and apocalyptic—background has not yet ap-

peared. The ethical view of socialism and criticism of it are presented simply in terms of the principles concerned, albeit with
extraordinary thoroughness.

As mentioned earlier, when consciousness runs up against the
world governed by the mathematical laws of nature, the world as
"rational," it is pushed into "contemplation" and gradually grows
inert. This inertia means that *control by the laws of nature* is in fact the
product of consciousness and thus profoundly affects its workings.
The only resistance against it is despair and the pleasure in despair.
In this latter, one senses within, or puts into practice, "nasty and
base desires" of which the normal individual is not aware. In aban-
donment to these desires, one is then tormented by a guilty conscience, which in turn generates pleasure in humiliation. The
reason Dostoevsky emphasizes despair and humiliation, and the
pleasure in them, is that they constitute the last remaining declaration of an absolute refusal to acquiesce to or compromise with the
control of the *self* by "two times two is four."

A normal individual who does not possess the hyperconsciousness to think in contemplative inertia and enter into the underground world readily bows down before the "wall" of the
rational world, and with a sigh of relief sets back to work. Accordingly, he comes to think that his sound sense of justice and rational
interests can only stand up on the footing of such a rational world.
Along with the scientific-rational worldview go scientific-rational
ethics and social relations. This is where the "crystal palace" is
erected, in which the *laws of free will* themselves are discovered, and
all desires and behavior are regulated with precision and down to
the last detail, carefully catalogued, and submitted to the unchang-
ing calculus of a logarithmic table. One who has been guided by
science and reason becomes "as if he had never had free will or
caprice," no more than "the keyboard on a piano." By virtue of the
laws of nature one becomes spontaneously good and pure in a
frighteningly facile manner, fully apprised of what one's normal interests are. With that, the ideal of the "philanthropists" is realized.
This is, to be sure, ironical caricature, or distortion of the reality.
But caricature is in many ways truer than the real thing, the distortion more true to life than the actual state of affairs. The tacit pre-
sumption behind all socialist theories is the negation of freedom
which turns people into piano keys being struck by the fingers of
necessary laws.

For Dostoevsky, to be deprived of freedom is to die, and he
resists the tendency unreservedly. In the crystal palace one feels like
"sticking out one's tongue [or] thumbing one's nose on the sly," so

badly does one want to live as one wills. Even in the case of what goes against one's normal interests and contradicts the dictates of sound reasoning, in the case of "extremely uneconomical and silly nonsense," or of opposing the new patters of economic relations or intellectual enlightenment, the important thing when all is said and done is to be able to *desire* these things. "One must do it decisively, no matter what," says the underground man. Even in deliberately desiring the greatest disadvantage, my own *will* is more advantageous than all rational interests combined, and it is this *best interest* that the advocates of the welfare of humanity have left out of their calculations.

> You gentlemen may say to me that an enlightened and developed man, such, in short, as the future man will be, cannot knowingly desire anything disadvantageous to himself, that this can be proved mathematically. . . . But there is one case, one only, when man may purposely, consciously, desire what is injurious to himself what is stupid, very stupid—simply in order to *have the right* to desire for himself even what is very stupid and not to be bound by an obligation to desire only what is rational. . . . He would deliberately desire the most fatal rubbish, the most uneconomical absurdity, simply to introduce into all this positive rationality his fatal fantastic element. It is just his fantastic dreams, his vulgar folly, that he will desire to retain, simply in order to prove to himself that men are still men and not piano keys . . . (VIII)

Provisionally accepting the worldview according to which free will is governed by laws, and hence also the ethical view that we must voluntarily allow free will to be governed by laws, Dostoevsky considers the consequences of this position, until finally he is driven to the paradoxical leap of negating the whole thing all at once. This is the final form of his resistance against scientific rationality and his confrontation with the principles of socialism. Given a single "base" desire, "all systems and theories will be exploded into smithereens."

Behind all these ideas lies a *metaphysics*. Dostoevsky says that will normally contradicts reason, and that this is not only salutary but often admirable. A human being, he says, may even deliberately go insane to avoid giving the victory to reason. Will is opposed to reason because "two times two is four is no longer life but is merely

the beginning of death." In other words, *will to life* stands opposed
to reason. He writes of the "philosophy" of "the man who has lived
underground for forty years" as follows:

> Reason is an excellent thing, there is no disputing that, but
> reason is only reason and can only satisfy man's rational fac-
> ulty, while will is a manifestation of all life, that is, of all
> human life including reason as well as all impulses. And al-
> though our life, in this manifestation of it, is often worthless,
> yet it is life nevertheless and not simply extracting square
> roots. After all, here I, for instance, quite naturally want to
> live, in order to satisfy all my faculties for life, and not simply
> my rational faculty, that is, not simply one twentieth of all my
> faculties for life. What does reason know? Reason only knows
> what it has succeeded in learning (some things it will perhaps
> never learn; while this is nevertheless no comfort, why not say
> so frankly?) and human nature acts as a whole, with every-
> thing that is in it, consciously or unconsciously, and even if it
> goes wrong, it lives. (VIII)

Those who "come out of the lap of nature," we noted earlier,
are called normal people, and rationality is the measure of their
normalcy. Their nature is regulated by reason, such that they "easily justify" their actions, and on the basis of such justification are
able to act at peace with themselves. To this extent they are *covert
idealists;* should reason become self-conscious in them, and their activity self-conscious as the activity of freedom *with an ideal,* one
could then speak of their idealism as overt.

Once reason is in full control of one's nature, and necessity
governs the soul systematically inside and extends to society and
the world outside, then the socialist is able to appear on the scene
as the *realist* bearing blueprints for the crystal palace. The socialist
claims that there is freedom in the very act of erecting one's own
crystal palace and in submitting to the system of necessity. The
transition from the idealism of the normal individual to the realism
of the socialist is a natural shift, at least insofar as the control of
reason or the enlightenment of the intellect is concerned. As a matter of course, the normal individual "surrenders honestly."

But when things get this far, the *nihilist* living in the underground steps forth to reject absolute surrender. For one whose
home is the underground world within the heart, who knows what
it is to live at the bottom of intensified consciousness and contemplate with *the eye of nihility,* the only path is to assert the right to the

freedom to will, even to will the absolutely absurd. Only in this way can one take sides with life "as a whole," which lies beyond the pale of reason. The nihilist, a radical intellectual for whom the normal rationalist is obtuse, reveals himself as a champion of the "naturalness" of human activity as a whole against the radical rationalism of the socialists. The intensity of intellect born of contemplation with the eye of nihility comes together with the totally irrational "will to life" at a point beyond all rationalism. This will to life may be called a feral health. It may be in their grasp of "life" at this fundamental level that the remarkable closeness between Dostoevsky and Nietzsche has its roots.

Reason, a quality of the progressive "person of the future," is basically a thing of the past when compared the will within the phenomenon of life as a whole. It only "knows what has been learned up to now." This kind of paradox, which applies to all forms of rationalism, highlights the difference between rationalism and nihilism. The nihilist takes a stand on a metaphysical nihility that is beyond all rationalism and yet manifests itself as a will to capricious freedom or will to life on this side of all rationalism. In the words of the underground man: "For men like us, capriciousness may be truly more advantageous than anything else on earth." Stavrogin in *The Possessed* conducts an experiment by suddenly grabbing a man by the nose at a social gathering and pulling him around the room. Such capriciousness bears witness to an inner abyss of nihility that can erupt into one's daily life at any moment. The underground man, too, exposed to humiliation when the woman he loves visits him for the first time, thinks to himself: "Shouldn't I run away, dressed as I am in my dressing gown, wherever my feet may take me, and let come what may?" Caught in the entanglements of love, he reviles her with the words: "Let the whole world collapse as long as I get my tea every time." He orders her out: "As for me, I need peace" (Part Two, IX and X). Her disappearance and his leaving the house in his dressing gown are two aspects of the same nihility, a nihility at the ground of "life."

To say that life is the point at which rationalism is broken through to a dimension where the inner and outer are one means that life itself is in continual *process*. Dostoevsky expresses the idea paradoxically:

perhaps the only goal on earth to which mankind is striving lies in this incessant process of attaining, or in other words, in life itself, and not particularly in the goal which of course must always be two times two makes four, that is a formula, and after all, two times two makes four is no longer life, gentlemen, but is the beginning of death. (IX)

Actually to attain the goal would be terribly comical. "Two times two is four" is an unbearable state of affairs which makes a mockery of human beings. Nonetheless, to orient oneself directly toward the goal is normal and peaceful and safe. From Dostoevsky's perspective, human beings love suffering as much as peace and security. The human being is a *creative* animal, but one that loves destruction and chaos. That life is process means that it continually disrupts its own stability and does itself harm. Moreover, if the goal of life is in life itself rather than something external to life—if its aim lies *in* the process itself rather than at its end—then the work of building life up like a "civil engineer" and the work of tearing it down are equally fundamental. Suffering belongs to the creativity of life, and self-consciousness depends on life's being so structured. Pain is the origin of consciousness; herein lies the fundamental unity, recognized by Nietzsche as well as by Dostoevsky, of the healthiness of life and the disease of consciousness. Dostoevsky thus comes to the problem of the origin of consciousness by his own path, a problem touched on by Fichte, Novalis, Kierkegaard, Nietzsche and other recent "philosophers of life" in their respective ways. This "path" is the confrontation with the "crystal palace."

> In the crystal palace suffering is even unthinkable; suffering means doubt, means negation, and what would be the good of a crystal palace if there could be any doubt about it? And yet I am sure man will never renounce real suffering, that is, destruction and chaos. Why, after all, suffering is the origin of consciousness. . . . Consciousness is the greatest misfortune for man, yet I know man loves it and would not give it up for any satisfaction. Consciousness, for instance is infinitely superior to two times two makes four. Once you have two times two makes four, there is nothing left to do or to understand. There will be nothing left but to bottle up your five senses and plunge into contemplation. While if you stick to consciousness, even though you attain the same result, you can at least flag yourself at times, and that will, at any rate, liven you up. (IX)

"Contemplation with the five senses blocked" had been the heart of idealism from Plato to Hegel, but for the underground man who lives in the law-regulated heyday of science and socialism the technique represents a last resort for the resistance of self-consciousness—a radically paradoxical state of affairs. Here self-consciousness arises from the *bottom of nihility*, of which neither normal individuals nor science nor socialism can be aware, a nihility in which both doing and knowing have come to an end *in the essential sense*. The underground man calls the crystal palace an "ant-hill", suited better for domestic animals *(aux animaux domestiques)*: "I would rather my hand were withered than to let it bring a single brick to such a building" (X). The phrase recalls the remark of the nihilist Bazarov who tries to destroy the old social system and authorities but holds that "it is not for the gods to have to bake bricks." His egoistic self-consciousness planned a social edifice for himself and his followers, the new "gods," with bricks which they had "fools" bake for them. Self-consciousness in the underground nihilist, in contrast, counters this kind of edifice with contemplation through the eye of nihility and will to life. Here for the first time we see a truly nihilistic nihilism that leaps to a new dimension. André Gide was surely right in calling *Notes from Underground* the key to all of Dostoevsky's works.

Earlier on in this chapter, holding up Turgenev's Bazarov as a kind of prism, I attempted to analyze certain moments within the chaos that is Russian nihilism and provisionally distinguished four facets: the scientific spirit and its realistic worldview, socialist morality, egoism, and fanaticism. With *Notes from Underground*, however, we come upon a radical irony directed against all these elements. The scientific worldview and socialist morality try to transform people into piano keys and herd animals, as an ultimate resistance against which Dostoevsky proposes underground contemplation and absolutely irrational freedom of will. With respect to fanaticism he points out the necessity for all actions to be reduced to inert inactivity. The egoism of the desire for power, the desire to become the gods of a "new society" by having others disappear, is negated by an egoism based on true "nihility." In this manner the various facets of Russian nihilism that appeared in Bazarov are subjected to a paradoxical negation, resulting in a nihilism of greater and deeper proportions.

In the shift to a true nihilism which occurs within the protagonist of *Notes from Underground*, the escape from the world of iron laws through underground contemplation inhibits movement in the real world. The real world stands before the underground man as an obstacle, an impenetrable wall. Meantime, behind him the world of the ideal is no longer there to return to. The basement of nihility can only be a dead-end of "inactivity." The first step away fron nihilism as contemplative inertia and toward nihilism's trying to assert itself through breaking the laws of the real world, seems to come with the "action" of Raskolnikov in *Crime and Punishment*. There nihilism leaps out from the underground and into the real world. Nihility takes on the positive meaning of negation of the world and its laws, and the nihilist comes to stand on a deeper egoistic "selfishness." In other words, nihilism becomes more self-aware. At the same time, nihilism becomes a problem for itself, appearing as a complex of deeper self-assertion and deeper self-doubt, of limitless hope and despair, of an infinite sense of power and of helplessness.[8]

Chapter Eight

Nihilism as Philosophy: Martin Heidegger

1. Existentialism as a Discipline

With Heidegger, nihilism began to assume the form of a scientific metaphysics in the true sense. Against this backdrop, a standpoint of what Heidegger calls freedom in the transcendence beyond beings emerges, a standpoint that holds the promise of letting us be fully what we are as human beings.

What Heidegger means by a transcending of beings is not a transcendence *away from* human existence in the direction of another world beyond or behind the world we know. The transcendence he is speaking of is part and parcel of human being from the beginning; indeed it is what allows us to exist *actually* and allows the world to disclose itself as world. In this transcendence the totality of beings opens up from its own ground. There is no world apart at the ground of this ground but only an abyss—a ground of nothingness. In other words, the basic meaning of transcendence is that Nothing is revealed, and thereby the self becomes the *true* self, *freedom* becomes a genuine possibility, and beings are understood in their *truth*. Heidegger gives us nothing less than an ontology within which nihilism becomes a philosophy. By disclosing the nothing at the ground of all beings and summoning it forth, nihilism becomes the basis of a new metaphysics.

Thinkers like Kierkegaard and Nietzsche, despite their faith in Existence and life, lacked faith in "academic disciplines," casting their lot in with the most passionate adventures of thought. For them, the idea of a "science" that would demand objectivity in place of passionate subjectivity would fail to reach any kind of truth. Kierkegaard accused those who philosophize through "abstract speculation" of being dishonest, and Nietzsche dismissed the

157

"will to truth" as a sign of the impotence of life, *décadence*, and self-deception. The standpoint of Existence they took militated not just against metaphysics but against any "scientific" standpoint. They saw the positivistic and naturalistic philosophies that had moved in to replace Hegel's metaphysics as merely new forms of dogmatic metaphysics trumpeted under the banner of science. Hence their mistrust of a certain kind of "science."

Meantime, another battle broke out on a different front. The strategy here was to expose metaphysics and naturalistic philosophy as dogmatically academic and, pursuing the line of critique developed by Kant, to set up philosophy as a rigorous "science." The neo-Kantian schools, the phenomenology of Husserl, and Dilthey's philosophy of history belonged to this camp.[1] In opposition to attempts to absorb the standpoint of science directly into philosophy, they undertook a methodological critique of scientific knowledge of nature and history. Their aim was, on the one hand, to ground scientific knowledge philosophically, and on the other, to mark off its limits. In contrast to a naturalistic philosophy that promoted skepticism regarding the meaning of human life, a new philosophical idealism emerged affirming norms and values. This new idealism argued from the human capacity for science against despair in the human condition.

In their own way, each of these critiques was caught up in the attempt to understand human being objectively as the subject matter of a "scientific discipline," whether through an analysis of the workings of human consciousness or through an "understanding" of historical life. Subjectivity became reduced to the confines of scientific categories or supposedly universal structures. The more they pursued objectivity, the more the subjective nature of consciousness or life became diluted and distanced from *this*, my *self*. It was against this trend that the immersion of the self into passionate thinking, as we see it in Kierkegaard or Nietzsche, took shape.

Heidegger worked his way through the neo-Kantian school, Husserl, Dilthey and others, one after the other. Sharing with them the conviction that science is an essential ingredient of human existence, he seems to have realized the danger in the scientific standpoint of divorcing the self from subjectivity and Existence. Hence the need for a radical reconception of philosophy as a discipline that does not cut the self off from Existence but plants its roots firmly there. This is what Heidegger had in mind in making ontology existential, thus breaking completely with the metaphysics of the tradition from Plato to Hegel.[2] In Heidegger the passionate thinking of Kierkegaard and Nietzsche, who repudiated science in the name of

Existence, and critical philosophy in the broad sense of a scientific discipline aimed at safeguarding "human being" in the world of nature and history, come together to give his existential philosophy its unique character. This is also the framework within which nihilism reappears as the ground of philosophy.

2. The "Ontological Difference"

From the time of Plato and Aristotle, philosophy had been set up as the "science" of Being. Since then and up until Hegel, the problem of Being (*das Sein*) was at the foundations of philosophy. Indeed, Heidegger agrees that the question of Being is the only issue in philosophy. What does this mean? The Being that forms the subject matter of philosophy is the Being of beings (*das Sein des Seienden*), that is, the basic reason or ground on which a "thing that *is*" comes to be a "thing that *is*." But what does it mean to make an issue of this ground of being of a "thing that is"? To answer this question, we must look at what Heidegger calls the *ontological difference*, in virtue of which metaphysics as the study of Being comes about.

The things that surround us, no matter what they are, are all things that in some way *are*. For example, there *is* something before me now; it *is* a desk; it *is* in this room; it *is* made of wood; and so on. We talk about and experience this kind of thing every day. "Being," however, is not some "thing that is"; nor is any "thing that is" "Being."[3] "Being" (*Sein*) is not any kind of being or "thing that is" (*Seiendes*). But now, if what we call *beings* are all "things that are," then that is all there is. If not, there would only be "nothing." Thus when someone says "Being," we do not know what to think of. At the same time, we *are* constantly thinking and talking about "Being." We say things like: here *is* something (a thing that is) rectangular; it *is* a desk; it *is* in this room; and so forth. We already understand the "is." Or rather, understanding immediately takes place (*Verständnis versteht sich*).[4] The meaning of the "is" is not grasped conceptually (*begriffen*); somehow it is understood and yet its meaning remains hidden.

Without this kind of immediate understanding we would not be able to exist in the world of "beings." We ourselves are also "beings" who exist in the world amidst various other beings, but we differ from everything else in that we are beings who *have an understanding of* the *being* of things and of ourselves as "beings" in their midst. This kind of immediate understanding of Being is part and parcel of our very way of being as beings. Our being comprehends in its structure an understanding of Being, and this accounts for our way of being in the world.

The "world" is the place in which all beings are, but is itself neither a thing nor a being. The being of the world is not something "objective," as the being of beings is; if it were, we would have to be outside the world in order to understand it. The world is prior (in a non-temporal sense) to everything; it is the locus in which all beings come to be and which lets them be. Therefore, when we understand that all things are, and that we ourselves are, the world is already included. All these issues—that various things *are*, that in their being there is included the sense of "in-the-*world*," that we ourselves are actually in the world, and that our being includes an understanding of Being itself—are comprehended within the understanding of Being. The events and experiences of everyday life rest on this immediate, self-evident understanding of Being.

Philosophy—in particular, metaphysics as "first philosophy"—brings this self-evidence in question and makes an issue of Being. Ordinarily, what Being is, what the world is, what human being is, and so on, are roughly understood. In philosophy, it is precisely this rough understanding that gives these matters their deeply problematic nature. Our understanding is pregnant with "something" that lies hidden behind a smokescreen of self-evidence in what Heidegger calls "everydayness." The question of Being may arise when we try to look at ourselves and the world objectively. Or there may be times when the being of the self becomes the kind of question that breaks through our everydayness and brings into question the world and everything in it.[5] In such cases, "Being" is clearly differentiated from "beings" and may be questioned thematically. Unlike the ontical (*ontisch*) difference between one being and another, the difference between beings and Being is the *ontological* difference. In contrast, the immediate understanding of Being that belongs to everyday experience is pre-ontological (*vorontologisch*). Only when the ontological difference is developed out of the pre-ontological difference is the horizon of the discipline that takes Being thematically as the issue—namely, metaphysics—opened up.[6]

The significance of calling metaphysics a "discipline" is best grasped by contrasting it with what is called a "worldview."[7] A worldview makes an issue of things like God, nature, history, reason, spirit, and life. By understanding the connections among these things, it tries to think about the meaning of the world and our lives in it. In this case God, nature, and so on are all "beings," and our existence in relation to them is also understood as a "being." Here the knowledge attained within a worldview is all ontical knowledge; the "being" itself of the various beings discussed is not brought into question. A worldview demands an ontology at its basis. This is the place of philosophy in the true sense, of metaphysics as science. A worldview itself is not a philosophy; nor are the special sciences. Knowledge of God, nature, history, and so forth constitutes disciplines such as theology, natural science, and the study of history; but these are all sciences of "beings," and of special kinds of beings at that. Hence they are *all* dependent on ontology, which questions the being *itself* of all things that are. The question of ontological foundations does not arise from within the standpoint of science. "Being" itself is not one of the questions of science; nor, it goes without saying, is "Nothing."[8]

The ontological difference in which philosophical problems of Being and Nothing are set up forms the bedrock not only of daily life and experience but also of scientific inquiry and the construction of worldviews. Philosophy's question is precisely what to these latter is self-evident and therefore hidden from view. At the beginning of *What is Metaphysics?* Heidegger mentions Hegel's idea of the "inverted world." Hegel writes as follows:

> Philosophy by its very nature is esoteric; for itself it is neither made for the masses nor is it susceptible of being cooked up for them. It is philosophy only because it goes exactly contrary to the understanding and thus even more so to "sound common sense," the so-called healthy human understanding, which actually means the local and temporary vision of some limited generation of human beings. To that generation the world of philosophy is in and for itself a topsy-turvy, an inverted, world.[9]

For Heidegger, too, philosophy is an inverted world; it is a world in which the ontological foundation, hidden at the ground of everydayness and science, is turned inside out. The critical question is where to look for the clue to this inversion. Heidegger seeks it in the understanding of Being that is included in what he calls *Dasein*—namely, within human being. This is what provides his existential philosophy with its new standpoint.

3. Transcendence and Being-in-the-World

The ontological difference can come to light in the simple posture of placing *before* us everything that is, including ourselves.[10] Aristotle, for example, sought the clue for how to approach "Being" in questions like what a thing is, what kind of nature it has, where it is located, and so on—namely in the basic categories one draws on to let others understand what sort of thing one is talking about. In other words, out of all the predicates of a thing, he tried to isolate the basic forms that determine what a thing *is*. Kant took his clue from the various forms of judgment, and from them isolated the basic *a priori* structures of the understanding. He then extracted from these the "transcendental" formal structure of the ways in which the understanding relates to intuition. Both thinkers, however, set the world up as an object of contemplation. Such an approach, while admittedly one mode of human existence, in effect disengages one from the real self who *actually* is, as well as from the world. In the contemplative mode we place ourselves before ourselves but do not touch on who the *we* is who is doing the looking and thinking. The self who sees and the self who is seen are bifurcated.

The self who *actually* is has been thrown into the world and *is* in relation to the various things in it. To take this kind of actual existence as the clue to the human mode of being is to say that it is possible to question Being from within a mode of existence where the seeing self and seen self are truly one. In other words, it is to say that the ontological difference is understandable. This is the standpoint of Heidegger's existential philosophy.

To understand Being in this way is to see it as fundamentally temporal. Nietzsche says that "temporality" reaches to the very essence of human being; and Kierkegaard sees Existence in temporality as a synthesis of time and eternity. Heidegger's approach also exposes human existence as "*mood*-ish" being,[11] holding that the moods of boredom, anxiety, courage and the like uncover the true face of human being in its essential temporality. To be able to employ these moods as clues in this way, one must do so from within the "mood-ish" and *Affekt*ed way of being. Through this "moodish" opening up of the self to the temporality of Being, the ground of it all is discovered to be nihility[12]—and it is this sense that philosophy as existential understanding has nihilism in its foundations.

According to Heidegger, our way of being as the beings we are consists in our relating (*Verhalten*) to other things that are. At the ground of this kind of relating is an understanding of Being, through which all modes of relating become possible. Included, therefore, in our way of being as human beings is a sense that the things that are are encountered as a whole. What is it, then, that makes an understanding of Being possible in general? Within what kind of horizon can we understand Being?

In principle, when we distinguish Being from beings, we *transcend* the realm of things that are. It is not that we go to some other world beyond the world we know, or enter into some different realm of beings. Such notions constitute, for Heidegger, a vulgar form of metaphysics with which true philosophy (metaphysics as science) has nothing in common. Philosophy does not go beyond beings ontically to other beings that dwell beyond or behind. It transcends beings *ontologically* in the direction of Being.[13] In the act of transcending beings, human being at the same time goes beyond the self as a being, and thus for the first time reaches human existence as the "self" (*Selbst*). In this way, transcendence constitutes the "selfhood" (*Selbstheit*) of the self.[14] Or, to put it another way, in the act of transcending beings, a distinction is made between what is "self" and what is not, on this basis the self relates *itself* to the beings it has transcended. This is what it means for a self to "be"—insofar as everything it is to be a self is exhausted in relationships. It is not that there is first of all a self on one side and then a "thing" on the other, so that the self can then relate to what lies outside it. This kind of conceptualized schema has nothing to do with the self's basic mode of being. Basically, the self's mode of being is to be "outside" from the beginning.[15]

The next question concerning the human being's transcendence of beings becomes: where does it go to if not to some world beyond? The horizon up to which (*woraufhin*) human being transcends is what Heidegger calls "world."[16] This is not some pre-existent beyond, nor indeed any kind of object at all. When human being relates to beings from its situatedness in their midst, a horizon of beings-in-totality is revealed, and this horizon is the world. Thus transcendence is an understanding of beings in their totality, and this understanding is *transcendence-to-world*. In this transcendence, the being of beings is disclosed; and this kind of disclosure belongs essentially to human existence.

In this sense human being as transcendence is what Heidegger calls "being-in-the-world" (*In-der-Welt-sein*). This should not be thought of as something fixed or static, since every time one relates to something self-being is opened up and the world occurs—that is, the world "worlds."[17] In this sense transcendence to the world, together with the "worlding" of the world, arises in the essence of human existence. Being-in-the-world itself has the structure of arising, and this in turn is an indication of the fundamental temporality of Being itself, the very foundation upon which "time" is conceived.

That the being of human being is disclosed as "being-in-the-world" does not mean that existence is "known" as such. It is not a matter of theoretical knowledge or consciousness of the self. It is rather that the self grasps itself in the mode of being outside itself, that one "finds oneself disposed" (*sich befindet*) in the midst of beings.[18] Human existence discovers itself as something unclear, even to itself, as to where it came from and where it is going. It is as if *Dasein* has been handed over (*überantwortet*) to human beings, whose being is thereby revealed to be a burden (*Last*) with which they have been laden. Just *why* one has been so burdened is unknown, even to oneself; only the fact of the burden is clear.

The mood-ish self-disclosure of our being as a burden is a manifestation of what Heidegger calls "*thrownness*" (*Geworfenheit*).[19] That *Dasein* is "being-in-the-world" means that it is thrown—from where, one does not know—into the midst of beings. The mere "facticity" of being handed over points to the "fated" character inherent in human being—the fact that "it is so." And so while transcendence constitutes the *being-able-to-be* (*Seinkönnen*) in human being, its being-possible (*Möglichsein*) is always already thrown into a particular situation: "*Dasein* is being-possible which has been handed over to itself, it is through and through *thrown possibility*" (*SZ* 144). This kind of being-possible opens up a "free play space" (*Spielraum*)[20] in which human being is able to relate to things as being-in-the-world: "*Dasein* is . . . *thrown* out among beings *as free* being-able-to-be [*als freies Seinkönnen*]" (*ER* 129). Heidegger calls the structure of *Dasein* as being-possible "projection" (*Entwurf*)—and indeed always "*thrown* projection."[21]

Transcendence to world as being-in-the-world means projecting world on to beings through coming out beyond them; the world as the horizon within which beings are encountered is thrown over (*Überwurf*) beings.[22] This is the meaning of being-possible, or possibility. The possibility of relating to things rests on this projection of the "world," as does the sense of Existence as a going outside of oneself.[23] Here the being of the self comes to light as at once a transcendence of beings and an understanding of Being.

Given that there are no beings apart from beings-as-a-whole, the claim that transcendence is a going beyond and coming out above beings-as-a-whole means that *Dasein* is *being held out into Nothing* (*Hineingehaltenheit in das Nichts*).[24] In other words, human being is exposed to nihility in its very foundation and through this nihility is able to go beyond beings and to relate to them and to itself.[25] This gives *Dasein* the freedom that lets it be itself: "If it were not for the primordial revelation of Nothing there would be no self-being and no freedom" (*WM?* 106). The very transcendence that arises in the essence of human being is made possible by Nothing.

4. Being-toward-Death and Anxiety

That nihility lies at the ground of *Dasein* is evident from the phenomenon of *death*. Heidegger says that the ground of human being is its "thrownness into death" (*Geworfenheit in den Tod*) [*SZ* 251]. Death is already included within life; it is a way of being that human being takes upon itself as soon as it *is:* "As soon as a man receives life he is old enough to die" [*SZ* 245]. Death is the end of being-in-the-world. In its existing, in its projection as being-able-to-be, human being constantly (*ständig*) lets itself go beyond and run ahead of itself [*SZ* 303–23]. This is Existence as projection. To this extent human being constantly has "not yet" reached its end, and yet at the same time is "always already" at its end. This is not to say that *Dasein* has already ended, but rather that in the precursory[26] projection of the self ahead of itself, self-being is always "being-to-the-end" (*Sein-zum-Ende*). In standing out from itself, self-being runs ahead and hits the "end" of self-being; it comes up against death. In coming up against its end, self-being becomes *my* self-being: the self thereby comes to itself. *Dasein* is *Dasein* only as something "futured" by its end;[27] and to come up against the end of the uttermost possibility of being-able-to-be means both that the ground of one's being is revealed and that Nothing is revealed at the ground of self-being.

Since the being of human being is always a being-to-the-end, and death *is* such an end, Existence means a "being-toward-death" (*Sein zum Tode*). Earlier I mentioned that through the revelation of Nothing at the ground of human being, human being becomes itself—through coming to itself. The same holds true of human being as being-toward-death. That human being includes an understanding of Being, and is therefore the being that is aware of its own being, means that it grasps its own being from the Nothing that is its ground, as a being-toward-death. Human being comprehends its own being in the light of the end where all possibility of the self's being-able-to-be runs out. Being as Existence, as projection toward being-able-to-be, is always something that has not yet ended, something that has not yet exhausted the entirety of possibility, and which therefore maintains itself constantly while running ahead of itself. If *not-yet*-at-the-end is the ontological foundation of life and of all creative activity, then the self's living and being able to live from the ground of death must be included within its life. As "being-toward-death," the self becomes for the first time the source of being-able-to-be, a being-toward the being-able-to-be that is inherent and fundamental to the self.

Death is not a matter of indifference to human existence. One can "run ahead" to it before one dies, and in this way human being can be truly *individualized*. As being-toward-death *Dasein* is grasped for the first time as itself and as no other; willy-nilly, death makes *Dasein* individual *Dasein*. In this individualization *Existence* opens up the meaning of *being* truly *there* (*Da-sein*) (*SZ* 263). It is being-toward-death that makes possible projection or "world-forming" (*Weltbilden*),[28] so that world may "world" as the disclosure of the being of the self from the ground up.

Just as Nothing discloses the being of human being by making the transcendence of *Dasein* possible and letting the self come to itself, so in death the possibility of Being and therefore the possibility from which life and all activity become possible is revealed. Being-toward-death is being-toward one's ownmost being-able-to-be. At the same time, the "being-to-the-end" that makes freedom possible is not itself a free act; it belongs rather to *Dasein's* thrown-ness, to the essential finitude of human being, to which topic I shall return presently.

In everydayness, of course, this true way of being of the self is concealed. The human being flees from its self-being held out into nothing, from self-being as individualized, in order to exist as "the social one" (*das Man*)[29] within the "public" world. One exists in such a way that one can be anyone and no one. In the busi-ness of the social world one is oblivious of the death, or nothing, at the ground of the self and avoids thinking of self-being as being-to-the-end. This condition Heidegger calls "*falling*," intending the term in an ontological sense rather than in the sense of a *décadence* of civilization. Both the person who is living the healthiest of lives in the public sphere and the progressive who is working toward a hoped-for future society exist in this "falling." As *das Man*, one lives in the mode of care (*Sorge*) for the business of the so-called world, and feels at home (*zu Hause*) in the world. One's basic existence is at home in the world whether one rejoices or grieves, whether in joy or sadness.

In contrast, true being-in-the-world is "uncanny" (*unheimlich*); the fundamental mood (*Grundstimmung*) of our true way of being is *anxiety* [*SZ*, § 40]. Human being is in anxiety regarding the self's being-in-the-world and shudders from the anxiety of death—that is, in the face of the possibility that Existence may become impossible. In anxiety, human being "finds itself before the Nothing of the possible impossibility of its *Existence*" (*SZ* 266). Basically we are never truly at home in the world; the true being of the self is fundamentally *unheimlich*. And in this anxiety, Nothing is revealed.

As Heidegger says in *What is Metaphysics?*, nihility is not any existing thing given as an object and therefore cannot be grasped (*erfassen*) by the intellect. Anxiety does not mean a rational grasp of nihility. It means that we encounter nihility in the experience of having beings-as-a-whole gradually withdraw and slide away from us, assuming a strangely alienating aspect (*Befremdlichkeit*). And having withdrawn in this way, they return to press in upon us [*WM?* 103–05]. The attack of nihility does not signify the negating of beings: negating means power, whereas anxiety means a complete powerlessness in relation to beings. Thus in the attack of nihility and the falling away of beings-as-a-whole, it is not that we negate them, but rather that nihility reveals itself as the ground of beings-as-a-whole. "Nothing itself nothings [*nichtet*]" (*WM?* 105). Beings-as-a-whole become strange and alienating through being wrapped[30] in nothing. This is the "nothinging" of Nothing, in which the true form of our self-being is revealed as "the self individualized to itself in uncanniness and thrown into Nothing"; it is "*Dasein* in its uncanniness, primordially thrown being-in-the-world as not-at-home (*Unzuhause*), the naked 'that' (*Dass*) in the nihility of the world" [*SZ* 276–77].

Everydayness escapes from this kind of fundamental being-in-the-world into an inauthentic way of being which conceals the basic uncanniness of our being here. From the bottom of this being-in-the-world, Heidegger says, our being calls out to us with the voice of "conscience" [*SZ* §§ 56–60]. To respond to this call and return to the truth of our human being is what Heidegger calls "resolution" (*Entschlossenheit*), the decisive opening up of self-being. "*Dasein*, understanding the calling voice, *listens to and obeys its ownmost possibility of existing* [*Existenzmöglichkeit*]. It has chosen itself" (*SZ* 287). To choose oneself in the resolution to leave the inauthentic standpoint of "the social one" means that *Dasein* stands in "being-to-the-end" and totally immerses itself in the essential finitude of self-being.

Human being, we saw, is projective; it is the being that constantly stands out from itself and takes over its own being-able-to-be *precursorily.* Moreover, it is constantly limited in its being-able-to-be by death and its running up against death with every step. *Dasein* thereby becomes a finite and individualized "self." In projecting itself toward the ultimate possibility *Dasein* constantly comes up to itself (*auf sich zukommen*), and this is the *future* in the essential temporality of human being. The self "futures" itself in running ahead, thereby coming into its own futurally as being-toward-death.[31] But since all projection is "thrown projection," all future is in this sense already "been" (*gewesen*).[32] Thrownness is the *pastness* in temporality as human being, and this pastness is revealed in running ahead to the most futural, ultimate possibility. Thus human being, in relating to beings in this kind of thrown projection, is actually being-"there" (*Da-sein*). This is being-in-the-world, and the essential temporality or finitude of this being consists in its being thrown projection. Heidegger defines this thrown projection as care and sees anxiety as its basic mood. Anxiety is anxiety that existence as thrown being-in-the-world may become impossible. And it is here that metaphysics arises.

5. Finitude—Metaphysics—Existence—Freedom

Human beings exist in the midst of beings-as-a-whole as beings who exist in the way of transcendence. This means that human existence is being held out into Nothing and as such is thrown into the midst of the totality of beings as such. As transcendence *Dasein* encounters beings against the horizon of world as Being; as held out into Nothing, it encounters the Being of beings. Nothing "nothings" within the "being" of beings. In other words, the totality of beings shows itself as liable to collapse (*hinfällig*) [*WM?* 104], and human being, which exists in its midst, finds itself as itself in *anxiety*. In this sense, finitude constitutes our innermost essence— "Transcendence is the innermost finitude, the finitude which sustains *Dasein*"[33]—and therefore the "foundation" of metaphysics as fundamental ontology.

   That Dasein is essentially finite comes from the revelation of Nothing at its ground. To be suspended in Nothing is to go beyond and come out from beings-as-a-whole, albeit in a transcendence that is at the same time always "being-to-the-end." Moreover, the revelation of Nothing at the ground of human being means that the horizon of the understanding of Being is opened up. Therefore the finitude of human being and the understanding of Being are bound together within the revelation of Nothing: "Understanding of Being . . . appears as the innermost ground of human finitude. . . . It is itself the innermost essence of finitude" (*KM* 236–7/222). If transcendence and the understanding of Being are what establish the ontological difference, then finitude in the sense just mentioned belongs to the foundations of metaphysics. This means, Heidegger goes on, that metaphysics belongs to our inherent nature, echoing Kant's allusion to "metaphysics as a natural disposition."[34] In Heidegger, this idea is even more directly stated:

Human *Dasein* is able to relate to beings only if it holds itself out into Nothing. This going out beyond beings takes place in the essence [*Wesen*] of *Dasein*. But this going out beyond is metaphysics itself.

. . . Metaphysics is the fundamental occurrence within *Dasein*. It is *Dasein* itself. (*WM?* 111–12)

In other words, in being held out into Nothing, Existence has "broken into" the midst of the totality of beings, and this is already metaphysics.[35] The reason behind the questions asked in metaphysics is that human being is finite; for an infinite being, these questions would not arise. This is why Heidegger characterizes philosophizing as a "most inwardly *finite* of efforts [*zu innerst endliche Anstrengung*]" (*ER* 11).

It is not only the questions of metaphysics that derive from the finitude of Existence, but the fact that metaphysics should occur in the form of a question at all. This has two meanings. First, that metaphysics is a fundamental event within human *Dasein* because *Dasein* is itself a question for itself. In this sense, metaphysics is pre-ontological; despite its "ontological" disclosures, it remains ontical. The understanding of Being is the innermost essence of the finitude of Existence and is the most finite of finite things. But "the most finite thing in the finitude of *Dasein* is known (*bekannt*) but not yet grasped (*begriffen*)"; and this issue itself is "a metaphysical primordial fact (*Urfaktum*)" (*KM* 241/226).

But if metaphysics has already arisen in virtue of our finitude, then why are we all not always living in metaphysics? The reason, of course, is that we are not normally preoccupied with the finitude of our self-being. In other words, we have not become fully finite in the finitude of the self, in the innermost essence of self-being, in the "abyssal ground" that is the revelation of Nothing. Instead the revelation of the finitude of *Dasein*, the "nothingness" of Nothing, drives us toward beings, to relate and "submit" to them.[36] It makes us oblivious of the Nothing over which the true self hangs suspended:

Nothing in its nothinging precisely refers us to beings. Nothing nothings unceasingly, without our really knowing about this occurrence with the knowledge within which we move every day. (*WM?* 106)

This forgetting and concealment are inevitable, given our "thrownness" and radical finitude. That we are free in this condition is not a function of our free projection or free will; that is, we are not "creator and master" of ourselves.[37] Even projection is "thrown projection," and because of this thrownness our being is submitted to the beings into whose midst it has been cast. As Heidegger says:

> We are so finite that we are simply unable by our own deci-
> sion and will to bring about the fundamental encounter with
> Nothing. Finitude is so deeply entrenched in our *Dasein* that
> our freedom cannot reach our ownmost and deepest finitude."
> (*WM?* 108)

Thus our finitude is due not to our freedom but to the nothinging of Nothing which is the "ground" even of our freedom.

In spite of the fact that metaphysics takes place at the ground of *Dasein* itself, and indeed is *Dasein* itself radically questioning itself, we are not normally aware that this is going on. *Dasein* forgets to question itself fundamentally, which brings us to the second mean- ing of metaphysics as a question. Metaphysics has to arise from the ground of our being as an inquiry into Being itself. To question our *Dasein* fundamentally, we have to philosophize—and philosophize *existentially*. Only thus can we be authentically ourselves.

In our everyday, public way of being, we have fallen away from the innermost ground of our being, and the most finite thing in our finitude has been concealed from us. The radical nullity of *Dasein*, of being held out into Nothing, is forgotten in the course of relating to beings; with great peace of mind we hurry to the super- ficial domains of *Dasein* and busy ourselves with the public life [*WM?* 106]. "The finitude of *Dasein*—the understanding of Being— lies in oblivion" (*KM* 241/226). Metaphysics consists in *Dasein*'s wresting its fundamental finitude from oblivion and disclosing the nothinging of Nothing at its ground so that *the self completely becomes its own finitude*. This disclosure of Nothing means that *Dasein* is grasped as "being-to-the-end" or "being-toward-death." This is the *individualization* of *Dasein* mentioned earlier, in which we revert from the public self to the true self, to the self as individual.

From this is is clear that metaphysics is not merely an idle pas- time of the intellect but a practice based on a resolution in which we risk our very being. The question is whether we *authentically* hold ourselves out into Nothing, become completely finite, and thus become ourselves; or whether we exist inauthentically as mem- bers of the public, and lose ourselves by deceiving ourselves with regard to our finitude. To opt for the former, it is imperative that our *Dasein* return to the anxiety of being held out into Nothing, that the totality of beings become brittle and uncanny, and that all our projection, all free, creative activity, be carried out resolutely upon our "ownmost being-able-to-be" as being-toward-death.

These are matters with which "the sciences" are unequipped to deal. Scientific *Dasein* is concerned exclusively with beings. "Nothing" is not a concern of the sciences, and yet "scientific thinking" itself is possible only because it is already inserted into Nothing. If science regards its refusal to take "Nothing" seriously as an indication of its quality and superiority, its claims become ludicrous. As Heidegger says:

> For this reason the rigor [*Strenge*] of a science cannot match the seriousness [*Ernst*] of metaphysics. Philosophy can never be measured by the standard of the idea of science. (*WM?* 112)

Metaphysics, as just discussed, has to do with "the disclosing of the entire realm of the truth of nature and history" (*WM?* 111), as well as of the finitude that belongs by nature to the Being of beings. Because "Being itself is in its essence finite and reveals itself only in the transcendence of *Dasein* which is held out into Nothing," it follows that: "It is only in the Nothing of *Dasein* that the totality of beings comes to itself in its own most possibility that is, finitely" [*WM?* 110].

Heidegger has attempted to restructure Kant's standpoint of "transcendental grounding" from the standpoint of the disclosure of Being within transcendence. When Nothing is revealed and beings press in upon us in their true nature as something uncanny, unfamiliar, or alien, the wonder this experience evokes in us raises the question "Why?" Once Nothing has been revealed and the question Why has been raised, the sciences can begin to raise questions in their respective fields of inquiry. Meanwhile, "the inquiry into Nothing puts us ourselves the inquirers into question. This inquiry is a metaphysical inquiry" (*WM?* 111). Here the abyss (*Abgrund*) of *Dasein* itself is opened up. "The truth of metaphysics resides within this abyssal ground (*abgründigen Grunde*)" (*WM?* 112).

Just as human being reaches authentic self-being by seeing itself as finite at the abyssal ground, so does the totality of beings "come" to itself as finite in being grounded ontologically on the same abyssal ground. These two events are one and the same. This is precisely the standpoint of metaphysics as a "ground-event" or basic occurrence (*Grundgeschehen*) within Dasein, and as such represents the standpoint of freedom. Freedom is the abyss of Dasein itself; it is "the ground of ground" for all things (*ER* 127), and also "the source of ground in general" (*ER* 105). Freedom opens up the ground that grounds beings as "freedom for ground." In other words: "The sudden breaking open (*Aufbrechen*) of the abyss in transcendence which grounds is the primordial movement (*Urbewegung*) that freedom perpetrates upon us" (*ER* 129). Freedom, as this kind of abyss, is what integrates the totality of beings from the ground of their being; Heidegger calls this "grounding in world-projection" (*Gründen in Weltenwurf*) [*ER* 107–109]. The projection of world opens up a "world-horizon" for the totality of beings and as such is transcendence. What Heidegger calls fundamental "world-content" takes form at the ground of *Dasein:* "the more primordially the content of the world (*Weltgehalt*) is grounded, the more simply it touches the heart (*Herz*) of *Dasein* and its selfhood in its activity" (*ER* 129). In other words, the abyss that opens up at the ground of *Dasein* is the bedrock on which the world-content rests and at the same time the depths of the heart and the place where action becomes action of the *self.*

It seems reasonable to suggest that here we have a view similar to Nietzsche's idea of the world as perspectives of will seen in terms of will to power, and also to Stirner's idea of "world-enjoyment" (*Weltgenuss*) see in terms of "creative nothing." Of course, Heidegger differs from both of them in maintaining to the end a stand on metaphysics as ontology and, like Kant, making transcendental grounding a central issue.

To sum up: for Heidegger, "projection of world" (the fundamental unity of the totality of beings) and "thrownness" (the essence of finitude) come together in the transcendence peculiar to human being. If we grant that this reveals Nothing at the ground of human being, we may see here a distinctively Heideggerian approach to the *fundamental unity of creative nihilism and finitude* mentioned earlier in connection with Stirner and Nietzsche. Projection of world is a standpoint that brings together the totality of beings and renders possible all "creative" activity as the activity of the *self.* For Heidegger, metaphysics means to assume this kind of standpoint.

Chapter Nine

The Meaning of Nihilism for Japan

1. The Crisis in Europe and Nihilism

Nihilism is a recognition of the presence of a fundamental and universal crisis in modern Europe. It is a *crisis* in the sense that people began to feel a quaking underfoot of the ground that had supported the history of Europe for several thousand years and laid the foundations of European culture, thought, ethics, and religion. More than this, it means that life itself is being uprooted and human "being" itself turns into a question mark. Since the latter half of the nineteenth century this sense of crisis or nihilism, combined with a sense of pessimism and *décadence*, has been attacking Europe sporadically. In fact, this sort of thing can and does occur regardless of time or place. The sense that life is groundless and human existence without meaning can arise in connection with the religion and philosophy of any era of history. Here we have focused on the nihilism connected with the historical consciousness of Europe.

Nihilism is not restricted to religion and metaphysics, but reaches over to culture and ethics as well, bringing into question the historical ground of the entire human endeavor, diachronically and synchronically. The confrontation it promotes with the whole of previous history occurs at the metaphysical ground of history. In short, nihilism is a historical actuality in the absolute sense. This accounts for its momentous importance, and it also explains why the attempt to come to grips with nihilism in the form of a personal experiment means to preempt the destination of history and strike down to its very bottom.

The encounter with nihility at the base of historical actuality was the turning point in which Nietzsche's "counter-movement" emerged from nihility: the shift away from a nihility of death to a nihility of life, or to what Stirner calls "creative nothing." Through this shift, nihility unexpectedly took on a new life that could not be beaten down by wind or rain.[1] For the thinkers who cleared the ground for it, this life represented a unity of *creative nihilism and finitude*. Nihilism in the true sense appears when not only the world of all finite beings (the world of "phenomena") is seen to be fundamentally null and thus transcended negatively, but also when the world of eternal being (the world of "essences" conceived after this negative transcendence) is negated. This double negation elicits a standpoint in which finitude and eternity are one against the backdrop of nothingness. Here finitude becomes a full and final finitude. This is what Nietzsche meant by speaking of "*this* life, this *eternal* life." Such a life lives time temporally, as something primordially given as self-being and "ripening with time." Finite self-being, though *in* the world, embraces the world *within* at the ground of its nihility. Eternal recurrence in Nietzsche, the world as property of the individual in Stirner, and the standpoint of transcendental grounding in Heidegger all carry this sense.

Affirmative nihilism began to emerge from an awareness of the fundamental crisis in Europe as a way to overcome this crisis at its roots.

2. The Crisis Compounded

If "nihilism" is the historical actuality of Europe, and if under these circumstances it becomes a historical-existential standpoint, how are we to determine its meaning for us in Japan? It is true: our culture and ways of thinking have become Europeanized; our culture is a recent offshoot of European culture and our thinking a shadow-image of European-style thinking. Still, our importation of European culture never went to the extent of including the Christian faith that has served as the basis and formative power of the European spirit, not to mention the ethics and philosophy that have been developing since the age of the Greeks. Unlike objective realities like institutions and cultural artifacts, or academic disciplines and technologies having to do with objective things, these things of the spirit are directly rooted within the subject and not readily transferable from one place to another. The spiritual basis of Europe has not become our spiritual basis; and in that sense a crisis generated from the shaking of those foundations is not a reality for us. There seems to be no way for nihilism to become a vital issue for us. Does that mean we can do no more than eye it with curiosity as "someone else's business"? The enduring popularity of Nietzsche and the current popularity of existentialism may seem to strengthen this suspicion.

What makes the issue still more complicated is the fact that we do not have any spiritual basis whatsoever at present. The West still has the faith, ethics, ideas, and so forth that have been handed down from Christianity and Greek philosophy, and the integration of these various elements is still the dynamic force behind the formation of the person. No matter how much this basis is now being shaken, it is still very much alive, and one battles against it only at the cost of fierce determination. For us in Japan, things are different. In the past, Buddhism and Confucian thought constituted such a basis, but they have already lost their power, leaving a total void and vacuum in our spiritual ground. Our age probably represents the first time since the beginning of Japanese history that such a phenomenon has occurred.

Up until the middle of the Meiji period a spiritual basis and highly developed tradition was alive in the hearts and minds of the people. Indeed, the reason Japan was able to take in western culture with such unprecedented alacrity was that people then were possessed of true *ability* born of spiritual substance. However, as Europeanization (and Americanization) proceeded, this spiritual core began to decay in subsequent generations, until it is now a vast, gaping void in our ground. The various manifestations of culture at present, if looked at closely, are mere shadows floating over the void. The worst thing is that this emptiness is in no way an emptiness that has been won through struggle, nor a nihility that has been "lived through." It is the natural result of our having been cut off from our tradition. Before we knew what was happening, the spiritual core had wasted away completely.

From the perspective of political history, Japan's being cast on to the stage of world politics during the Meiji Restoration was the greatest change in the history of the nation. But if we look at the change from the point of view of spiritual history, the greatest spiritual crisis in the nation's history was also taking place. What is more, we went through this crisis without a clear realization that it *was* a crisis; and even now the crisis is being compounded by our continuing lack of awareness of our spiritual void. This is why we find it so difficult subjectively to make European nihilism a serious issue, although objectively it ought to become the most pressing problem for us. Hence nihilism tends to be seen as a passing fad, and not something acutely urgent for us. This is the paradox of our situation.

Karl Löwith's superb essay, "European Nihilism," contains an appendix for Japanese readers.[2] In it he writes as follows:

> The time at which the Europeanization of Japan began coincided, unfortunately, with the period when Europe began to experience itself as an insoluble problem. In the latter half of the nineteenth century, when Japan began to make contact with Europe, it took in European "progress" with admirable energy and zealous speed. European culture, however, while it had advanced and conquered the entire world on the surface, had itself actually decayed internally. But, unlike the Russians in the nineteenth century, the Japanese at that time did not confront Europe in a critical manner. And what the leading figures of Europe from Baudelaire to Nietzsche saw through and sensed a crisis in, the Japanese at the beginning adopted *tout court*, naively and uncritically. And when they came to know the Europeans better it was already too late; the Europeans had already lost faith in their own civilization. Moreover, the Japanese never paid any attention to self-criticism—which is the best thing about the Europeans.

Löwith compares the undiscriminating nature of the Japanese with the free mastery of the ancient Greeks when they adopted neighboring cultures: they felt free among others as if they were at home, and at the same time retained their sense of self. There is no such unity of self and others in the case of Japan. Löwith says that modern Japan is itself a "living contradiction." What he says is true—but how are we then to resolve such a contradiction? As a European, Löwith let the question lie there. It is *our* problem, a problem of *will*.

From the beginning, the westernization of Japan was clearly a national resolution, of a kind rarely found in the history of the world. It was forced on us from outside by the enormous progress of world history, and at the same time it was impelled by a powerful will from within. This distinguishes it from the Europeanization of other non-European nations, and no doubt accrues to the greatness of those people who led Japan around the time of the Meiji Restoration. Such individuals were the products of the high quality of traditional oriental culture, of the national "moral energy" cultivated in that culture, and of the vitality of a nation not yet weakened by over-saturation with culture. As westernization progressed, however, this moral energy and spiritual core began to weaken and disappear, and a self-splitting began to take place in the will of the subject.

On the one hand, the ideas of the "cultured person" and the "civilized life-style" that began to appear during that period harbored at bottom some measure of self-contempt vis-à-vis the overwhelming influence of European culture. There was a tendency to a mood of resignation about having been born Japanese. Löwith says that the Japanese are all patriots, but this was the case only up until the turn of the century. Löwith himself says of contemporary students that "they no longer extract from their study of Europe anything to enrich their own Japanese selves,"which is an indication of the loss of spiritual self among modern intellectuals. Thus "culture" forgot itself in being among others, and eventually lost itself.

On the other hand, national moral energy gradually metamorphized into the violence of exclusionist and uncultured "patriots" as a reaction against this loss of self. The self was clung to without consideration for others, or for the historical context. In another sense, this, too, was a loss of ties to the historical ground. Both extremes are one-sided, and represent a falling away from the spirit of "free mastery," of being able to be oneself among others. Löwith further remarks that Japanese intellectuals "do not return to themselves from others and are not free." Where free will—or Nietzsche's primordial will—should be, there is only a deep and cavernous hollowness.

Nietzsche stresses a sense of responsibility toward the ancestors, a "thinking through the succession of the generations," and bearing the accumulation of every possible spiritual nobility of the past.[3] His nihilism, a radical confrontation with history, was backed up by responsibility toward the ancestors to redeem what is noble in the tradition. His standpoint calls for a returning to the ancestors in order to face the future, or to put it the other way around, a prophesying toward the tradition. Without a will toward the future, the confrontation with the past cannot be properly executed; nor is there a true will toward the future without responsibility toward the ancestors. For us Japanese now, the recovery of this primordial will represents our most fundamental task. It is here that European nihilism will begin to reveal its fundamental significance for us.

3. The Significance of European Nihilism for Us

As noted above, our crisis is compounded by the fact that not only are we in it but we do not know that our situation is critical. Thus our first task is to realize that the crisis exists in us, that modern Japan is a living contradiction with a hollowness in its spiritual foundations. To awaken to this fact is to place it in the context of the

spiritual history of modern Japan. In other words, we need to reflect historically and ask how it is that we have become unable to
"think in terms of the succession of generations." What teaches us
to pose the question in this fashion is precisely European nihilism.
It can make us aware of the nihility within—a nihility, moreover,
that has become *our historical actuality*. And this in turn can bring us
to Nietzsche's "positive nihilism," or so-called "pessimism of
strength." This is the first significance of European nihilism for us.

The essential thing is to overcome our inner void, and here
European nihilism is of critical relevance in that it can impart a radical twist to our present situation and thereby point a way toward
overcoming the spiritual hollowness. This is the second significance
that nihilism holds for us. The reason the void was generated in the
spiritual foundation of the Japanese in the first place was that we
rushed earnestly into westernization and in the process forgot ourselves. When Löwith says that the Japanese adopted western culture indiscriminately, he means both that we adopted it without
realizing that "the Europeans themselves had already ceased to believe in their own culture," and also that we Japanese had lost touch
with ourselves. These are two sides of the same coin.

The reason why the Japanese at the time were not aware of the
extreme anxiety the leading European thinkers were feeling about
themselves and about Europe was that they were not interested in
spiritual depth but only with more or less external matters (such as
politics, economics, military concerns, and so forth) such as might
redound to the strength of the country. The result was an oblivion
of the problem of inner spirtual depth. This was not so much of a
problem as long as the wisdom and spiritual "energy" that had
been cultivated in the tradition still held sway. The high achieve-
ments of Meiji culture which drew on that power represented a zenith in Japanese cultural history. Now we find ourselves in the exact
opposite situation, radically different from that of the Japanese of
the Meiji era. And this is not simply because the war put an abrupt
end to the process of becoming a strong nation. It is rather due to
the fact that the wisdom and moral energy that people in the Meiji
era had inherited from the tradition were no longer there, and that
the Western civilization in which they had innocently believed began to show conspicuous signs of an inner crisis, even to their eyes.

Nietzsche did not succeed in eliciting any response during his
lifetime. He ended up in solitude, shouting in a vacuum as it were.
Toward the end of his life he said: "People will come to understand
me after the coming European war is over." The prophecy proved to

be true. The First World War exposed the profound crisis of Europe, and at the same time Nietzsche's nihilism came to attract more attention than the ideas of any other thinker. Those of our generation learned about this self-criticism of the Europeans, and of their nihilism in particular, at the same time as our own spiritual substance was slipping away from us. European nihilism thus wrought a radical change in our relationship to Europe and to ourselves. It now forces our actual historical existence, our "being ourselves among others," to take a radically new direction. It no longer allows us simply to rush into westernization while forgetting ourselves. Nihilism teaches us, first, to recognize clearly the crisis that stands in the way of Western civilization—and therefore in the way of our westernization—and to take the analysis of the crisis by "the best thinkers in Europe," and their efforts to overcome the modern period, and make them our own concern. This may entail pursuing the present course of westernization to term. Secondly, European nihilism teaches us to return to our forgotten selves and to reflect on the tradition of oriental culture. This tradition has, of course, been lost to us moderns, and is thus something to be rediscovered. There is no turning back to the way things were. What is past is dead and gone, only to be repudiated or subjected to radical criticism. The tradition must be rediscovered from the ultimate point where it is grasped in advance as "the end" (or *eschaton*) of our westernization and of Western civilization itself. Our tradition must be appropriated from the direction in which we are heading, as a new possibility, from beyond Nietzsche's "perspective." Just as European nihilism, the crisis of European civilization, and the overcoming of the modern era become problematic, so must our own tradition. In other words, it cannot be divorced from the problem of overcoming nihilism.

Creative nihilism in Stirner, Nietzsche, Heidegger and others was an attempt to overcome the nihilism of despair. These attempts, conducted at varying depths, were efforts (in Nietzsche's words) "to overcome nihilism by means of nihilism." The tradition of oriental culture in general, and the Buddhist standpoints of "emptiness," "nothingness," and so on in particular, become a new problem when set in this context. Herein lies our orientation toward the future—westernization—and at the same time our orientation toward the past—reconnection with the tradition. The point is to recover the creativity that mediates the past to the future and the future to the past (but *not* to restore a bygone era). The third significance of European nihilism for us is that it makes these things possible.

4. Buddhism and Nihilism

Nihilism in Europe culminated, we said, in a standpoint of "transcendence *to* the world" as "the fundamental integration of creative nihilism and finitude." Taken as a general perspective on the human way of being, this is remarkably close to the standpoint of Buddhism, and in particular to the standpoint of emptiness in the Mahāyāna tradition, if we look at it from the general perspective of the way of being of humankind. Following on Schopenhauer's profound concern with Buddhism, Nietzsche makes constant reference to Buddhist ideas in his discussions of nihilism. He also picked up Schopenhauer's biases and oversights, however, especially regarding the Mahāyāna tradition.[4] As I mentioned earlier, he referred to the most extreme nihilism of "nothing (meaninglessness) eternally" as "the European form of Buddhism," and dubbed the nihilistic catastrophe about to befall Europe "the second Buddhism" (*WP* 55). Furthermore, based on the idea that the sincerity cultivated by Christianity reveals the falseness of Christianity itself, he called the standpoint of "everything is false" a "Buddhism of doing" (*Tat*), and considers such "longing for nothingness" a quasi-Buddhist characteristic (*WP* 1). In Nietzsche's view Buddhism is the culmination of what he calls *décadence:* a complete negation of life and will.

Ironically, it was not in his nihilistic view of Buddhism but in such ideas as *amor fati* and the Dionysian as the overcoming of nihilism that Nietzsche came closest to Buddhism, and especially to Mahāyāna.[5] For example, as mentioned earlier, he spoke of the Dionysian as a "great pantheistic sharing of joy and suffering" and a "feeling of the necessary unity of creation and annihilation" (*WP* 1050). It is beyond the compass of these pages to go into a comparison with Buddhism. What is clear, however, is that there is in Mahāyāna a standpoint that cannot be reached even by nihilism that overcomes nihilism, even though this latter may tend in that direction. For this standpoint:

> By virtue of emptiness everything is able to arise,
> but without emptiness nothing whatsoever can arise.[6]

In other words: everything is possible in a person in whom the nature of emptiness arises. As a master once said to his students, or "followers of the Way":

> he, who at this moment, before my eyes is shining alone and clearly listening to my discourse—this man tarries nowhere;

he traverses the ten directions and is freely himself in the three realms. Though he enters the differentiations of every state, no one of these can divert him. In an instant of time he penetrates the dharmadhatus: on meeting a buddha he persuades the buddha, on meeting a patriarch he persuades the patriarch . . .[7]

For the present this standpoint remains buried in the tradition of the past, far from historical actuality. One way to retrieve it and bring it back to life is, as we have been saying, to grasp in advance the point at which our Europeanization is to culminate, and make European nihilism an urgent problem for ourselves.

Today non-European powers like the United States and the Soviet Union are coming to the fore; in any event, they are the players who have stepped on to the stage of history to open up a new era. But neither "Americanism" nor "communism" is capable of overcoming the nihilism that the best thinkers of Europe confronted with anxiety, the abyss of nihility that opened up in the spiritual depths of the self and the world. For the time being they are managing to keep the abyss covered over, but eventually they will have to face it In this regard, Dostoevsky may be a prophet whose time is coming in the Soviet Union, much as Nietzsche's time is coming in Western Europe. Nietzsche referred to himself as "the spirit of the bird of prophecy," and his sharp cry still echoes in the ears of thinking Europeans. Stefan Zweig, for example, says that Nietzsche's ideas are "deeply decisive for our spiritual world"; and Heidegger calls him the last of the determinative thinkers, the one in whom the history of Western philosophy since Plato turned into a question. Both Dostoevsky and Nietzsche anticipated the nihilism that was to come, and dared to descend to the depths of history and humanity to struggle desperately against it. They can even lead us Japanese to the nihilism lurking in the ground of our historical actuality. But in order for us to take up the struggle, we need our own means. The way to overcome it must be of our own creation. Only then will the spiritual culture of the Orient which has been handed down through the ages be revitalized in a new transformation.

The Problem of Atheism

1. Marxist Humanism

As is commonly known, Marxism looks on religion as a way for those unable to come to terms with the frustrations of life to find satisfaction at the ideal level by imagining a world beyond. In so doing, the argument goes, they nullify the self and transpose the essence of their humanity into the image of "God" in the other world. In this act of religious "self-alienation" both nature and humanity become nonessential, void, and without substance. Atheism consists in the negation of this nonessentiality. By denying God it affirms the essence of the human. This emancipation of the human in turn is of a single root with human freedom.

This variety of atheism is connected with Marx's characterization of the essence of the human individual as *worker:* humanity is achieved by remaking the world through work. The process of self-creation by which one gradually makes oneself human through work is what constitutes history. Seen from such a perspective, atheism is unavoidable. For since the source of religious self-alienation lies in economic self-alienation (the condition of being deprived of one's humanity economically), once the latter is overcome, the former will fall away as a matter of course. According to Marx, then, atheism is a humanism wrought through the negation of religion.

Now insofar as Marx's atheistic humanism is a humanism that has become self-conscious dialectically—its affirmation rests on the negation of religion—it clearly strikes at the very heart of religion. In it we find a clear and pointed expression of the general indifference, if not outright antagonism, to religion in the modern mind. From its very beginning, modern humanism has combined the two facets of maintaining ties to religion and gradually breaking away from it. In a sense, the history of modern philosophy can be read as a struggle among approaches to humanism based on one or the other of these aspects. At present the debate over humanism—what it is that constitutes the essence of the human—has become completely polarized. The responses provided by the various religious traditions show no signs of being able to allay the situation. Questions such as freedom, history, and labor, in the sense in which Marx discusses them in relation to the essence of humanity, paint a picture of the modern individual that had until recently escaped the notice of religion. To come to grips with such questions, religion will have to open up a new horizon.

Even if we grant that Marx's thought touches the problem of religion at some depth, it is hard to sustain the claim that he understood its true foundations correctly. Matters like the meaning of life and death, or the impermanence of all things,[1] simply cannot be reduced without remainder to a matter of economic self-alienation. These are questions of much broader and deeper reach, indeed questions essential for human being.

The problem expressed in the term "all is suffering"[2] is a good example. It is clearly much more than a matter of the socio-historical suffering of human individuals; it belongs essentially to the way of being of all things in the world.[3] The problem of human suffering is a problem of the suffering of the human being as "being-in-the-world," too profound a matter to be alleviated merely by removing socio-historical suffering. It has to do with a basic mode of human being that also serves as the foundation for the pleasure, or the freedom from suffering and pleasure,[4] that we oppose to suffering.

Or again, we might say that the issue of "the non-self nature of all dharmas"[5] refers to "the nonessentiality of nature and humanity," but this does not mean that we can reduce the claim to a self-alienating gesture of projecting the essence of our humanity on to "God." It refers to the essential way that all things in the world *are:* depending on each other and existing only in interdependency. It is meant to point to the essential "non-essentiality" of all beings, and hence to a domain that no society can alter, however far it may progress. It is, in short, the very domain of religion that remains untouched by Marx's critique. Marx argues emphatically that through work human beings conquer nature, change the world, and give the self its human face. But deep in the recesses behind the world of work lies a world whose depth and vastness are beyond our ken, a world in which everything arises only by depending on everything else, in which no single thing exists through the power of a "self" (or what is called "self-power"[6]). This is the world of human beings who exist as "being-in-the-world."

As for religion itself, whose maxim all along has been "all is suffering," the idea that this has to do with "historical" suffering has not often come to the fore. (In this regard, Christianity represents an exception.) The idea of "karma" is supposed to relate concretely to the historicity of human existence, but even this viewpoint has not been forthcoming. The human activities of producing and using various things through "self-power," of changing nature and society and creating a "human" self—in short, the emancipation of the human and the freedom of the human individual—would seem to be the most concrete "karma" of humanity and therefore profoundly connected with modern atheism. But none of these ideas has been forthcoming from the traditional religions. Even though for Christianity the fact that we must labor by the sweat of our brows is related to original sin, the germ of this idea has not, to my knowledge, been developed anywhere in modern theology.

2. Sartrean Existentialism

Modern atheism also appears in the form of existentialism. The same sharp and total opposition that separates existentialism and Marxism in general applies also to their respective forms of atheism. Unlike Marxism, which understands the human being as an essentially social being, existentialism thinks of the human being essentially as an individual; that is, it defines the human as a way of being in which each individual relates to itself. Marx's critique of religion begins from the self-alienation of human beings in religion, redefines it as an economic self-alienation, and then deals with religion in terms of its social functions. In contrast, the existentialist Sartre, for example, understands the relationship between God and humanity as a problem of each individual's relating to the essence of "self"-being itself. In other words, he begins from something like an ontological self-alienation implied in seeing human beings as creatures of God. For all the differences between the standpoints, they share the basic tenet that it is only by denying God that we can regain our own humanity. As is the case with Marx's socialist individual, for Sartre's existentialist individual humanism is viable only as an atheism—which is the force of Sartre's referring to existentialism as a humanism.

According to Sartre, if God existed and had indeed created us, there would be basically no human freedom. If human existence derived from God and the essence of human existence consisted in this derivation, the individual's every action and situation would be determined by this essential fact. In traditional terms, "essential being" precedes "actual being" and continually determines it. This means that the whole of actual human being is essentially contained within the "Providence" of God and is necessarily predetermined by God's will. Such predestination amounts to a radical negation of human freedom. If we grant the existence of God we must admit God's creation; and if we grant God's creation, we must also allow for God's predestination—in other words, we are forced to deny that there is any such thing as human freedom. If human freedom is to be affirmed, the existence of God must be denied.

Human "existence" (a temporal and "phenomenal" way of being) does not have behind it any essential being (a supratemporal and "noumenal" way of being) that would constitute its ground. There is nothing at all at the ground of existence. And it is from this ground of "nothing" where there is simply nothing at all that existence must continually determine itself. We must create ourselves anew ever and again out of nothing. Only in this way can one secure the being of a self—and exist. To be a human being is to humanize the self constantly, to create, indeed to have no choice other than to create, a "human being." This self-being as continued self-creation out of nothing is what Sartre calls freedom. Insofar as one actually creates the self as human, actual *existence* precedes essence in the human being. In essence, the human individual is existence itself. This way of being human is "Existence," and Existence can stand only on an atheism.

Of late we are beginning to see a turn in the standpoint of Heidegger, in that he no longer refers to his thought as an "existentialism."[7] Still, it seems important to point out what his thinking up until now has shared in common with the existentialism of Sartre. That human beings continually create themselves out of nothing is meant to supplant the Christian notion of God's *creatio ex nihilo*. To this extent it is not the standpoint of "self-power" in the ordinary sense. Self-creation out of nothing is not brought about simply by the inner power of a being called *human* and hence is not a power contained within the framework of human *being*. This "being" is continually stepping beyond the framework of "being." Nothingness means transcendence, but since this transcendence does not mean that there is some transcendent "other" apart from self-being, it implies a standpoint of "self-power," not of "other-power." In contrast to Christianity, it is a view in which nothingness becomes the ground of the subject and thereby becomes subjective nothing—a self-power based on nothing. Here the consciousness of freedom in the modern mind finds a powerful expression and amounts to what is, at least in the West, an entirely new standpoint. It seems doubtful that this standpoint can be confronted from within the traditional horizons that have defined Christianity so far. It is quite different with Buddhism.

From the perspective of Buddhism, Sartre's notion of Existence, according to which one must create oneself continually in order to maintain oneself within nothing, remains a standpoint of attachment to the self—indeed, the most profound form of this attachment—and as such is caught in the self-contradiction this implies. It is not simply a question here of a standpoint of ordinary self-love in which the self is willfully attached to itself. It is rather a question of the self being *compelled* to be attached to itself willfully. To step out of the framework of being and into nothing is only to enter into a new framework of being once again. This self-contradiction constitutes a way of being in which the self is its own "prison,"[8] which amounts to a form of karma. Self-creation, or freedom, may be self-aware, but only because, as Sartre himself says, we are "condemned to be free." Such a freedom is not true freedom. Again, it may represent an exhaustive account of what we normally take freedom to be, but this only means that our usual idea of freedom is basically a kind of karma. Karma manifests itself in the way modern men and women ground themselves on an absolute affirmation of their freedom. As Sartre himself says, his standpoint of Existence is a radical carrying out of the *cogito, ergo sum* of Descartes, for the Cartesian *ego* shows us what the modern mode of being is.

That Sartre's "Existence" retains a sense of attachment to the self implies, if we can get behind the idea, that the "nothingness" of which he speaks remains a nothingness to which the self is attached. It was remarked earlier that in existentialism nothingness became subjective nothingness, which means that, as in the case of Greek philosophy or Christianity, it is still bound to the human individual. Again looked at from behind, we find that human subjectivity is bound up inextricably with nothingness and that at the ground of human existence there is nothing, albeit a nothing of which there is still consciousness at the ground of the self. No matter how "pre-reflective" this consciousness is, it is not the point at which the being of the self is transformed existentially into absolute nothingness. Sartre's nothingness is unable to make the being of the self (Existence) sufficiently "ek-static," and to this extent it differs radically from Buddhist "emptiness." The standpoint of emptiness appears when Sartrean Existence is overturned one more time.

The question is whether Buddhism, in its traditional form, is equal to the confrontation with existentialism.

Sartre thinks that to be a human being is to "human-ize" the self continually and to create the self as human out of nothing. Pushing this idea to the extreme, and speaking from the standpoint of emptiness in Buddhism, it is a matter of continually assuming human form from a point where this form has been left behind and absolutely negated. It is, as it were, a matter of continued creative "accommodation," a never-ending "return"[9] to being a new "human." Taken in the context of Buddhist thought as a whole, there is some question as to whether this idea of "accommodation" really carries such an actual and existential sense. Does it really, as Sartre's idea of continual humanization does, have to do with our actual being at each moment?

When Sartre speaks of ceaseless self-creation out of nothing, he refers to an Existence that is temporal through and through. It does not admit of any separate realm of being, such as a supra-temporal (or "eternal") essence, but is simply based on "nothing." But for Sartre Existence is self-created within a socio-historical situation, which demonstrates his profound appreciation of the social and historical dimensions of the human way of being. In the case of the standpoint of Buddhist emptiness, in which human being is understood as arising out of emptiness and existing in emptiness, we need to ask how far the actual Existence of the human being at each moment is included. How much of the Existence within the actual socio-historical situation, and completely temporalized in this actuality, is comprehended? To the extent that the comprehension is inadequate, the standpoint of Buddhism has become detached from our actuality, and that means that we have failed to take the standpoint of emptiness seriously enough and to make it existential. In this case, talk of "accommodation" is merely a kind of mythologizing.

3. Atheism in the World of Today

A crisis is taking place in the contemporary world in a variety of forms, cutting across the realms of culture, ethics, politics, and so forth. At the ground of these problems is that fact that the essence of being human has turned into a question mark for humanity itself. This means that a crisis has also struck in the field of religion, and that this crisis is the root of the problems that have arisen in other areas. We see evidence of this state of affairs in the fact that the most recent trends of thought in contemporary philosophy which are having a great influence—directly and indirectly—on culture, ethics, politics, and so on, are all based on a standpoint of atheism. This applies not only to Marxism and existentialism, especially as represented by Sartre, but also to logical positivism and numerous other currents of thought.

Involved in the problem of the essence of human being are the questions, "What is a human being?" and "By what values should one live?" These are questions that need to be thought through in terms of the totality of beings, the "myriad things" of which human beings are only one part. It is a question, too, of the place of human beings in the order of the totality of beings, and of how to accommodate to this position (that is, how to be truly human). For the order of being implies a ranking of values.

For example, even if "man" is said to be the lord of creation, this places him in a certain "locus"[10] within the totality of things, and therefore refers to how one ought to live as a human being. In the Western tradition the locus of human being has been defined in relation to God. While we are said to have been created from nothing, our soul contains the *imago dei*. This divine image was shattered through original sin, to be restored only through the atonement of God's Son, Jesus, and our faith in him as the Christ. Here the locus of human beings in the order of being and ranking of value takes a different form from the straightforward characterization of man as lord of creation, a form consisting of a complex interplay of negation and affirmation. This locus of human being is well expressed in Augustine's saying: "Oh God, you have created us for you, and our hearts are restless until they rest in you." Needless to say, the basic dynamism behind the forming of this locus came from Greek philosophy and Christianity.

Modern atheism, Marxism, and existentialism share in common the attempt to repudiate this traditional location of the human in order to restore human nature and freedom. The seriousness of this new humanism is that such a restoration is possible only through a denial of God. At the same time, the new humanism harbors a schism in its ranks between the standpoints of Marxism and existentialism. The axis of the existentialist standpoint is a subjectivity in which the self becomes truly itself, while Marxism, for all its talk of human beings as subjects of praxis, does not go beyond a view of the human being as an objective factor in the objective world of nature or society. Each of them comprehends human being from a locus different from the other.

In the Western tradition the objective world and subjective being—the natural and social orders on the one hand, the "soul" with its innate orientation to God on the other—were united within a single system. The two main currents in modern atheism correspond respectively to these two coordinates, the soul and the world, but there is little hope of their uniting given the current confrontation. There is no way for modern men and women simply to return to the old locus, and the new atheism offers only a locus split into two. Confusion reigns in today's world at the most basic level concerning what human beings are and how they are to live.

Each of these two standpoints seeks to ground itself from start to finish in actual being. This is related to the denial of God, in that full engagement of the self in actual being requires a denial of having already been determined within the world-order established by God, as well as a denial of having been fitted out in advance with an orientation to God in one's very soul. Both standpoints stress the importance of not becoming detached from the locus in which one "actually" is, of remaining firmly grounded in one's actual socio-historical situation, or more fundamentally, in actual "time" and "space." But do these standpoints really engage actual being to the full?

Earlier on I suggested that as long as Marxism and existentialism continue to hold to the standpoint of the "human," they will never be able to give a full account of actual human being. These new forms of humanism try to restore human beings to actual being by eliminating from the world and the soul the element of divine "predetermination." The result is that they leave a gaping void at the foundations, as is evidenced by the lack of a locus from which to address the problem of life and death. Since the human mode of being consists in life and death, we must pass beyond the human standpoint to face the problem of life and death squarely. But to overcome the human standpoint does not necessarily mean that one merely returns to the "predetermination" of God, nor that one simply extinguishes freedom or actual being. It is rather a matter of opening up the horizon in which the question can be engaged truly and to its outermost limits.

Earlier I also proposed consideration of the locus of Buddhist "emptiness" in this regard. In the locus of emptiness, beyond the human standpoint, a world of "dependent origination"[11] is opened up in which everything is related to everything else. Seen in this light, there is nothing in the world that arises from "self-power" and yet all "self-powered" workings arise from the world. Existence at each instant, Sartre's self-creation as "human," the humanization in which the self becomes human—all these can be said to arise ceaselessly as new accommodations from a locus of emptiness that absolutely negates the human standpoint. From the standpoint of emptiness, it is at least possible to see the actuality of human being in its socio-historical situation in such a way that one does not take leave of "actual" time and space. In the words of the Zen master Musō:

> When acting apprehend the place of acting, when sitting apprehend the place of sitting, when lying apprehend the place of lying, when seeing and hearing apprehend the place of seeing and hearing, and when experiencing and knowing apprehend the place of experiencing and knowning.[19]

Notes

Introduction

1. The essay "Nietzsches Wort 'Gott ist tot' " was originally published in *Holzwege* in 1950; an English translation by William Lovitt is available in *The Question Concerning Technology* (New York, 1977).

2. A comprehensive account of the beginnings of modern European nihilism is to be found in the Introduction to Dieter Arendt, ed., *Nihilismus: Die Anfänge von Jacobi bis Nietzsche* (Cologne, 1970). See also the articles by Th. Kobusch and W. Müller-Lauter on "Nichts" and "Nihilismus" in J. Ritter and K. Gründer, eds., *Historisches Wörterbuch der Philosophie* (Darmstadt, 1984). A fine discussion of nihilism in the context of German Idealism is Otto Pöggeler, "Hegel und die Anfänge der Nihilismus-Diskussion," *Man and World* 3 (1970). Also helpful are the texts of Karl Löwith already mentioned.

3. "Hegel und die Anfänge der Nihilismus-Diskussion," p. 166. Another passage from Jacobi's letter to Fichte is interesting for the way it anticipates themes from both Stirner and Nietzsche which Nishitani will discuss: "Everything gradually dissolves into its own Nothing. The human being has but a single choice—the only choice: Nothing or a God. In choosing Nothing one makes oneself into God; that is, one makes God a ghost" ("Jacobi an Fichte," in *Werke* III, p. 49). For another helpful discussion of the importance of Jacobi and Hegel in this story, and an illuminating perspective on the topic generally, see Stanley Rosen, *Nihilism* (New Haven and London, 1969), especially chapter three, "History and Nihilism."

4. Karl Löwith, *Kierkegaard und Nietzsche, oder theologische und philosophische Überwindung des Nihilismus* (Frankfurt, 1933). Karl Jaspers devotes the first of his 1935 lectures "Vernunft und Existenz" to a consideration of the "Historical Significance of Kierkegaard and Significance of Kierkegaard and Nietzsche" (*Vernunft und Existenz* [Groningen, 1935], pp. 6–33). Jaspers's idea of *Existenz* appears to have influenced Nishitani's understanding of "Existence" in the present text (see below, the first endnote to chapter one).

5. It is interesting to note that this text of Löwith's was translated into Japanese in 1952, twelve years before it appeared in English. Löwith's

studies of figures and issues from the period between Hegel and Heidegger have always been better appreciated in Japan than in the West, in part, no doubt, because he spent five years there (from 1936 to 1941) as a professor of philosophy at Sendai University. Given the overlap of his interests in the Western philosophical tradition with those of Nishitani, his work was bound to influence the latter's thinking.

6. Much of the material for this essay, "Yōroppa no nihirizumu," comes from the 1943 text "The Historical Background of European Nihilism," reprinted in Karl Löwith, *Nature, History and Existentialism* (Evanston, 1966). Nishitani discusses the appendix to the essay in chapter nine, sec. 2, below.

7. Walter Bröcker, "Nietzsche und der Europäische Nihilismus," *Zeitschrift für Philosophische Forschung* 3 (1948).

8. Ernst Benz, *Westlicher und östlicher Nihilismus* (Stuttgart, 1949).

9. Helmut Thielicke, *Der Nihilismus* (Pfullingen, 1951). It is another indication of the interest in the topic of nihilism in Japan that Thielicke's book was translated into Japanese long before an English translation appeared: *Nihilism: Its Origin and Nature—with a Christian Answer* (New York, 1961).

10. Albert Camus, *The Rebel*, trans. Anthony Bower (New York, 1954). The synoptic view of Stirner and Nietzsche is anticipated by Löwith in *From Hegel to Nietzsche* as well as by Nishitani's treatment (see the discussion of Stirner in chapter six, below).

11. "Watakushi no tetsugakuteki hossokuten" ("My Philosophical Starting Point"), in Tanaka Michitarō, ed., *Kōza: Tetsugaku taikei* (Kyoto, 1963). Jan Van Bragt discusses this piece in an essay entitled "Nishitani on Japanese Religiosity," in Joseph Spae, *Japanese Religiosity* (Tokyo, 1971).

12. "Gendai Nippon no tetsugaku," quoted by Van Bragt on p. xxviii of the Introduction to his translation of Keiji Nishitani, *Religion and Nothingness* (Berkeley and Los Angeles, 1982).

13. *Beyond Good and Evil*, aphorism 6.

14. For the reader unfamiliar with Nishitani's thought there are two introductions available in English. One is Hans Waldenfels's *Absolute Nothingness*, the first part of which provides background in the history of Buddhist thought which is helpful for an understanding of the philosophy of the Kyoto School in general (*Absolute Nothingness: Foundations for a Buddhist-Christian Dialogue*, trans. J. W. Heisig [New York, 1980]). The second part, entitled "Keiji Nishitani and the Philosophy of Emptiness," is a fine exposition of many aspects of Nishitani's thinking (with pertinent references to Heidegger and, to a lesser extent, Nietzsche) which contains

translations of passages from a variety of his works. There is also a comprehensive bibliography which includes most of the English translations of Nishitani's essays.

More valuable, because more direct, is Jan Van Bragt's superb translation of Nishitani's major work, *Religion and Nothingness*. The Translator's Introduction is informative and illuminating, and amplifies Waldenfels's account of Nishitani as a thinker. The original Japanese text of *Religion and Nothingness* was first published in 1961, and in many ways it represents the culmination of certain themes first developed in *The Self-Overcoming of Nihilism*.

15. As translated by Van Bragt in his Introduction, pp. xxxiv–xxxv. Later in this essay Nishitani writes of his enthusiastic reading of Plotinus, Eckhart, Boehme, and the later Schelling. Another autobiographical piece, "The Time of My Youth," mentions the author's avid readings of Tolstoy, Dostoevsky, Ibsen, and Strindberg, as well as of Nietzsche's *Thus Spoke Zarathustra*.

16. See the relevant papers in Graham Parkes, ed., *Nietzsche and Asian Thought* (forthcoming, 1991).

17. The breadth of Nishitani's understanding of the Western philosophical tradition is first made manifest in a long essay from 1939 on Meister Eckhart and Nietzsche's *Zarathustra*. The essay appears as the first section of Nishitani Keiji, *Shūkyō to bunka (Religion and Culture)* (Tokyo, 1940).

18. Stanley Rosen's *Nihilism* is an engaging exception to this general rule.

19. Watsuji Tetsurō, *Niichie kenkyū* (Tokyo, 1913); Abe Jirō, *Niichie no Zarathustra* (Tokyo, 1918).

20. See the first chapter of Nishitani's study *Nishida Kitarō*, an English translation of which by Yamamoto Seisaku and James Heisig has just been completed.

21. Tanabe Hajime, *Philosophy as Metanoetics*, trans. Takeuchi Yoshinori et al. (Berkeley and Los Angeles, 1986), chapter 3, "Absolute Critique and History."

22. A detailed discussion of some of these parallels is to be found in Okōchi Ryōgi, "Nietzsches *Amor Fati* im Lichte des Karma des Buddhismus," in *Nietzsche-Studien* 1 (1972).

23. See below, chapter four, sec. 4. For a discussion of the idea of eternal recurrence from the perspective of the "moment," see Graham Parkes, "Nietzsche and Nishitani on the Self through Time," *The Eastern Buddhist* 17/2 (1984).

24. The two years (1936–38) Nishitani spent in Freiburg studying with Heidegger made a great impression on him, and he speaks to this day of Heidegger's charisma in the lecture hall and seminar room.

25. It is interesting to note the change in Nishitani's attitude toward Nietzsche that has taken place by the time he writes *Religion and Nothingness*, where Nietzsche's achievement is seen to fall considerably short of the insights of Buddhism. Since a major ground for this evaluation is Nietzsche's purported hypostatization of the will to power, it looks as if Heidegger's reading might after all have exerted a delayed influence on Nishitani's understanding of Nietzsche.

26. This was the chapter the author most wanted to revise and expand in the light of Heidegger's later writings on nihilism, but he realized that an adequate treatment would require a whole new book.

27. In spite of the reviewer's expressed admiration for Heidegger as "a thinker of real importance," Ryle's concluding reservation to the effect that he had "fallen [far] short of understanding this difficult work" is, unfortunately, well taken. He approaches the book from a narrow historical perspective and an inadequate understanding of the project of phenomenology as carried out by Husserl, as well as a lack of appreciation for the complex architechtonic that informs *Being and Time*. In focusing too much on what he denigrates as "the countless 'nursery' terms which Heidegger is trying to build up into a new philosophical vocabulary," Ryle fails to appreciate the features of the book that are truly revolutionary. One suspects that the appearance of this review allowed a number of people in the Anglophone philosophical community to breathe deep sighs at being relieved of the obligation to tackle such a difficult and initially unrewarding text themselves.

28. Carnap's sterile misreading of some paragraphs from Heidegger's *What is Metaphysics?* purports to nullify Heidegger's entire enterprise—as well as that of Hegel, author of the monumental *Wissenschaft der Logik*—by showing that these so-called metaphysicians were simply incapable of understanding the syntax of terms such as *"das Nichts."*

29. The only treatment of this topic in English so far is Yuasa Yasuo, "Modern Japanese Philosophy and Heidegger," in Graham Parkes, ed., *Heidegger and Asian Thought* (Honolulu, 1987).

30. See the references in Hans-Martin Sass, *Heidegger-Bibliographie* (Meisenheim/Glan, 1968).

31. Again, a look at the list of translations of Heidegger's works in the Sass bibliography shows that all Heidegger's major works were translated into Japanese, usually before any English translation appeared; and even today the Japanese lead the field in the enterprise of translating the volumes of the new Heidegger *Gesamtausgabe* as they appear.

32. While working on the translation of the Stirner chapter, I was intrigued to come across special tables in bookstores in Tokyo with promi-

nent displays of a new Japanese translation of *The Unique One and Its Own* in a handsome two-volume set.

33. Nishitani also points out more ideas in Nietzsche that are antici-pated by Stirner, and suggests grounds for their genesis, than any Anglo-phone commentator had done at that time. To enumerate them briefly, they are: the ideas of creative nothingness and the relativity of good and evil (chapter 6, section 3, below); the dialectical emergence of nihilism from the Christian virtue of "sincerity" (sec. 5); the notion of power *(Macht)* and the relations between the wills to truth and to deception (sec. 7); and the con-ception of the I *(Ich)* as self-dissolving and ultimately unnameable (sec. 8).

34. Kōsaka Masaaki, Nishitani Keiji, Kōyama Iwao, Suzuki Shigetaka, *Sekaishiteki tachiba to Nihon* (Tokyo, 1943).

35. I have dealt with this question, which is too complex to go into here, in a forthcoming essay entitled "Nihilism and Nationalism: Prescrip-tions for Recovering from One without Contracting the Other."

36. Among recent studies in this genre are: Thomas L. Pangle, "The Roots of Contemporary Nihilism and its Political Consequences according to Nietzsche," *The Review of Politics* 45 (1983); Robert Eden, *Political Leader-ship and Nihilism: A Study of Weber and Nietzsche* (Tampa, 1983); Peter Berg-mann, *Nietzsche, "the Last Antipolitical German"* (Bloomington, 1987); and Mark Warren, *Nietzsche and Political Thought* (Cambridge MA and London, 1988). And while Allan Bloom may be less sensitive to the positive aspects of Nietzsche's response to nihilism than is Nishitani, he has at least brought the issue to the attention of a wider audience by devoting the ma-jor part of *The Closing of the American Mind* to the topic of "Nihilism, Amer-ican Style."

37. *Religion and Nothingness*, pp. 50–52.

Preface

1. In the author's Preface to the 1966 Edition, which has been omit-ted here, Nishitani mentions that he would like to have revised the chapter in *Nihirizumu* on Heidegger in the light of the lectures on nihilism which Heidegger published after *Nihirizumu* was written—namely, "Nietzsches Wort 'Gott ist tot'," in *Holzwege* (1950); *Was Heisst Denken?* (1954); "Überwindung der Metaphysik" and "Wer ist Nietzsches Zarathustra?," in *Vorträge und Aufsätze* (1954); *Zur Seinsfrage* (1946); and *Nietzsche* (1961).

2. Nietzsche himself would have approved of this conjunction: in *Twilight of the Idols* he writes of Dostoevsky as "the only psychologist from whom I had something to learn: he counts among the most beautiful

strokes of fortune in my life, even more so than my discovery of Stendhal" ("Skirmishes of an Untimely Man" 45).

3. *Kū* is the traditional translation of the Sanskrit Buddhist term *śūnyatā;* it is translated uniformly as "emptiness." The character originally connotes the openness of the empty sky or heavens. Of the many words in this text which refer to various kinds of nothingness, *kū* carries the most "positive" connotation. Nishitani elaborates his central idea of "the standpoint of emptiness" *(kū no tachiba)* in *Religion and Nothingness.* For a discussion of *kū* and the numerous other words and compounds Nishitani uses in connection with the notion of nothing, see Hans Waldenfels, *Absolute Nothingness,* chapter 6.

4. Nicholas Berdyaev, *Dostoevsky,* chapter 2, "Man."

5. The idea of exploring the overlap between Buddhist ideas and the thought of the European nihilists philosophically was ahead of its time when Nishitani first raised it in this book forty years ago. In an important sense it sets the agenda for Nishitani's thinking during the subsequent decade or so, culminating in the publication of *Religion and Nothingness* in 1961. The only major work on this topic in a western language, as far as I know, is Freny Mistry's *Nietzsche and Buddhism* (New York and Berlin, 1981). Mistry offers a comprehensive account of Nietzsche's (rather limited) acquaintance with Buddhism and an illuminating comparison of his ideas with those of early (Hīnayāna and Theravāda) Buddhism.

6. The word "standpoint' *(tachiba)* occurs in this text more than any other technical term, so often in fact that "view" or "perspective" has occasionally been substituted. As the alert reader will observe, however, Nishitani's use of spatial metaphors has its own philosophical import, and I have therefore tried to retain the term "standpoint" as often as is feasible.

Chapter One

1. *Jitsuzon*—a key (and, to some extent, "technical") term in Nishitani's text. He sometimes adds the German *Existenz* in parentheses, suggesting an allusion to the idea developed by Karl Jaspers. In what follows, *jitsuzon* will be translated "Existence," with the upper-case "E" marking the special nature of the term, in the expectation that its meanings will become clear as the discussion unfolds. Since the Japanese translation of "existentialism" is *jitsuzonshugi,* it will not be misleading if the special marking of the term connotes "existence" as generally understood in existential philosophy.

2. Nishitani's frequent use of the idiom "to become a question mark" *(gimonfu to naru)* is surely an allusion to Nietzsche's references to the self as a question and a problem (see, for example, BGE 1, 235). His expres-

sion "to become an X" (*X to naru*) recalls Kant's use of the "unknown object = X" to refer to the "thing-in-itself" in the *Critique of Pure Reason*.

"Nihility"—*kyomu*. *Kyomu* is one of the various "grades" or aspects of "nothing" as Nishitani has developed it. The translation of "nihility" follows the precedent set by Jan Van Bragt in his translation of *Shūkyō towa nani ka*. It means literally "hollow *[kyo]* nothingness *[mu]*," generally with a negative connotation. Only when confronted and realized in oneself does this void open up into "absolute nothing" *(zettai mu)*, or "emptiness' *(kū)*. The experience of this transformation, to be discussed in detail in what follows, corresponds to the transition from passive or negative nihilism to active or affirmative nihilism.

3. *Gensonzai*—the usual Japanese rendering of the term *Dasein* in Heidegger's *Being and Time*. Nishitani clearly has this allusion in mind when he uses the word, but until we reach the explicit discussions of Heidegger it seems best to render it more literally as "actual existence."

4. The "final destination" is chapter nine in the present translation, "The Meaning of Nihilism for Japan," which was the last chapter of the book as it was originally published. The final position gave the chapter a prominence it rightfully deserves, and which should not be overlooked in this edition.

5. *Kūkyo*. This term combines the emptiness of *kū* with the hollowness of *kyo*.

6. Nishitani's use of "world" in quotation marks here is no doubt an allusion to Heidegger's description of the way in which the "nothing of the world" *(das Nichts der Welt)* obtrudes upon us in the experience of *Angst (Being and Time*, §68b). Indeed the whole passage here is reminiscent of Heidegger's accounts of the experience of anxiety in both *Being and Time* and *What Is Metaphysics?*. See the discussion of Heidegger below, in chapter seven.

7. *Tsuitaiken suru*—presumably an allusion to the notion of historical *Verstehen* as elaborated by Wilhelm Dilthey, which exerted a considerable influence on the thinking of the Heidegger of *Being and Time*.

8. *Mappō*—the degeneration of the Buddhist dharma, or law. There were thought to be three stages of the degeneration of the dharma after the death of Śākyamuni Buddha: the periods of the "true law" *(shōbō)*, "imitation law" *(zōhō)*, and "final law" or "ending dharma" *(mappō)*. It was believed that the first two would last for a thousand years each, or for five hundred and a thousand years respectively, and the final period of degeneration for ten thousand years. Toward the end of the Heian period, just prior to the Kamakura period, the idea emerged that the *mappō* would begin in 1052 C.E. rather than in the sixth century as the Chinese had thought. The idea was reinforced by the increasing prevalence in Japan of internecine strife and natural disasters as the date drew nearer.

For detailed discussions of the idea of *mappō*, see the references to "Final Law" and "Final Age" in Delmer M. Brown and Ichirō Ishida (trans. and eds.), *The Future and the Past: A Translation and Study of the Gukanshō, An Interpretive History of Japan Written in 1219* (Berkeley and London, 1979); and also the references to *mappō* in Daigan and Alicia Matsunaga, *Foundation of Japanese Buddhism*, vol. 2 (Los Angeles and Tokyo, 1976).

9. Karl Jaspers, *Psychologie der Weltanschauungen* (Berlin, 1919). A major section of the third chapter deals with the issue of nihilism.

10. Two helpful accounts of the emergence of the philosophy of history and of its connection with nihilism are to be found in Karl Löwith, *From Hegel to Nietzsche*, and in Stanley Rosen, *Nihilism*, especially chapter three.

11. *Mu*—a key word in Japanese Buddhism for "nothing," also used to translate the Sanskrit *śūnyatā*. It is rendered here either as "Nothing" or, when ambiguities would result from that term, as "nothingness."

Chapter Two

1. From the *Vorrede* to the *Grundlinien der Philosophie des Rechts;* see *Hegel's Philosophy of Right*, trans. T. M. Knox (Oxford, 1952), pp. 10, 12.

2. Nishitani adds *realisieren* in parentheses here to encourage the play on the ambiguity of the term "realize"—between the senses of "become aware of" and "make real."

3. The Japanese term Nishitani uses here is the standard translation of Hegel's notoriously untranslatable term *aufheben*. In Hegel's usage, the German term connotes *negating* a thing in its limited individuality, *preserving* it in its essential being, and *raising* it *up* to a higher level of reality.

4. The verb translated "collapse" here, *botsuraku suru*, can also refer to the decline of a dynasty or a family, a connotation we bring out by rendering the term by "decline" in the following sentence. The Japanese term is a more felicitous translation of the German *zu Grunde gehen* (literally: to go to ground) than can be found in English. (It is also the verb generally used in Japanese translations of Nietzsche's *Zarathustra* to render the idea of *untergehen*, "to go under, perish.")

5. *Parerga and Paralipomena* I, "Sketch of a History of the Doctrine of the Ideal and the Real." Translations of the quotations from this text are based on the original texts in Schopenhauer, *Sämtliche Werke* (Stuttgart/Frankfurt, 1960) vols. IV and V. The work is available in an English translation by E. F. J. Payne (Oxford, 1974) in two volumes.

6. The quotations are taken from the Appendix to the first essay in *Parerga and Paralipomena*. In speaking of Fichte's having "eliminated" the real entirely, Schopenhauer uses the Hegelian term *aufheben*. With reference to Hegel's philosophy as "the nadir," Nishitani has in fact softened Schopenhauer's language, which speaks of "the spiritless and tasteless charlatan Hegel."

7. Nishitani is using—as the majority of Japanese scholars have done—a German translation of Kierkegaard's works, *Werke* (Jena, 1922–29), which accounts for his occasional insertion of German terms in parentheses when discussing Kierkegaard. In translating the author's Japanese translations of this German translation, I have "triangulated," as it were between the German text and the English translations that have appeared in the definitive edition, *Kierkegaard's Writings*, under the general editorship of Howard V. Hong (Princeton University Press). References to this edition will be abbreviated as *KW* followed by the numbers of volume and page.

8. *Kierkegaard's Concluding Unscientific Postscript*, trans. David F. Swenson and Walter Lowrie (Princeton, 1941), p. 376.

9. This is the central idea in Kierkegaard's *Fear and Trembling* (published two years earlier than the *Postscript*, in 1844), as developed in "Problema I"; see *Kierkegaard's Writings* VI, pp. 62, 70, 81. In this work Kierkegaard develops a reading of the story of Abraham and Isaac which understands Abraham's faith as lifting him as a "single individual" higher than "the universal" (the level of the ethical) and putting him, paradoxically, in an "absolute relation to the absolute" (that is, to God—whom Johannes de Silentio, the pseudonymous author of this text, understands as being "that all things are possible"). It is an interesting coincidence that this text, with its emphasis on "the single individual," was written at the same time as the greatest apotheosis of the "unique individual" *(der Einzige)*, Max Stirner's *The Ego and his Own* (see below, chapter six).

10. "Rotation of Crops: A Venture in a Theory of Social Prudence," the penultimate section of Volume I of *Either/Or*, which contains the papers of the young aesthete named "A" and was published in 1843; see *Either/Or*, I, ed. and trans. Howard V. Hong and Edna H. Hong (Princeton, 1987).

11. This and the following four brief quotations are from Kierkegaard's *Concluding Unscientific Postscript*, pp. 377–78.

12. The *locus classicus* for Kierkegaard's ideas about irony is *The Concept of Irony: With Constant Reference to Socrates*, trans. Lee M. Capel (New York, 1965). The book, published in 1841, was Kierkegaard's academic dissertation and is as much an *Auseinandersetzung* with Hegel as with Socrates (see, especially, the section in Part Two entitled "The World-Historical Validity of Irony").

13. *The Concept of Anxiety*, ed. and trans. Reidar Thomte (Princeton, 1980), p. 61. Although these two sentences are set within quotation marks, Nishitani's rendering of the last part of the first sentence is actually a para-

phrase of the German text. Kierkegaard's elaboration of the phenomenon of *Angest* anticipates Heidegger's treatment of *Angst* as a crucial notion in *Being and Time* to such an extent that the latter's cursory acknowledgement (*SZ* 190) of Kierkegaard's ideas in *The Concept of Anxiety* is strikingly inadequate. Nishitani discusses Heidegger's notion of *Angst* below, in chapter seven, sec. 4.

14. See *The Concept of Anxiety*, pp. 74–80. To link the word *Schuld* with "indebtedness," as Nishitani does here, may perhaps be more appropriate to Heidegger's use of the term in *Being and Time* than to Kierkegaard's in this text.

15. "If . . . time and eternity touch each other, then it must be in time, and now we have come to the moment [*Øiblikket*]. . . . A blink [of the eye: *Øiets Blik*] is a designation of . . . time in the fateful conflict when it is touched by eternity (*The Concept of Anxiety*, p. 87). And again: "Only with the moment does history begin. . . . The moment is that ambiguity in which time and eternity touch each other, and with this the concept of *temporality* is posited, whereby time constantly intersects eternity and eternity constantly pervades time" (p. 89). It is a taxing but rewarding study to compare Kierkegaard's notion of the moment (*Øiblikket*) with Nietzsche's idea of the moment (*Augenblick*) as the crucial point of the eternal recurrence—and both with Heidegger's characterization of the *Augenblick* in *Being and Time* (see, especially, *SZ* 328–50). Nishitani discusses the eternal recurrence below (chapter four, secs. 4–6), and in *Religion and Nothingness*, pp. 211–37, where he also briefly touches again upon the notion of the moment in Kierkegaard (p. 161).

16. *The Concept of Anxiety*, p. 88. This "paradoxical dialectics" which Nishitani finds in Kierkegaard, in which despair itself—as long as one lets oneself sink down into it totally—turns out to be "the medium for redemption," is the paradigm for his understanding of nihilism in general, and as elaborated by Nietzsche in particular. The idea is that one can overcome nihilism properly only by *experiencing* (literally: "going through") it to the utmost.

17. Compare the remark from Kierkegaard's *Repetition*, which he footnotes twice in *The Concept of Anxiety* (pp. 18 and 151), to the effect that "eternity . . . is the true repetition."

18. Ludwig Feuerbach, *Grundsätze einer Philosophie der Zukunft*, in *Gesammelte Werke* (Berlin, 1970), §30; English translation by Manfred Vogel, *Principles of the Philosophy of the Future* (Indianapolis, 1986).

19. Ludwig Feuerbach, *Lectures on the Essence of Religion*, trans. Ralph Manheim (New York, 1967), lecture 22. The ideas from Feuerbach Nishitani discusses in the next several paragraphs are developed in a number of the *Lectures*, which date from 1849, after the publication of the two revolutionary works *The Essence of Christianity* and *The Essence of Religion*. Feuer-

bach's penetrating analysis of the roles played by human desire and phantasy in the development of religion anticipate—especially in these later formulations—many of both Nietzsche's and Freud's ideas on the topic; indeed, many of the similarities are so striking that one begins to feel that Nietzsche in particular ought to have acknowledged Feuerbach's insights explicitly.

20. Nishitani is referring here to Feuerbach's idea that sensation—or sensuousness *(Sinnlichkeit)*—is the primordial and most important human faculty. Löwith paraphrases a passage from one of Feuerbach's letters on the topic as follows: "ideas should not remain above the sensuous in the realm of the universal, but should descend from the 'heaven of their colorless purity' and 'unity with themselves' to observable particularity, in order to incorporate themselves in the definiteness of phenomena" (*From Hegel to Nietzsche*, p. 72). Feuerbach's emphasis on the senses as our primary access to the real (see the *Grundsätze*, §§25 and 32) is accompanied by a corresponding emphasis on the body *(Leib)* which anticipates Nietzsche's emphasis and also constitutes a major theme of Nishitani's text: "the new philosophy begins with the proposition: *I am an actual, a sensuous being: the body belongs to my essential being; in fact the body in its totality is my I, my very essence*" (§36). See Nishitani's discussion of Nietzsche's understanding of the body as the true "Self" in *Zarathustra* chapter five, sec. 10.

21. This passage appears to be a selective paraphrase of parts of Karl Marx and Friedrich Engels, *Die Deutsche Ideologie*, chapter I (entitled "Feuerbach"), part B, sec. 3. The Japanese translation of this text from which Nishitani is quoting here is by Miki Kiyoshi, an important figure in twentieth-century Japanese philosophy. While Miki's translations are renowned for being "free," they are backed up by an intelligent philosophy of translation adumbrated in an essay from 1931 entitled "Disparaging Translations" in which Miki argues for a greater fidelity to the philosopher's thought than to literal accuracy of style. The quotation from *The German Ideology* which follows is a rather accurate translation of a paragraph from part A, sec. 2 of the same chapter on Feuerbach.

Chapter Three

1. Nietzsche does not mention nihilism in any published work before 1886, when the term appears in *Beyond Good and Evil* (aph. 10). Most of his remarks on the phenomenon are to be found in the unpublished notes from the years 1886–89. A helpful discussion of the various meanings and uses of the term in Nietzsche is to be found in Alan White, "Nietzschean Nihilism: A Typology," *International Studies in Philosophy* 19/2 (1987).

2. For an English translation of the selections from Nietzsche's notebooks from the years 1883 to 1888, see the edition by Walter Kaufmann, *The*

Will to Power, trans. Walter Kaufmann and R. J. Hollingdale (New York, 1968). Kaufmann's Introduction and notes "On the Editions of The Will to Power" (pp. xiii–xix) provide helpful background on the nature and history of this unusual text. The notes that constitute this "Preface" date from winter/spring 1887–88.

3. *The Will to Power*, Preface sec. 3. With respect to the term *Versucher-Geist* Nishitani is sensitive to Nietzsche's fondness for playing on the verb *versuchen* and its cognates. *Versuchen* means to try, to attempt; but a *Versucher* is a tempter, or seducer; while the noun *Versuch* often connotes scientific research or experiment—this last being a theme that is especially developed in the present chapter.

4. A powerful statement of Nietzsche's idea of "tackling things experimentally [*versuchsweise*]" is to be found in aphorism 432 of *Dawn*, which is entitled "Researchers and Experimenters." In *GS* 324 Nietzsche speaks of "the thought that life must be an experiment of the one who seeks knowledge" as "the great liberator." One of Nietzsche's fullest and richest statements of what it means "to experience the history of humanity as one's own history" is to be found in *GS* 337.

5. The first and most famous formulation of the idea of the "death of God" is put into the mouth of "the madman" in *The Gay Science*, aphorism 125. It is surprising that Nishitani never discusses this passage, which is one of Nietzsche's best known in the English speaking world.

6. Nishitani is referring to what are actually numbered sections 2, 3 and 4 in *The Will to Power*.

7. See *WP* 13, 15.

8. In this instance I have followed Nietzsche's *"Nichts" (nothingness)* rather than Nishitani's *kyomu*, which is otherwise rendered as "nihility."

9. See also *WP* 765 and *AC* 42, 62.

10. See *WP* 339, 345; *BGE* 62.

11. In *Twilight of the Idols* Nietzsche excoriates what he calls "Rousseau-ean morality" in these unequivocal terms: "The doctrine of equality! There is no poison more poisonous: for it *seems* to be advocated by justice itself, whereas it is the *end of justice*. . . . 'To equals give what is equal, to unequals what is unequal—*that would be the true speech of justice:* and, what follows that, never make what is unequal equal' " ("Skirmishes of an Untimely Man," 48).

12. See *BGE* 260; *GM* I, 10 and 11.

13. *The Antichrist* 7. The image of the Hyperboreans is introduced in the first aphorism of *The Antichrist*, and also appears much earlier in *Human, All-Too-Human*, "The Wanderer and His Shadow," 265.

14. Nishitani uses several Japanese expressions here which play on the literal meaning of the German *auslegen*, "to interpret," which is "to lay out." The idea is that Nietzsche's experience of nihilism led naturally to his expressing his understanding of it by "laying it out." This is something that Nishitani himself experienced personally: in "My Philosophical Starting Point" he speaks of his early encounter with nihilism as being "pre-philosophical" but as including essentially a move to a philosophical dimension. In an early aphorism entitled "Quiet Fruitfulness," Nietzsche writes: "Born aristocrats of the spirit are not over-zealous; their creations appear and fall from the tree on a quiet autumn evening unprecipated, without being pushed aside by something new" (*MA* I, 210). He then adds a sentence whose Taoist overtones would surely appeal to Nishitani: "If one is something, one doesn't really need to do anything—and yet does a great deal."

15. The verb rendered here as "expressed" is *hakidasu*, which also means "to spit out," or "to vomit forth." Nishitani may have in mind the episode in "On the Vision and the Enigma" from *Thus Spoke Zarathustra* (discussed below, at the end of chapter four) in which the young shepherd who is a "mask" of Zarathustra (who is a mask of Nietzsche) bites off the head of the black snake of passive nihilism and "spits it forth" (*Za* III, 2).

16. *Kyomō*—in which the hollowness of the *kyo* of *kyomu* is combined with the character *mō* which connotes falsehood and delusion.

Chapter Four

1. *Kyoka*—a rather unusual word combining the *kyo*, or "hollowness," of *kyomu* with *ka*, meaning "temporary." A number of compounds using the character *kyo* appear in the first page or two of this chapter, all of which may be heard to resonate with the *kyomu*, the "nihil," of "nihilism."

2. *WP* 585A. One gains a better understanding of Nishitani's interest in this theme of Nietzsche's if one understands the creative force in a non-individualistic way as the impotence of the personal will to create. This note begins: "Tremendous *self-reflection:* to become conscious of oneself not as an individual but as humanity. *Let us reflect, let us think back: let us take the small and the great paths.*" (See also note 4, below.)

3. See also *WP* 798. Although Nishitani quotes a passage from the *Nachlass* here, the *locus classicus* for the interplay between the powers of Apollo and Dionysus is, of course, *The Birth of Tragedy*.

4. *WP* 617. The idea of creation is again presented as non-individualistic in being linked with self-negation, self-overcoming, and the non-existence of the subject.

5. See *Meister Eckhart, Sermons and Treatises*, trans. and ed. M. O'C. Walshe (Shaftesbury, Dorset, 1987), vol. 1, sermon 16.

6. This is a common dictum in Zen, referring to the "just-as-it-is-ness" or "suchness" of things as they are.

7. *Hōen Zenshi goroku*, T. XLVII, no. 1995, p. 658b21.

8. *WP* 586A. Nietzsche uses the Hegelian term *aufheben* to characterize the way in which the conception of an other world "annuls" necessity and fate. In fact the new critical edition of the *Nachlass* has *das Faktum* instead of *das Fatum*—which would anticipate Heidegger's idea of "facticity" in asserting the factical nature of all becoming. In any case, Nishitani's argument does not depend on reading "fate" instead of "fact."

9. *WP* 1005. Nishitani emphasizes the phrase "being-able-to-be-different" in his translation, though it is not emphasized in the original. The central importance of the idea of "difference" in Nietzsche has come to be appreciated in the West only in the last decade or two, with the work of Gilles Deleuze, Jacques Derrida, and other contemporary French philosophers. The "God" referred to in this passage is—as is made clear by the first part—Dionysus.

10. "Dieser . . . *lähmendste* Glaube"—while Nishitani translates this by a word which means "anesthetizing" I have chosen "crippling" so that the phrase will resonate with Nietzsche's referring later to the eternal recurrence as "the most crippling thought" *(der lähmendste Gedanke)*.

11. It is interesting that Nishitani appears to have reversed his position on this issue by the time he wrote *Religion and Nothingness*. See pp. 215–16, where the "moment" in relation to eternal recurrence "cannot signify the point where something truly new can take place." For a detailed discussion of Nietzsche's idea of *amor fati* in relation to the Buddhist notion of *karma*, see Ōkōchi Ryōgi, "Nietzsches *Amor Fati* in Lichte des Karma des Buddhismus," *Nietzsche-Studien* 1 (1972). The idea of the interconnectedness of all things is common to many forms of Buddhism.

12. In case Nishitani's use of the term "ego" in this discussion should invite an overly individualistic interpretation of his reading of this theme in Nietzsche, one should bear in mind that the context is Nietzsche's paradoxical equation of *ego* with *fatum*. Also, will to power is far from being anything like "will power": it is precisely because it is an interpretive force on a cosmic scale—not confined to human beings—that the self can "turn the necessity of the world into its own will."

13. See also *WP* 1041. It is surprising that Nishitani does not adduce the first aphorism of Book Four of *The Gay Science* in his discussions of *amor fati* (especially since he quotes the poem that stands as the epigraph to the Book; see chapter five, note 15). It contains one of Nietzsche's most beautiful evocations of the idea, and harmonizes perfectly with the passages

Nishitani quotes from the *Nachlass*. The aphorism is entitled "For the New Year," and in it Nietzsche speaks of the first thought to "run across [his] heart" that year:

> I want more and more to learn to see what is necessary in things as being beautiful: in this way I become one of those who make things beautiful. Amor fati: that will be my love from now on! I do not want to wage any kind of war against what is ugly. I do not want to accuse, I do not want to accuse even the accusers. *Looking away* shall be my only negating! And, all in all and on the whole: I want some day to be only a Yes-sayer! (*GS* 276)

14. *Nietzsche contra Wagner,* Epilogue, sections 1 and 2. Much of this passage is Nietzsche's quotation from sections 3 and 4 of the Prologue to *The Gay Science.*

15. Nishitani's amplification of this image touches on an important point of contact between Nietzsche and Zen. When one's inner creativity is able to burst through the overlay of conventional values and conceptualizations, the resultant condition is not one of pristine purity but rather one in which the pool of the psyche is still polluted by debris from the barriers that have been breached. The point is that such debris need not be rejected, but may rather be used in the reconstruction of the "new" self. Compare the first section of Nietzsche's third *Untimely Meditation,* "Schopenhauer as Educator," in which he speaks of how "it is an excruciatingly dangerous undertaking to dig into oneself and to force one's way down into the shaft of one's being . . . Culture [*Bildung*] is liberation, the removal of all the weeds, debris and vermin that want to attack the tender buds of the plants, a streaming forth of light and warmth, a gentle swishing of nocturnal rain . . ."

16. *Zarathustra* III, 14; cf. also I, 22, §1 and III, 12, §30, where Zarathustra addresses his *will* as *Wende der Not*. Nietzsche exploits the ambiguity of the German *Not*, which embraces a range of meanings between "need"—in the sense of "want" or "lack"—and "necessity," and he coins the phrase *Wende der Not* ("turn of need") to play it off against *Notwendigkeit,* meaning "necessity." Nishitani is the first commentator, as far as I know, to explicate the implications of this play in Nietzsche's text. It takes some effort since the word he uses for *Not* is *konkyū,* which connotes only "basic want" and not "necessity." The results seems to me to be not only hermeneutically but also psychologically enlightening.

17. I have chosen this rather archaic word as a compromise to convey the senses of encircling and enveloping and wrapping which Nietzsche's *Umfang* and Nishitani's *hōkatsu* connote.

18. Nishitani is bringing into relief here an important aspect of the idea of the soul in *Zarathustra* which has been for the most part overlooked.

As early as the Prologue Zarathustra speaks of his love for "him whose soul is overfull, so that he forgets himself, and all things are in him: thus all things become his perishing [*Untergang*]" (sec. 4). A fuller discussion of this theme can be found in Graham Parkes, "The Overflowing Soul: Images of Transformation in Nietzsche's *Zarathustra*," *Man and World* 16/3 (1983).

19. *Zarathustra* IV, 19. In the new critical edition of Nietzsche's *Werke* this song is entitled "The Night-Wanderer Song" (*Das Nachtwandler-Lied*).

20. *Ecce homo* III, "Thus Spoke Zarathustra" 1.

21. There is actually no mention of the "spirit of melancholy" in this section of *Zarathustra*, but only of the "spirit of gravity" (*Geist der Schwere*); the two are, nevertheless, linked by their common heaviness (*Schwere*). The spirit of melancholy does not appear until "The Song of Melancholy," which is sung by the Magician in Part IV.

22. Nishitani's text has "the spirit of resistance" (*hankō no sei*)— but there is no such idea in this speech or elsewhere in the text. It is presumably a misreading of the first phrase of the speech, "Dem Geist zum Trotz"—"in defiance of the spirit."

23. Cf. *Za* I, 7 and II, 16, §7.

24. *Dionysus Dithyrambs*, "Amid Birds of Prey." This unparalleled paean to the abyss contains several images that figure in Nishitani's text: it addresses Zarathustra as "bored into yourself" (*in dich selber eingebohrt*) and as "laboring bowed in your own mine-shaft, self-excavated, digging into yourself" (*im eignen Schachte/gebückt arbeitend,/in dich selber eingehöhlt,/dich selber angrabend*). An English translation of this collection of poems appears in R. J. Hollingdale, *Nietzsche: Dithyrambs of Dionysus* (Redding Ridge, 1984). Most of the poems were written in 1888, but the collection was not published until 1891, when it was issued with the first public printing of Part IV of *Zarathustra*. Much of the imagery in these poems is relevant to Nishitani's discussion, and especially the latter half of "Fame and Eternity" (*Ruhm und Ewigkeit*) which concerns *amor fati*.

25. The opposition between courage and melancholy is more significant in German—especially since Nietzsche can associate the latter (*Schwermut*) with the spirit of gravity (*Schwere*).

26. Nishitani develops this theme of the "moment" as the opening out into the horizons of past and future in *Religion and Nothingness*. For a discussion of Nishitani's engagement with this theme in Nietzsche, see Graham Parkes, "Nietzsche and Nishitani on the Self through Time," *The Eastern Buddhist* 17/2 (1984).

27. Nishitani's rendering speaks of the "ring" rather of the "wheel" of Being, and of the "annual ring" of Being (as of a tree) rather than the "year" of Being. This repeated emphasis on the "ring"-like aspect of eternal recurrence is salutary; too many interpretations understand the idea as referring to a *circle* of time. Nishitani's language concerning cyclical accu-

mulation puts into relief the important third dimension of Nietzsche's image of the ring. Compare Jacques Derrida's comment on Nietzsche's speaking of his birthday in the "exergue" to *Ecce homo:* "The anniversary is the moment when the year turns back on itself, forms a ring or annulus with itself, annuls itself and begins anew" (*The Ear of the Other* [New York, 1985], p. 11).

28. Augustine, *Confessions* Book XI, chapter 77; the rest of Book XI develops the relationship between time and eternity.

29. XII 67. The German text reads "your . . ." rather than "this eternal life . . ."

30. *Hekiganroku,* T. XLVIII, no. 2003, pp. 161b28, 161c8, 161c10.

31. Birds "shining in the sunlight" is an image from the series of poems that forms a supplement to *The Gay Science* entitled "The Songs of Prince Vogelfrei." (*Vogelfrei* means, literally, "free as a bird.") In connection with "fliers of the spirit" see *Dawn* 575, the title of which is "We Air-Ship-Sailors of the Spirit" (see next note), and also *GS* 293 which is entitled "Our Air." This air is, significantly, "science" (*Wissenschaft*), but the conclusion of the aphorism is pure poetry:

> Let us then do what we [who are born for the air] alone can do: bring light to the earth, be "the light of the earth"! And for that we have our wings and our speed and severity; for this we are virile and even terrifying, like fire. May those fear us who do not know how to gain warmth and light from us!

(See also *Dawn* 574 and *GS* 294).

32. Lou Andreas-Salomé reports that Nietzsche wrote this poem as a dedication in the copy of *The Gay Science* which he presented to her in November 1882; see her important book, originally published in 1894, *Friedrich Nietzsche in seinen Werken* (Frankfurt, 1983), pp. 168–69. (An English translation of this book, entitled simply *Nietzsche,* by Siegfried Mandel, has just been published by Black Swan Press, Redding Ridge, Ct.) The original text of the poem reads as follows:

> Freundin!—sprach Columbus—traue
> keinem Genueser mehr!
> Immer starrt er in das Blaue—
> Fernstes lockt ihn allzusehr!
> Wen er liebt, den lockt er gerne
> Weit hinaus in Raum und Zeit—
> Über uns glänzt Stern bei Sterne,
> Um uns braust die Ewigkeit.

Lou Salomé quotes these verses in the context of the conclusion of *Dawn* 575 (which is the conclusion of the entire book):

> Do we want to go *over* the sea? Where does this powerful longing draw us, that is worth more to us than any pleasure? Why precisely in this direction, where all suns of humanity hitherto have *gone down?* Will it perhaps be said of us one day that we too, *steering westward, hoped to reach an India—* but that it was our fate to be wrecked upon infinity? or, my brothers? Or?—

She sees Nietzsche as the reverse of Columbus, who discovered the New World in searching for the Old, in that in his search for the new he rediscovered the old. A similar poem concerning a Genoese ship can be found in *Dionysus Dithyrambs* p. 9.

33. For a discussion of this idea of Heidegger's, see chapter seven, section 3.

34. *Zarathustra* III, 1 and IV, 19, §10.

35. *Vollendung*. Nishitani has *kannen*, which means "idea"—presumably a misreading of *Vollendung* as *Vorstellung*.

36. This kind of paradoxical formulation is common in Mahāyāna—and especially Zen—thought, and occurs frequently in *Religion and Nothingness*.

37. Nietzsche actually calls it *"der* lähmendste *Gedanke,"* "the most *laming* [or crippling] thought." This echoes Zarathustra's reference ("On the Vision and Enigma") to the spirit of gravity's sitting on his shoulder as "half-dwarf, half-mole; lame; laming; dripping lead through my ear, lead-drop-thoughts into my brain."

38. "Hammer": XIV, 321; *KGW* VII 27[80]; see also VIII 2[129]. Nietzsche uses the phrase "the great *disciplining* thought" twice in the first few notes of the final section of *The Will to Power* (*WP* 1053 and 1056). Nishitani refers to the thought as a *tanrensha*, a drill-master. The Japanese characters *tan* and *ren* translate Nietzsche's idea of *Züchtung* perfectly, and they have the additional connotation of forging metal or tempering steel, which connects nicely with the image of the hammer.

39. *WP* 1059. Nietzsche calls the thought "der *schwerste* Gedanke," which connotes the heaviness of its weight, its specific gravity, as well as its difficulty. The Japanese *konnan na* has rather the connotation of "troubling" as well as "difficult."

40. Nishitani is insightful in pointing out that the hammer is to be applied not only to the world but also—and perhaps *primarily*—to oneself. In the section "Upon the Blessed Isles," Zarathustra speaks of the need for

taking a hammer to the stone of the self in order to release the image of "the beauty of the *Übermensch*" that sleeps within (II, 2).

41. *Beyond Good and Evil,* "From High Mountains: Aftersong."

42. Another passage, from *Ecce homo,* which exemplifies a great deal of what Nishitani has been saying about the connection between *amor fati* and eternity, reads:

> My formula for greatness in a human being is *amor fati:* that one wills to have nothing other than it is, neither forwards, nor backwards, nor in all eternity. Not merely to tolerate what is necessary, far less to conceal it—all idealism is mendacity concerning the necessary—but to *love* it. ("Why I Am So Clever," §10)

43. See Kierkegaard's *The Concept of Anxiety* (as discussed in chapter two, above), and also *Philosophical Fragments,* for a discussion of the Moment *(Øiblikket)* in which eternity enters into time. In view of Nishitani's discussion of folly at the end of this section, it is interesting to recall Kierkegaard's comment in the latter text concerning the absurd paradox of eternity's entering time, to the effect that "the moment is foolishness" (*Philosophical Fragments,* trans. Howard V. Hong and Edna H. Hong [Princeton, 1985], p. 52).

44. *UdW* II, sec. 1343. The note continues: "This thought [of recurrence] contains more than all the religions that have despised this life as something fleeting and taught people to look toward some indeterminate other life."

45. *Kōtei suru;* Nietzsche actually uses the term *rechtfertigen* in this context, which has the somewhat different sense of "to justify."

46. *Zarathustra* I, 7; IV, 11; IV, 13, §20; IV, 13, §18; III, 4.

47. *Keitoku Dentōroku,* T. LI, no. 2076, p. 312b22–27.

48. *Keitoku Dentōroku,* p. 266a18.

49. *Hekiganroku,* T. XLVIII, no. 2003, p. 198b17–18.

50. Nietzsche's poem is the first of the "Songs of Prince Vogelfrei" (see note 31, above). The first and third stanzas of the poem are a close parody of the famous *Chorus Mysticus* that ends the Second Part of Goethe's *Faust.* I have followed the original German here (without attempting to render it into rhymed verse) rather than Nishitani's Japanese translation. The interplay of folly and wisdom is a major theme in *Zarathustra.* Compare also *BGE* 55, where Nietzsche writes of "sacrificing God for Nothing" and of worshipping "stone, stupidity, gravity, fate, Nothing." Nishitani discusses another aphorism from *Beyond Good and Evil* which employs similar imagery (231) in section 8 of the following chapter.

Chapter Five

1. The reference here is to Heidegger's essay "Nietzsches Wort 'Gott is tot'," which is based on lectures Heidegger gave on Nietzsche from 1936 to 1940 (the first two semesters of which Nishitani attended when he was in Freiburg). The subsequent two quotations are from Martin Heidegger, *Holzwege* (Frankfurt am Main, 1952), pp. 204, 196. For an English translation of this essay, see "The Word of Nietzsche: 'God is Dead' " in Martin Heidegger, *The Question Concerning Technology,* trans. William Lovitt (New York, 1977); see pp. 61, 65, 58.

2. *Twilight of the Idols,* "The Four Great Errors," §3.

3. This refers back to the discussion of pity in chapter three, sec. 3. Nietzsche's best argued criticism of pitying—which renders Nishitani's endorsement of it more understandable—is to be found in *GS* 338. This aphorism, entitled "The Will to Suffer and Those Who Pity," ends with Nietzsche's affirming his desire to make people "bolder, more persevering, simpler, gayer! I want to teach them what so few people today understand, and the preachers of pity [*Mitleiden*] least of all: the sharing of joy [*Mitfreude*]!"

4. *UdW* I, 625. "Fichte, Schelling, Hegel, Feuerbach, [David] Strauss—all of them smell of theologians and Church Fathers."

5. *Mu e*—a Buddhist term meaning "not relying on anything," and connoting the "untroubledness" or impassivity of *nirvāṇa*. The term is used by the Zen master Rinzai, whom Nishitani greatly admires, to characterize the "True Human of the Way." See, for example, *The Record of Lin-chi,* trans. Ruth Fuller Sasaki (Kyoto, 1975), Discourse 14.

6. The word Nishitani uses here, *datsuraku,* is used frequently by the thirteenth-century philosopher Dōgen in connection with the "sloughing off" of body and mind in the practice of Zen.

7. Nishitani plays here on the literal meaning of *erinnern,* which is "to internalize"; the usual meaning is "to remember," which suggests— appropriately in the context of this aspect of Nietzsche's thought—a memorial dimension to the encounter with fate.

8. XIII 34. Nishitani refers to this analogy again in *Religion and Nothingness,* p. 55.

9. XIII, 39; *KGW* VII 26[47] (1884).

10. *Jōhari*—a crystal mirror located in one of the Buddhist hells, which reflects all the good and bad actions performed by a person during his or her lifetime.

11. Goethe, "Über den Granit." This very short essay, a gem among Goethe's geological writings, contains several passages which it is not hard to imagine appealing to both Nietzsche and Nishitani. Goethe speaks of

"the ancient discovery that granite is both the highest and the deepest . . .
the solid ground of our earth," and of "the serene tranquility afforded by
that solitary, mute nearness of great, soft-voiced nature." In contrast to the
fertile valleys, the granite peaks "have never generated anything living nor
devoured anything living: they exist prior to and superior to all life." The
idea of the immutable nature of the will as the innermost core of a person's
character is a major theme in Schopenhauer, whose thought had a profound impact on the young Nietzsche; see, especially, *The World as Will and
Representation*, vol. I, §55, and also his *Essay on the Freedom of the Will*, ch. 3.
Compare the opening section of Nietzsche's "Schopenhauer as Educator"
where he speaks of the "true primal sense and basic material" of a person's
being as "something absolutely ineducable and unmoldable." This view of
Nietzsche's is, however, somewhat modified by the time of *Dawn*, where he
calls the doctrine of the unalterability of the character "a prejudice," and
emphasizes the extent to which we are free to cultivate the various drives
that constitute our nature in a variety of different ways and styles.

12. The allusion is to the verse attributed to Bodhidharma:

A special transmission outside the scriptures,
Not founded upon words and letters;
By pointing directly to [one's] mind
It lets one see into [one's own true] nature and [thus] attain
Buddhahood.

Cited from Heinrich Dumoulin, *Zen Buddhism: A History* (New York, 1988),
vol. 1, p. 85). The source can be found in *Mumonkan*, T. XLVIII, no. 2005, p.
293c15, or *Hekiganroku*, T. XLVIII, no. 2003, p. 154c5.

13. *Keitoku dentōroku*, T. LI, no. 2076, p. 322c26.

14. *Daitōgoroku*, T. LXXXI, no. 2566.

15. The poem stands as the epigraph to Book Four of *The Gay Science*.
The full text runs as follows:

Der du mit dem Flammenspeere
Meiner Seele Eis zertheilt,
Dass sie brausend nun zum Meere
Ihrer höchster Hoffnung eilt:
Heller stets und stets gesunder,
Frei im liebevollsten Muss:—
Also preist sie deine Wunder,
Schönster Januarius!

—Genoa, January 1882

In his paraphrase, Nishitani omits the last two lines, in which Nietzsche's soul is said to praise the miracles of January. The miracle of Sanctus Januarius refers to the annual liquefaction of the saint's blood on his feast day.

16. See, for example, *WP* 126, 229, 230, 233, 255, 258.

17. The German word Nietzsche uses here, *Vernunft*, has a connection with the verb for "to perceive" *(vernehmen)* that cannot be paralleled by the Japanese *risei* any more than by the English "reason."

18. Nishitani's choice of the term *shijisha*, meaning "pointer" or "indicator," to translate the German *Weiser* points up an important play on the word which English-speaking translators and commentators have missed. The English translations have only "wise man" or "sage," ignoring the second way of taking the term.

19. *GS* 371; see the similar passage, equally rich in significance, in Zarathustra's speech "On the Tree on the Mountainside" (*Za* I, 8).

20. Compare the image in Plato's *Timaeus* (90a) of the human soul as an inverted tree with its roots in the heavens (the intelligible realm).

Chapter Six

1. Max Stirner (real name: Johann Kaspar Schmidt), *Der Einzige und sein Eigentum* (Stuttgart, 1981); English translation by S. T. Byington, *The Ego and His Own* (New York, 1963). A more recent English edition of selections from the text is the volume by John Carroll, *Max Stirner: The Ego and His Own* in the "Roots of the Right" series edited by George Steiner (New York, 1971), which appeared the same year as the only recent book-length study of Stirner in English: R. W. K. Paterson, *The Nihilistic Egoist: Max Stirner* (London and New York, 1971). The classic study locating Stirner's work in the more general development of nineteenth-century German philosophy is Karl Löwith, *From Hegel to Nietzsche*. I retain the translation of the title as "The Ego and His Own" only because the book is so widely known under this name. The German title is admittedly difficult to translate, but "Ego" is not a happy rendering of *Der Einzige*— Stirner's espousal of (a peculiar form of) egoism notwithstanding. "The Unique One and Its Own" would not only be a better translation of the German but also of Nishitani's rendering of it as *Yuiitsusha to sono shoyū*.

2. On the question of Stirner's influence on Nietzsche, see Carroll, pp. 24–25, and Paterson, chapter 7. For a recent treatment of Lange's influence on Nietzsche, see George J. Stack, *Lange and Nietzsche* (Berlin, 1983).

3. Löwith points to the source of this motto in one of Goethe's *Gesellige Lieder* entitled "Vanitas! vanitatum vanitas!" which begins with the lines: "I have founded my affair on nothing./That's why I feel so well in the

world." I have to thank my friend Eberhard Scheiffele of Waseda University for pointing out that Goethe is here parodying a Pietistic hymn which begins: "I have founded my affair on God . . . " Löwith notes that Kierkegaard was also acquainted with the line from Goethe and thought it interesting as "the nihilistic 'summation of life' of a very great individuality (*From Hegel to Nietzsche*, p. 411, note 155).

4. *Kyomu tentan*—Chinese: *hsü-wu t'ien-t'an*. Although this term does not actually appear in the *Lao-tzu* it is a quintessentially Taoist phrase, and appears frequently, for example, in the *Huai Nan Tzu*, a later Taoist text from the Han dynasty. In chapter 15 of the *Chuang-tzu* the phrase *hsü-wu t'ien-t'an* occurs in a description of the Taoist sage, of whom it is said: "in emptiness and nothingness, calm and indifference, he joins with Heaven's Power"—see A. C. Graham, *Chuang Tzu: The Inner Chapters* (London, 1981), p. 266. This joining with the power *(te)* of heaven *(t'ien)* involves emptying the self in such a way that the forces of the natural world can operate through it unobstructedly—which may result in a condition not unlike the one Stirner is talking about, though from an opposite direction.

5. *The Ego and His Own*, p. 4; *Der Einzige und sein Eigentum*, p. 4. References to Stirner's book, separated by a slash, refer to the page numbers first of *The Ego and His Own* and then of the German edition. For the German text I have given references to the new Reclam edition rather than to the 1901 edition used by Nishitani, since the latter is no longer readily available. As usual I have translated from the original German while "leaning" toward Nishitani's Japanese rendering, but the results are similar enough to Byington's to enable the reader to locate passages in his translation.

6. 9/8; I have translated Nishitani's phrase rather literally; a more idiomatic rendering of *"hinter die Dinge kommen"* would be simply "to get to the bottom of things."

7. 5/5. The German reads: "Ich bin [nicht] Nichts im Sinne der Leerheit, sondern das schöpferische Nichts, das Nichts, aus welchem Ich selbst als Schöpfer alles schaffe." Nishitani translates *Leerheit* as *kūkyo*, which is here rendered, as usual, as "void." *Nichts*, with its obviously "positive" meaning, he translates as *mu*, "nothing." This is a remarkable passage, which surprisingly anticipates both Nietzsche and Heidegger and resonates deeply with a whole range of Buddhist and Taoist ideas. A couple of sentences later, in response to his own rhetorical question concerning the need for his *Sache* at least to be "good," Stirner exclaims: "What is good or evil! . . . I am neither good nor evil. Neither of them has any sense for me."

8. *Psychologie der Weltanschauungen*, pp. 296–300.

9. See above, chapter 3, sec. 4.

10. 43/46. "Du hast einen Sparren zu viel" means literally "you have one rafter too many," equivalent to the English expression "to have a screw loose."

11. At the end of the Preface to *The Essence of Christianity*, written shortly before Stirner's book was published, Feuerbach referred to Christianity as a *"fixed idea."*

12. The word "fanatic" comes from the Latin *fanum*, meaning "temple." *Enthusiasmus* has a similarly religious connotation, being derived from the Greek *entheos*, which means "having god or divinity in one."

13. 128/141. Nishitani translates *Eigenheit* as *gasei*, literally "I-ness," which emphasizes its connection with *jiga*, or "ego."

14. Hegel had earlier pointed to the significance of the connection between *Meinung*, "opinion," and "mineness"; see *The Phenomenology of Spirit*, section A, chapter I, which bears the title: "Sense-Certainty: or the 'This' and 'Meaning' [*Meinen*]."

15. On Nishitani's use of the verb *datsuraku* for "removes and discards," see chapter five, note 6. The idea of "casting off all robes" of any kind figures prominently in the ideas of Rinzai; see *The Record of Lin-chi*, Discourse 18. Stirner's admonition to strip away everything that is alien to oneself, everything that is not truly one's own, is a remarkable anticipation of the respects in which the "existential" aspects of Kierkegaard, Nietzsche, and Heidegger are congruent with later Buddhist ideas.

16. 157/173. Stirner's use of *Macht* and *mächtig* here and elsewhere gives the entire text a quite different illumination when read—as Nishitani reads it—in the light of Nietzsche's *Wille zur Macht*, as a power that is not primarily physical.

17. I have translated Stirner's *Nichts* here as "nothing," even though Nishitani uses *kyomu*; for *Nichtigkeit* later in the sentence he uses *kūmusei*, which is rendered, as usual, "nullity."

18. 183/201; 245/271. This anticipates another important theme in Kierkegaard and Nietzsche: the identity of each individual with the entire race.

19. *Jijuyō zammai* and *tajuyō zammai*; on the idea of the *samādhi* of self-enjoyment, see Dōgen, *Shōbōgenzō*, "Bendōwa," 15 i. Nishitani discusses "self-joyous *samādhi*" in the context of the "dropping-off [*datsuraku*] of body-and-mind" in chapter 5 of *Religion and Nothingness*.

20. *Jiririta kakugyokyuman*. This idea is another expression of "the bodhisattva ideal" of Mahāyāna Buddhism, in which a person's enlightenment conduces to the enlightenment of all sentient beings.

21. 182/200. Through a slip of the tongue, or pen, Nishitani translates the penultimate phrase as: "insofar as he remains what he is."

22. See Karl Marx and Friedrich Engels, *The German Ideology*, III "Sankt Max," sec. 1.

23. "Philosophy had not yet become *gaku*"—this word, which appears many times in the course of the next several pages, has the connotations of "learning, study, scholarship, science." It is often an apt translation of the German *Wissenschaft*, which has a much broader range of meaning than the English "science"; I have consequently rendered it variously through terms like "discipline" and "scholarship" as well as "science" and other cognates.

24. The reference is to Heidegger's project of "the destruction *(Destruktion) of the history of ontology*" as announced in §6 of *Being and Time*— a taking apart of the tradition, with what Heidegger calls a "positive intention," which is an important forerunner of the contemporary movement of "deconstruction."

Chapter Seven

1. This idea is expressed in Dostoevsky's *The Brothers Karamazov*. The slogan, "Nothing is true, everything is permitted," occurs in Nietzsche's *Zarathustra* (IV,9), and again in *On the Genealogy of Morals* (III, 24) where Nietzsche identifies it with the *secretum* of the Order of Assassins.

2. The terms "nihilism" and "nihilist" were apparently first used in Russia in a political or philosophical context by N. E. Nadezhdin in the year 1829. Direct quotations from *Fathers and Sons* are taken from the English translation by Rosemary Edmonds in the Penguin Classics series (Harmondsworth, 1975). References allude to the numbers of the short chapters, so that the passages can be found in any edition. The Edmonds edition offers as a bonus "*Fathers and Children*, the Romanes Lecture 1970" by Isaiah Berlin, which provides an illuminating complement to Nishitani's chapter in that it discusses such figures as Belinsky, Chernyshevsky, Dobrolyubov, and Herzen. Berlin brings out the quintessentially "existential" aspect of Turgenev in a way that makes Nishitani's attraction to him quite understandable:

> [Turgenev] knew that the Russian reader wanted to be told what to believe and how to live, expected to be provided with clearly contrasted values, clearly distinguishable heroes and villains. When the author did not provide this, Turgenev wrote, the reader was dissatisfied and blamed the writer, since he found it difficult and irritating to have to make up his own mind, find his own way. . . . the reader is left in suspense, in a state of doubt; the central problems are left unanswered. (p. 20)

3. In the Prologue to *Thus Spoke Zarathustra*, Zarathustra says to the people gathered in the marketplace, "You must have much chaos within you to give birth to a dancing star."

4. Nietzsche was familiar with the work of both Turgenev and Dostoevsky, though he did not discover the latter until early in 1887. He writes of this discovery to Franz Overbeck and Peter Gast in letters from February 23 and March 7 respectively. In the latter he has the following to say about *Notes from Underground:* "the first [part] is a kind of unfamiliar music, the second a stroke of true psychological genius—a terrifying and cruel piece of mockery of *gnōthi sauton* [know yourself] . . . " Some interesting accounts of Nietzsche's impact on Russian thinkers and literary and artistic figures are to be found in Bernice Glatzer Rosenthal, ed., *Nietzsche in Russia* (Princeton, 1986).

5. *Notes from Underground,* Part One, sec. III. Quotations are from the translation by Ralph E. Matlaw (New York, 1960). Unless otherwise indicated, the quotations are from Part One, with references to the section numbers in Roman numerals.

6. *The Will to Power* 12A. Nishitani has discussed this passage above, in chapter 3, sec. 2.

7. See the last two lines of the poem entitled "Sils Maria" in the appendix to *The Gay Science:*

> Then suddenly, friend, one became two—
> and Zarathustra passed before me . . .

There are two passages in *Zarathustra* in which Nietzsche plays with the connection between the word *Einsiedler* for "hermit" and his neologism *Zweisiedler* (literally: "two-settler"): at the end of section 9 of the Prologue and in "The Greeting" in Part Four. Compare also the penultimate stanza of "From High Mountains," which speaks of "the mid-day friend" and ends with the line: "At mid-day it was that one turned into two." (This stanza immediately precedes the one Nishitani quoted in chapter four above, concerning "friend Zarathustra, the guest of guests.")

8. When "Nihilism in Russia" was first published as a volume in the *Atene Bunko* series the following epilogue was added:

> This monograph is based on several talks which were delivered beginning in May of this year. The section on Dostoevsky's nihilism had to be divided, because of its length, into three parts. My major intention was to distinguish nihilism as "contemplation" in *Notes from Underground,* nihilism as "action" in *Crime and Punishment,* nihilism as "being" in Stavrogin in *The Possessed,* and nihilism as "spirit" in Ivan Karamazov, in order to trace the gradual deepening of Dostoevsky's nihilism. The present volume contains the Introduction to the whole work and the section on "contemplative" nihilism, but in view of the nature of this series I have tried to make it stand in its own.

Regarding the questions discussed at the beginning of this chapter, I relied on Maurice Bering's *The Russian People*, Karl Netzel's *Social Movements in Russia*, and the Japanese translation of *Russian History* by Richard Moeller. The quotations from Dostoevsky are taken from the Japanese translation by Yonekawa, as well as from English and German translations.

Chapter Eight

1. The neo-Kantian school, Husserl, and Dilthey were among the major influences on the early work of Nishida, Nishitani's teacher. Nishida's major engagement with the neo-Kantian tradition has recently appeared in English translation: *Intuition and Reflection in Self-Consciousness*, trans. Valdo H. Viglielmo with Takeuchi Yoshinori and Joseph S. O'Leary (Albany, 1987). Nishitani discusses this period in the history of philosophy at greater length in chapter five of his book *Nishida Kitarō* (English translation forthcoming).

2. The *locus classicus* for Heidegger's views on "scientific philosophy" is in *The Basic Problems of Phenomenology*, trans. Albert Hofstadter (Bloomington, 1982), which is the text of a lecture course Heidegger gave at Marburg in 1927. In the Introduction, Heidegger calls phenomenology "the method of scientific philosophy in general" (p. 3), and in a section entitled "Philosophy as science of being" (*Philosophie als Wissenschaft vom Sein*) he writes: "For the future we shall mean by 'philosophy' scientific philosophy and nothing else" (p. 13).

3. In introducing the ontological difference Nishitani uses the verb *aru*, "be" or "is" for Heidegger's *Sein*, "Being," and the compound *arumono*, "something (that is)" for *Seiendes*, "beings." A more literal translation of *aru* in these introductory sentences would be "is," but it is rendered as "Being" in order to preserve a continuity with the later terms of the distinction. Subsequently Nishitani uses the less usual word *sonzai* for "Being" (though this is the customary Japanese translation of the term in Heidegger), and *sonzaisurumono* for "beings," or "that which is."

4. The German phrase Nishitani has put in parentheses here means literally: "understanding understands itself." I have not come across this phrase in Heidegger, though it is clear that Nishitani is referring to the "pre-ontological" understanding of Being of which Heidegger speaks in the first chapter of *Being and Time*.

5. Heidegger describes these kinds of breakthrough in unusually accessible and "existential" terms in the first twenty or so pages of *Introduction to Metaphysics*, trans. Ralph Manheim (New Haven, 1959), which consists of lectures Heidegger gave in 1935.

6. Nishitani is presenting here the position of the early Heidegger, who attempted to "existentialize" metaphysics in such works as *What is Metaphysics?*, *Kant and the Problem of Metaphysics*, and *Introduction to Metaphysics* (1929–1935), as opposed to the the the later Heidegger who totally repudiates metaphysics in favor of a more primordial mode of thinking which he calls *Denken*.

7. For Heidegger's distinction between "scientific philosophy" and "philosophy as world-view [*Weltanschauung*]," see *The Basic Problems of Phenomenology* §2.

8. See the first section of the 1929 lecture *What is Metaphysics?* in David Farrell Krell, ed., *Martin Heidegger: Basic Writings* (New York, 1977).

9. The third paragraph of *What Is Metaphysics?* begins as follows: "From the standpoint of sound common sense philosophy is, in Hegel's words, the 'inverted world.' Thus the peculiar nature of our approach requires a preliminary characterization." There is in fact no further mention of Hegel's idea of the *verkehrte Welt*, the "topsy-turvy world," in *What Is Metaphysics?*; the passage Nishitani says Heidegger quotes from Hegel actually appears in §3 of *The Basic Problems of Phenomenology* (p. 14). It comes from an early essay of Hegel's entitled "On the Essence of Philosophical Criticism," whereas the *locus classicus* for the idea of the *verkehrte Welt* is section A3 of *The Phenomenology of Spirit*.

10. The verb Nishitani uses here, *hikisueru*, is a literal translation of the German *vorstellen*, meaning to "set before . . . " The noun *Vorstellung* means "idea" in the sense of "representation," but Heidegger is fond of playing on its literal meaning of "to place before" or "in front of." It is a recurrent theme in Heidegger's thinking that "representational thinking" (*vorstellendes Denken*) falsifies, impoverishes, and alienates us from the world by setting up things as objects (*Gegenstände*), as things that "stand over against" us as subjects. It is not surprising that Nishitani should disparage this way of setting the world up a few sentences later, since it has always been a major thrust of Zen to break down this way of relating to things.

11. This refers to Heidegger's idea that the world is disclosed to us more primordially in "moods" (*Stimmungen*) than in intellectual understanding. The Japanese *kibunteki* is not the awkward neologism that "moodish" is, although it fails to convey the connotation of being "attuned" to the world that *Stimmung* carries. For the importance of *Stimmung* and the more general structure, *Befindlichkeit* ("disposition"—rendered misleadingly as "state-of-mind" in the Macquarrie and Robinson translation of *Being and Time*), of which moods are particular manifestations, see *Being and Time* §29. Nishitani goes on to discuss *Befindlichkeit* and that aspect of our being which it discloses, our "thrownness" (*Geworfenheit*) into the world, later in this section.

12. Nishitani is alluding here to Heidegger's discussion in §58 of *Being and Time* of the connections between the disclosure of our thrownness through moods and the sense of existential "indebtedness" *(schuldig sein)* and nullity *(Nichtigkeit)* implicated in our being thrown into the world. To say that we are "thrown" into the world points up a nullity, or "notness," at the ground of our being insofar as it is *not* through ourselves that we come to be here in the first place: "Although [*Dasein*] has *not* itself laid the ground [of its own being], it rests in its heaviness which is manifest through mood as a burden" (*SZ* 284). (References to *Being and Time* follow the pagination of the German edition, *Sein und Zeit*, abbreviated as "*SZ*", which is also given in the margins of the English translation by Macquarrie and Robinson.)

13. Nishitani is referring here to Heidegger's discussion of the idea of *Transzendenz* in the 1929 essay *Vom Wesen des Grundes*, which is available in English translation (with German on the facing page) in *The Essence of Reasons*, trans. Terrence Malick (Evanston, 1969). In the Preface to the third edition, which was published in 1949 (the same year as Nishitani's book), Heidegger writes:

> The treatise *On the Essence of Ground* was written in 1928 at the same time as the lecture *What Is Metaphysics?* The latter ponders the problem of Nothing, the former discusses the ontological difference.
> Nothing is the "not" of beings [*Das Nichts ist das Nicht des Seienden*] and thus is Being as experienced from the side of beings. The ontological difference is the "not" between beings and Being. (*ER* 3)

In quoting passages from this text by way of supplementary explanation I have worked, as usual, from the original German, leaning toward Nishitani's rendering of related passages, though all references are paginated to the Malick translation (abbreviated "*ER*" and followed by the page number).

14. See the beginning of section II of *On the Essence of Ground*, entitled "Transcendence as the Realm of the Question concerning the Essence of Ground." Heidegger writes: "*In* surpassing, *Dasein* comes for the first time to the being that *it is, to it as* it'self.' Transcendence constitutes selfhood" (*ER* 39). The idea is that one can understand one's being as a "self" only insofar as one has gone beyond oneself and other things and come back to oneself in such a way as to experience the difference between beings and Nothing, and between oneself and others. The entire argument of this essay is heavily influenced by Heidegger's reading of Schelling's *Treatise on the Essence of Human Freedom* (1809), which was later published as the text of lectures given between 1936 and 1943. This work is available in English translation: *Schelling's Treatise on the Essence of Human Freedom*, trans. Joan Stambaugh (Athens, Ohio, 1985). One reason Nishitani was attracted to the themes of transcendence, ground, and freedom in Heidegger is

that he himself engaged in intensive study of Schelling early in his career, and translated the *Treatise on Human Freedom* into Japanese. The difficulty of Heidegger's discussion in *On the Essence of Ground*, and of Nishitani's discussion of Heidegger here, derives in part from the difficult nature of Schelling's *Treatise* which, though profound, is hardly a paradigm of lucidity.

15. Nishitani emphasizes Heidegger's "relational" and "non-substantial" conception of the self from the perspective of the long tradition in East Asian (Taoist and Buddhist) thought of viewing the self as a matrix of relations rather than as a substance. One of the ways in which Heidegger tries to explode the idea of the encapsulated self is by characterizing our awareness as an all-encompassing field or "clearing" (*Lichtung*) rather than an "inner" sphere of consciousness, and by emphasizing that, phenomenologically, we are "outside" far more than "inside":

> In orienting itself toward something or in apprehending something *Dasein* does not first go out from some inner sphere in which it is encapsulated, but rather it is in its primary mode of being always already "outside" with whatever beings it encounters in a world already discovered. . . . in this very "being-outside" with the object *Dasein* is in the proper sense "inside" that is, being-in-the-world. (*SZ* 62)

Heidegger goes on to emphasize that we are "outside" not only in the perception of the "external" world, but also in other cognitive activities which we are even more inclined to think of as "internal":

> In "merely" knowing about some interconnection of entities, in "only" imagining such a thing, in "simply thinking" about it, I am no less outside in the world with the entity in question than in an *original* apprehension of it.

Again, Nishitani is sensitive to this important theme in Heidegger, discussed only briefly in *Being and Time*, because it resonates with the way the Zen tradition understands the nature of human awareness.

16. The relevant passage reads:

> However, if beings are *not that up to which* the stepping beyond goes, how is this "up-to-which" to be determined or even investigated? We call that *up-to-which* Dasein as such transcends the *world*, and now characterize transcendence as *being-in-the-world*. (*ER* 41)

Heidegger goes on to distinguish two senses of "world": a "prephilosophical, vulgar" one and a "transcendental" one. The former understands the world as the totality of what there is, whereas the latter conceives it as the ultimate horizon within which any being can be what it is. This is prefigured in the distinction Heidegger makes in §14 of *Being and Time* between the "ontical" and "ontological" senses of *Welt*.

17. Because "world" in the transcendental/ontological sense is not a being or entity of any kind, it is not possible, strictly speaking, to say of it that it "is": "World never *is*, but rather *worlds* [*Welt* ist *nie, sondern* weltet]" (*ER* 103). This notion of world is, like Heidegger's ideas of Being, Nothing, and Thing, more or less impossible to grasp conceptually. Rather than trying to make simple what is inherently profoundly complex by offering a definition in other, simpler terms, of the form: "World is a, b, c, etc.," Heidegger keeps the reader focused on the difficulty by repeating the *explicandum* in the form of a verb: "World worlds," "Nothing nothings" (*das Nichts nichtet*), "the thing things" (*das Ding dingt*). The effect on the reader who takes this word-play seriously is not unlike that of a Zen kōan assiduously worked on. I have suggested elsewhere that Heidegger's fondness for this trope may have stemmed from his acquaintance (which he kept well concealed) with Zen ideas; see Graham Parkes, "Dōgen / Heidegger / Dōgen," *Philosophy East and West* 37 (1987), pp. 439–440. In fact Nishitani was a major source for Heidegger's knowledge of Zen, and reports that when he was studying in Freiburg, Heidegger frequently invited him over to his house in order to quiz him about ideas and images in the Zen corpus. See, in this context, the remarks of Nishitani quoted in the Introduction to *Heidegger and Asian Thought*, pp. 9–10.

18. The exposition has reverted to *Being and Time*, and to the idea of *Befindlichkeit*, or disposition, through which we find ourselves situated in the midst of the totality of beings-as-a-whole (see *SZ* §29).

19. See *SZ* §§29, 38, 58, and 68b.

20. The Japanese *katsudōkūkan* means "activity-space," and with its connotations of vital energy it perhaps better captures the "play" of the German *Spiel* than does "free space." While the idea of *Spielraum* plays an important role in Heidegger's later thinking, possibly under the dual influence of Nietzsche's emphasis on play and of its role in the East Asian traditions with which Heidegger became increasingly familiar, it nevertheless figures importantly, if not frequently, in *Being and Time*: see *SZ* 145, 355, 368–69; and also *ER* 109, (where it is translated "leeway"), and *Kant and the Problem of Metaphysics* §17 (where it is rendered as "free-space").

21. See *SZ* 145, 148 and 285. The idea of our being *geworfener Entwurf* is that although we always find ourselves *thrown* into a situation not of our own choosing, there is a "momentum" to this throw which we can take up and use to help us *project* (this works better in German, where the verb *werfen*, "to throw," is also the "-ject" of pro-ject) further possibilities of ourselves.

22. The verb Nishitani uses here for "throw over," *nagekabuseru*, has the connotation of covering whatever is the object of the throwing over. The relevant passage in *On the Essence of Ground* reads:

> The projection of world, while it does not explicitly grasp what is projected, is always also a *projection (Überwurf)* of the projected world *over beyond* beings. This prior projection is what makes it possible for beings as such to manifest themselves." (*ER* 89)

In a subsequent passage Heidegger writes: "The letting-world-hold-sway by projecting and throwing beyond is freedom" (*Das entwerfend-überwerfende Waltenlassen von Welt ist die Freiheit*). (*ER* 105—Malick adds "over being" to "by projecting and throwing world." This is misleading on an important point, insofar as Heidegger's idea is not that beings are there already and we then project world over them: the point is rather that the prior projection of world is what lets beings be what they are in the first place.)

23. This is a reference to Heidegger's frequent playing on the roots *ek-histemi* and *ex-sistere* which link the idea of "existence" to "ek-stasis," or "stepping out from."

24. This phrase occurs in *What is Metaphysics?*, and the rest of the paragraph is a paraphrase of and commentary on Heidegger's elaboration of the idea in that essay. (See the translation in *Basic Writings*, pp. 105–106; further references to this essay will be abbreviated *WM?* followed by the page number in *Basic Writings*.) This idea also occurs in Heidegger's first book on Kant (also 1929): see *Kant and the Problem of Metaphysics*, trans. James S. Churchill (Bloomington, 1962), p. 246. Subsequent references to this last work will be abbreviated "*KM*" and followed by the page numbers of the English translation and the German original, *Kant und das Problem der Metaphysik* (Frankfurt, 1973), respectively.

The idea that we are constantly "held out into Nothing" is one of Heidegger's most striking expressions of one of his central ideas. Coming from the perspective of later Buddhist thought, Nishitani is obviously struck by the image and refers to it again and again in this chapter. His translation, *sashikakerarete aru koto*, is interesting in several respects. The verb *kakeru* means "to hang," or "suspend," and is used here with the intensifier *sasu*, which means primarily "to hold up" (of an umbrella), but also "to insert" (a hairpin into the hair, or a skewer into food). This would lend to the image of our being held out into nothing, and hanging out over the abyss, a sense of being held *up* into nothing or *inserted* into it. The connotation concerning the umbrella enhances the feeling of contingency: when the rains stops the umbrella is taken down and put away, perhaps to be left somewhere by mistake. One thinks of Derrida's reading of Nietzsche's note, "*Ich habe mein Schirm vergessen*" (*Spurs/Éperons*, trans. Barbara Harlow [Chicago, 1979], pp. 122–43). A Derridean reading of Nishitani's translation of Heidegger's phrase would also remark that the character used for the *sa* of *sasu* means "difference"—although this is an artifact of the assigning of Chinese characters to native Japanese words, and thus the allusion to the ontological difference (which is what "being held up and out into nothing" is about) would not be heard in listening to speech, but only seen in reading Nishitani's written text.

25. While neither Heidegger nor Nishitani makes this connection explicit, a little reflection on the two texts from 1929 makes clear that "world" in *On the Essence of Ground* and "nothing" in *What is Metaphysics?* are equivalent. According to the former text, a being can only make sense to us if we have already projected a horizon of intelligibility in the form of a world; we can encounter a being only insofar as we have already gone beyond ("transcended") it to an empty horizon, against which it can appear as *not-nothing*—that is, as *something*. The common root of both ideas is to be found in *Being and Time*, in the discussion of the collapse of all intelligibility in the experience of *Angst* (which Nishitani treats in the next section), where Heidegger refers to "the nothing of world" *(das Nichts der Welt)* (SZ 343; see also SZ 276–77).

26. The Japanese *zensōteki* is a neologism that is less inelegant than the English one chosen here to translate the German *vorlaufend:* literally, "running-ahead."

27. There is a link between the talk of *Dasein's* "coming to itself" and being "futured" that is lost in the translation, and which is effected in both Japanese and German by the significant presence of the verb "to come" in the word for "future." In German, *Dasein* "kommt *auf sich zu*" in its "Zu-kunft"; Nishitani speaks of the way in which in "coming" *(tōrai)* to myself, I am "futured" *(shōrai sareru)* by my end.

28. Heidegger does not actually use the term *Weltbilden* (world-forming/imaging) in the discussion of being-toward-death in *SZ*, though it occurs in *On the Essence of Ground:*

> "*Dasein* transcends" means that it is essentially *world-forming/imaging (weltbildend)*, and "forming/imaging" in the sense that it lets world happen and with the world gives itself an originary view (image) which does not grasp explicitly, yet precisely serves as a pre-image for all manifest beings, among which the particular *Dasein* itself belongs. *(ER 89)*

In the Kant book from the same year, Heidegger elaborates the idea of the projection of world in strikingly similar terms, except that the term "horizon" is used instead of "world," in a discussion of Kant's notion of the transcendental imagination:

> The transcendental imagination effects the formation *(Bilden)* of the horizon-aspect. Not only does it "form" *(bildet)* the intuitive percepti-

bility of the horizon . . . but it also is "formative" *(bildend)* in another sense, insofar as it provides for the possibility of anything like an "image" in general.

It is only in the occurrence of this doubled forming/imaging that the ground of the possibility of transcendence becomes visible . . . *(KM* 95–6)

29. *Seken no hito*— this translation of Heidegger's *das Man*, a term difficult to translate satisfactorily into English, means literally "one in the social world." The relevant sections in *SZ* are §§25–27.

30. *Matowareta*—literally: "robed" or "clothed." This metaphor conveys a somewhat different feeling from Heidegger's talk of Nothing's being encountered "at one with" *(in eins mit)* beings-as-a-whole *(WM?* 104). Heidegger goes on to say that in anxiety "beings-as-a-whole become brittle *hinfällig),"* a powerful image which rather suggests that the totality of beings is *permeated* by Nothing. (The English translation here is totally misleading when it says "In anxiety beings as a whole become superfluous.")

31. The Japanese again retains the link between "coming" and the future, which is there in the German but is lost in the English. The verb translated here as "come into its own" is *genjō suru;* the term *genjō* figures prominently in Dōgen, and might also be translated "presencing."

32. Nishitani's reading of Heidegger here suggests an intriguing parallel between his ideas about temporality and Nietzsche's ideas of eternal recurrence and *amor fati.*

33. I am unable to find this exact phrase in the German original; there is, however, toward the end of §43, a sentence that reads: "The being of beings is, however, at all comprehensible—and herein lies the deepest finitude of transcendence—only if *Dasein* in the ground of its being holds itself out into Nothing" *(KM* 246/231).

34. *KM* 4/1 and 213/200. Kant speaks of metaphysics as a *"Naturanlage des Menschen"* in *The Critique of Pure Reason,* B 21.

35. Nishitani alludes here to a passage in the Kant book:

Metaphysics is not something that is merely "created" by human beings in systems and doctrines, but rather the understanding of Being, its projection and rejection, *occurs* in *Dasein* as such. "Metaphysics" is the basic occurrence in the irruption into beings which occurs with the factical Existence of a being such as human being. *(KM* 251/235)

A passage closer to Nishitani's paraphrase is to be found near the beginning of *What Is Metaphysics?* where, in speaking of the "pursuit of science," Heidegger writes:

In this "pursuit" there occurs nothing less than the irruption *(Einbruch)* of one [kind of] being, human being, into the totality of beings, and indeed in such a way that in and through this irruption beings break open into what and how they are. The irruption that breaks open *(der aufbrechende Einbruch)* is what helps in its way beings to themselves. *(WM?* 97)

36. Heidegger takes up this question in *What Is Metaphysics?* (pp. 106–108).

37. At *KM* 235/221 Heidegger writes that with all our culture and technology we can "never become master" of the beings upon which we are dependent: "Dependent upon beings other than themselves, [human beings] are at the same time not in control [*nicht mächtig*] of the beings which they themselves are." And at *ER* 129–131 he connects thrownness with the "powerlessness" *(Ohnmacht)* that "conditions the being of *Dasein's* being as such."

Chapter Nine

1. The allusion is to the first lines of "November 3rd," a poem by Miazawa Kenji (1896–1933), whose work is deeply informed by Zen ideas.

2. The reference is to an monograph by Karl Löwith entitled *Yōroppa no nihirizumu,* trans. Jisaburō Shibata (Tokyo, 1948). Löwith has addressed this theme in a number of his essays; see, especially, "The Historical Roots of European Nihilism," in Karl Löwith, *Nature, History, and Existentialism* (Evanston, 1966), and *Kierkegaard und Nietzsche: oder theologische und philosophische Überwindung des Nihilismus* (Frankfurt, 1933). While the Afterword to the Japanese monograph has not been published in English or German, some of the author's insights into the Japanese psyche are contained in "Japan's Westernization and Moral Foundation," *Religion and Life* 12/1 (1942/ 43), "The Japanese Mind," *Fortune* 28/6 (1943), and "Unzulängliche Bemerkungen zum Unterschied von Orient und Okzident," in Dieter Henrich, ed., *Die Gegenwart der Griechen im neueren Denken* (Tübingen, 1960).

3. This is an important theme in Nietzsche, and one generally neglected by the secondary literature in the West. Nishitani is referring to a passage in *The Gay Science* that merits quoting since it contains a number of themes with which the present text has dealt. In speaking of the "historical sense" as the "peculiar virtue and sickness" of contemporary humanity, Nietzsche continues:

Anyone who knows how to experience the history of humanity as *his own history* . . . [and could] endure this immense amount of grief of all kinds . . . as a person with a horizon of millennia in front of and behind him, as the heir of all the nobility of all previous spirit and an heir with a sense of obligation . . . : if one could take all of this upon one's soul . . . this would have to produce a happiness that up until now humanity has not known . . . (*GS* 337)

The theme of responsibility to the tradition appears early in Nietzsche's work, in the second *Untimely Meditation*, "On the Use and Disadvantage of History for Life," in which he speaks of our being "the heirs and descendants of the astonishing powers of classical antiquity, and seeing in that our honor and our spur" (sec. 8). Other important passages dealing with our responsibilities toward the ancestors are to be found in this essay on history, as well as in *The Gay Science* 54–57 and *The Will to Power* 969.

4. For a comprehensive account of Nietzsche's acquaintance with Buddhism and an extensive comparison of his ideas with Hīnayāna and Theravāda philosophy, see Freny Mistry, *Nietzsche and Buddhism*. See also Mervyn Sprung, "Nietzsche's Trans-European Eye" in Graham Parkes, ed., *Nietzsche and Asian Thought*. Arguing from a scrutiny of Nietzsche's correspondence with Paul Deussen and of the books in his personal library, Sprung concludes that Nietzsche had far less acquaintance with Indian sources than is commonly thought. For another perspective, see also Johann Figl, "Nietzsches frühe Begegnung mit dem Denken Indiens," *Nietzsche-Studien* 18 (1989), as well as Professor Figl's related essay in *Nietzsche and Asian Thought*.

5. Nishitani is surely right here, and this suggestion needs to be explored—contrary to Mistry's claim that with the development of Mahāyāna the parallels with Nietzsche's ideas (which he demonstrates convincingly with respect to Hīnayāna and Theravāda philosophy) break down.

6. Nāgārjuna, *Mūlamādhyamikakārikā* 24/14. This central idea of Nāgārjuna's Mādhyamika philosophy is seminal for the subsequent development of Mahāyāna Buddhism. Its centrality for Zen thought is a factor in Nishitani's interest in the issue of Nothing in Heidegger.

7. This is a passage from the *Rinzai-roku*, the Japanese name for a Ch'an Buddhist text from ninth century China; see *The Record of Lin-chi*, Discourse 13. The "three periods" are the three horizons of past, present, and future; the "ten directions" are the eight points of the compass together with the zenith and the nadir. The *dharmadhātu* (Jap., *hokkai*) means "dharma realm" and refers both to the totality of all things and to the underlying "ground" of all things.

Appendix

1. *Shogyōmujō*. The idea of impermanence (Sanskrit: *anitya*) is one of the three basic characteristics of existence according to Buddhist thought,

the other two being *muga* (Skt. *anātman*), not-self or non-ego, and *ku* (Skt. *duḥkha*), unsatisfactoriness, frustration, or suffering.

2. *Issai kaiku*—this phrase is a play on the nearly homophonous term *issai kaikū*, a common expression in Buddhism to denote the "emptiness" of all things.

3. *Sekai banbutsu*—literally: "the ten thousand things of the world," an expression that comes originally from classical Taoism.

4. *Fuku furaku*—This is the third of the "three states of sensation" *(sanju)*, the first two being pain and pleasure.

5. *Shohōmuga*—This expression refers to the insubstantiality of all phenomena, insofar as their existence is always dependent upon other phenomena and conditions.

6. *Jiriki*—an important idea in Shin ("True Pure Land") Buddhism. D. T. Suzuki offers the following explanation in the Glossary to his translation of Shinran's *Kyōgyōshinshō* (Kyoto, 1973):

> Shinran states that self-power is when a man counts upon his body, his mind, his power, or any of his various "good roots," and says that "to attain the true faith you must be free from the limitations of your discriminating intellect, and the roots of the self-power's working must be overthrown."

This is opposed to the "other-power" of *tariki* which

> denotes the power of Amida's Prayer. Although "other-power" is the apparent antithesis of "self-power," essentially, as a working force, "other" is beyond any such dualistic notions.
>
> (If we say that other-power issues from a personality named Amida, we somehow feel it to be something possessed of the nature of human conduct. But the working of Amida's great Compassion is free from all human agency, severed from discriminations and arguing; it is natural and not calculated. Therefore, this power of the Original Prayer is like Asura's harp, from which it is said the music comes out naturally without anyone playing on it. Here is the transcendental aspect of Shin teaching.) (pp. 243–44)

7. Nishitani is no doubt thinking of the essay Heidegger published in 1947 entitled "Letter on 'Humanism'," in which he argues forcefully against "humanistic" misreadings of *Being and Time* and at the same time emphasizes the anti-anthropocentric standpoint of all his thinking since then. The whole essay is a polemic against Sartre's notion of existentialism as "humanism," and argues for the priority of Being—especially as "housed" in language—over human being.

8. *Arijigoku*—literally: "antlion lair." The antlion digs a pit in the sand into which it pushes its prey, which is then caught and devoured by the larva lying in wait at the bottom.

9. The word translated here as "returning" is *gensō*, a Shin Buddhist term meaning, literally, "returning transfer." This has to do with the idea of "transference of merit" *(ekō)* between Amida Buddha and human beings—with which the word translated "accommodation," *ōgen*, is also connected. *Ōgen* refers to the two phases of merit transference, the "outgoing" *(ōsō)* and the "returning" *(gensō)*. Suzuki explains this merit-transference as follows:

Mahāyāna Buddhism holds that merit created anywhere by any being may be turned over to any other being desired or towards the enhancement and prevalence of Enlightenment in the whole world. A Bodhisattva practices asceticism not only for the perfection of his own moral and spiritual qualities but for the increase of such qualities among his fellow-beings. Or he suffers pains in order to save others from them and at the same time to make them aspire for Enlightenment.

With Shin, the source of this activity lies with Amida, and from Amida alone as the center starts the spiritual vibration known as merit-transference. The transference starts from Amida to all beings and not from all beings to the realization of Enlightenment. When this merit-transference is made to originate exclusively from Amida, we see where the idea of *tariki* comes from. We can almost say that the entire structure of the Shin teaching is dependent upon Shinran's interpretation of the principle of merit-transference, as he states at the outset of the section on *Teaching of the Kyōgyōshinshō*: "As I respectfully reflect on the true doctrine of the Pure Land, there are two forms of *ekō:* the outgoing *ekō,* and returning *ekō.*"

Personally, [Amida] is Dharmākara the Bodhisattva who is deeply engaged in the work of self-perfection so as to accumulate the stock of merit for the sake of all beings. This stock of merit is stored in the Name which is now the most efficient agent in leading all beings to the awakening of Enlightenment. The dynamism of this mysterious event is due to Amida's *mahākaruṇā* which produces a circular movement, outgoing and returning. The outgoing one called *ōsō-ekō* passes over to all beings and makes them turn toward the Pure Land, while the returning movement is what makes beings once awakened to Enlightenment wish to go back to their fellow-beings in the *sahālokadhātu,* this world of limitation and finitude. This is technically known as *gensō-ekō.* (pp. 213–14)

Also relevant in this context is the final chapter of Takeuchi Yoshinori, *The Heart of Buddhism*, ed. and trans. James W. Heisig (New York, 1983). In Part II of this text Takeuchi (who was a graduate student of Nishitani's at Kyoto University in the late thirties) presents an illuminating exposition of the idea of dependent origination in Pure Land Buddhism with frequent reference to the work of Heidegger. In chapter seven in particular he discusses *ōsō* and *gensō* in the context of several of the Heideggerian ideas discussed by Nishitani in chapter eight, above.

10. *Ba*—the ordinary word for "place." As part of the compound *basho*, the term alludes back to one of the key ideas in Nishida's later thought, as well as forward to Nishitani's more frequent use of the term in *Religion and Nothingness*.

11. *Engi*. This is the Japanese term for the central Buddhist idea of *pratītysamutpāda*, the idea that every phenomenon arises only as a result of other phenomena.

12. Musō Kokushi (1275–1351), whose monastic name was Sōseki, was the leading Zen master of the early Muromachi period. (The name *Kokushi* means "Teacher of the Nation," and is a title given to priests held in the highest esteem.) He was responsible for a revival of interest in the Neo-Confucian philosophy of the Chinese thinker Chu Hsi, and was also an enthusiastic and accomplished practitioner of the arts. Several of Japan's greatest Zen gardens are attributed to him.

Index